AF552496

UNDERSTANDING PLANT ECOLOGY

By

Dr. Pooja

Dept. of Botany
R.C.C. College
Ghaziabad (U.P.)
(India)

DISCOVERY PUBLISHING HOUSE PVT. LTD.
NEW DELHI-110 002

First Published-2010

ISBN 978-81-8356-545-5

© Author

Published by:

DISCOVERY PUBLISHING HOUSE PVT. LTD.
4831/24, Ansari Road, Prahlad Street
Darya Ganj, New Delhi-110002 (India)
Phone: 23279245 • Fax: 91-11-23253475
E-mail: parul.wasan@gmail.com
info@discoverypublishinggroup.com
Website: www.discoverypublishinggroup.com

Printed at:
Sachin Printers
Delhi

Preface

The present title "Understanding Plant Ecology" has been written for those students interested in careers in diverse fields of biological sciences. It provides a structured approach to learning by covering all the important topics in a uniform, systematic format. The book has been comprehensively designed incorporating recent advances in this fast moving field. It also provides accessible information on molecular biology in compact form for undergraduate students in biology and related life sciences. It is intelligible to the educated layman, though it deals with some complex ideas. It is an adequate text for all the requirements of students in this area. In addition, busy lecturers who require a quick reference compendium will find it useful, particularly for tutional planning. Simple, yet hopefully clear figures and tables are provided throughout the book.

The over-riding goal of this book, and indeed of the whole *Understanding series,* is to present the essential information concering molecular biology in a compact, readily accessible form which leads itself to student learning and revision. The convergence of various approaches has generated a rich panorama of detail, the significance of which we are still attempting to unraval. The present text has been written as an introduction to this rapidly growing field.

To make the work more comprehensive and informative, the author has consulted many authoritative books, research journals, abstracts, monographs etc., so there can be no claim to originality except in the manner of treatment.

The author expresses his thanks to his friends and colleagues whose continue inspirations have initiated him to bring out this book.

The author expresses his gratitude to Mr. Wasan and staff of M/s Discovery Publishing House Pvt. Ltd. for their whole hearted cooperation in the publication of this book.

In the mean time, the author will remain sincerely responsible for any shortcomings of the book and be grateful to the readers for their suggestions and constructive criticism for the continuous betterment of the book. He takes this opportunity to appeal to the readers to send their suggestions straightaway to his Publisher.

Author

Preface

[illegible] technology has been written for [illegible]

[illegible] Publishing House Pvt. Ltd. for the [illegible] cooperation in the publication of this book.

[illegible] the author will remain [illegible] responsible for [illegible] of the book and [illegible] grateful to the readers for their [illegible] and constructive criticism for the [illegible] of the book. He takes this opportunity to appeal to the readers to send [illegible] to the Publisher.

Contents

1

INTRODUCTION

At present ecology is among the most active and most *fascinating* of the biological sciences. It seems that a really general ecology is still in the *formative* stage and offers an alluring front for the advancement of knowledge. Most field studies of living organisms now have an ecological *orientation*.

Basic attitudes and principles of ecology have also *permeated* most of the biological sciences and some other sciences. Ecology is the special term for the *environment biology*.

The word ecology (*Oekologie*) is derived from the Greek word, "*olkos*" (meaning house, abode, *dwelling*) and logos. (meaning study or *discourse*). Thus literally, ecology is the study of "houses" or in a broader sense "environments".

As it is concerned especially with the biology of groups of organisms. and functional processes on the land, in the ocean as well as in fresh water, one may therefore define ecology as the study of structure and function of nature, including the living world. Thus ecology is the attempt to understand the relationship of plants and animals to their environments-where they live, how they live there and hopefully, why they live there.

According to Haeckel (1869) "ecology is the science treating of reciprocal relations of organisms and the external world." Elton (1927) called ecology "*scientific natural history*". According to Taylor (1936) "ecology is the science of all the relations of all organisms to all their environment." Abercrombie *et al.*, (1954) *opinioned* that the study of the relations of animals and plants, particularly of animal and plant communities, to their surroundings, both *animate* and *inanimate* is called ecology. Odum (1963) defined ecology as "study of the structure and function of nature." Hughes and Walker (1965) defined ecology .as "study of the relationships between organisms and their environment."

Ecology is that branch of science which deals with 'the relationship between living things and their physical renvironment together with all the other living organisms within it. General ecology deals with the biota (flora and fauna) and its environment. Ecology, as used to-day is a science which states organisms in relation to their *environment*: a *philosophy*—in which the world of life is described in terms of natural processes; an art requiring skill and having a plan and a pattern 'within which many *activities* may be centred.

The man emphasis of ecology is on the relationship between organisms and groups of *organisms* and their external environment.

HISTORY OF ECOLOGY

"The history of ecology can be traced back to *prehistoric* man who took into account the *environmental* factors for hunting, trapping animals, finding edible vegetation and finding out of shelter' to protect himself from *hardships* of nature. When man understood the importance of environment, it took a religious turn and man started *worshiping* sun, air, rains etc.

The early Greek' scientists and philosopheres also understood the importance of weather. First of all *Hippocrates* published a paper entitted "On *Air*, *Waters* and *Places*". After *Hippocrates*, '*Aristotle* studied the habits of animals and environmental conditions. Later Theophrastus, a student of Aristotle wrote about plants communities and the types of plants found in different areas.

Thus Theophrastus is considered to he first ecologist. Study of natural sciences was resumed by Reaumur (16831757) after centuries gap. He published about six volumes on the Natural History of Insects which contained ecological information about insects.

Baron Alexandert von Humbolt (1804) published about 26 volumes based on the data collected by him after exploring tropical and temperate South America. This gave an impaetus to other naturalists to study flora and fauna of South America.

Henry W-Bates published work on termites, warrior ants and parasol ants in relation to environment. Richard Spruce explored Amazon and Negro rivers 'while Alcide d' Orbigny (1826) collected specimens in Andes Mountains and Bolivia. Edward Forbes studied the *flora* and *fauna* of Mediterranean Sea. Joseph Hooker studied the flora and fauna of polar continent. Louis Agassiz (1846-1873) published "Contribution to the Natural History of the United States." He first founded Marine Laboratory in United States.

Darwin published "Journal of Researches into the Natural History and Geology of the Countries visited during the voyage of H.M.S. Beagle." Edward Forbes (1846) published a paper on palaeo-ecology of the British Isles. Alfred R. Wallace published three books:

(*a*) The Malaya Archipelago,

(*b*) Island life and

(*c*) The Geographical Distribution of animals.

Daven port (1903) published a paper on "The animal ecology of Cold Spring Harbor." S. A. Forbes (1907) described the distribution of Illinois fishes. E. Warming (1909) established the interdependence and close relationships between plant and animals. V.E. Shelford (1907, 1908) worked on Tiger Beetle. Allee, *et al.*, (1949) published 'Principles of Animal Ecology." In 1954 Andrewartha and Birch published scholarly work "The Distribution and Abundance of Animals."

Origin of Plant Ecology

While it is true that ecology as a science arose near the close of the last century, but there have always been a few naturalists.s interested to some degree in environmental relations. The *philosopher*, *Theophrastus* (370-285 B.C.) may well bė regarded as the first *ecologist* in history because he wrote and quite sensibly too, of the communities in which plants are associated, the relation of plants to each other and to their physical environment.

He also studied the features of water plants (swampy and marshy plants) and plants of dry and acid plants. There was an era of plant geography during which general studies of *vegetation* and *geographical distribution* of individual plants were made in eighteen century.

The works of Humboldt Schouw, A, de Candolle are the characteristics of this era. In the period 1838-1895 the study of plant formations was made. A plant formation was recognized as fundamental unit of vegetation. This period was the beginning of the study of plant succession.

The term ethology was proposed by the French zoologist named Hilaire in 1859 to designate the subject. The term ecology was, however, proposed in 1885 by Reiter, a zoologist. In 1886, Haeckel also another zoologist defined ecology as the study of the reciprocal relations between organisms and their environment.

The first general work devoted to ecology was by the Danish biologist J.E.B. Warming in 1895 followed by Swiss biologist A.F.W. Schimper in 1898. Warming published his book Oecology of plants and Schimper published a book named Plant geography upon a *physiological* basis. The period, 1895-1916 is the early part of modern plant ecology.

The contributions of Schimper, Drude and Warming are characteristics of this period. In this period the study of *habitat* along with the exact *determination* of *physical* factors was made. The plant ecology was divided into *autecology* and *synecology*.

After 1916, ecological research was greatly expanded by the establishment of ecological societies and publication of ecological journals. After world war 11, the United Nations Educational Scientific and Cultural Organisation (UNESCO) started desert and arid zone studies. Numerous regional ecological stations have been set up.

Indian Work Ecology

In India Ecological work has been started in the begining of the 20th century. In this century names of Prof. Dugdeon, Prof, Barucha, Prof. R. Misra may be mentioned as pioneer worker of ecology. "Indian forest Ecology" was published by Dr. G.S. Puri, Prof. R Misra, L.P. Mall, D. K. Tiwari etc., conducted Autecological studies of a number of plants. Prof. Misra, Pandeya and K.P. Singh contributed much to the Production Ecology. Still the work on Grass land Ecosystem is being done by Dr. K.C. Misra, J.S. Singh, L.P. Mall etc. Important Ecological Research centers in India are Banaras Hindu University, Saurastra Univ., Vikram Univ., Kurukshetra Univ., Punjab Univ. etc.

The environmental biology is called as Ecology which is a field of special interest these days. The term ecology, first of all described by Ernst Haeckel (1866), a German Zoologist, is derived from Greek word "Oikos" meaning "hose". Geoffroy -St. Hilaire (1859) a French Zoologist proposed the term "'Ethology" instead of ecology for the study of living being in relation to their environment.

Lankester in 1889 used the term "Bionomics" for the study of organisms and their relationship with the environment. The ecology is the study of biological interrelationship between organisms and their environment. In other words the ecology is concerned with the biology of groups of organisms and their relationship with the environment such as land, sea, fresh water etc.

The ecology is the combination of *biochemistry*, *biophysics*, *morphology* and *physiology*. Modern *ecologists* define ecology as "the study of the structure and function of nature." Here by nature we mean the animals and plants or organisms. An organism may be defined as "a self regulating and self perpetuating *physico-chemical* entity which is in state of perfect balance with the environment." The term environment includes the surroundings of the organism which .has a direct influence on it.

SUBDIVISIONS OF ECOLOGY

Early ecologists have recognized two major subdivisions of ecology in particular reference to animals or to plants, hence animal ecology and plant ecology. But when it was found that in the eco-systems plants and animals are very closely associated and *inter-related* then, both of these major ecological subdivisions became vague. However, when animals and plants are given equal emphasis, the term bioecology is used.

Further, *ecology* is often broadly divided into autecology and synecology. *Autecology* deals with the ecological study of one species of organism. Thus, an autecologist may study the life *history*, *population dynamics*, *behaviour*, home range and so on, of a single species, such as the Mexican free-tailed bat, Indian bull frog, or *maize-borer*, Chilo partellus, *Synecology* deals with the ecological studies of communities or entire ecosystems.

Thus, a synecologist might study deserts, or caves or tropical forests. He is interested in describing the overall energy and material flow through the system rather. than in concentrating on thefiner details of a particular organism. In the words of Herreid II (1977) "the two types of study, autecology and synecology, inter-relate, the synecolosist painting with a broad brush the outline of the picture and autecologist stroking in the finer details."

Besides these major ecological subdivisions, there are following specialized branches of ecology:

Habitat Ecology

It deals with ecological study of different habitats on planet earth and their effects on the organisms living there. According to the kind of habitat, ecology is subdivided into marine ecology (oceanography), estuarine ecology, fresh water ecology (limnology), and terrestrial ecology.

The terrestrial ecology in its turn is classified into *forest ecology*, *cropland ecology*, *grassland ecology*, *desert ecology*, etc., according to the kinds of study of its different habitats.

Palaeoecology

It is the study of environmental conditons, and life of the past ages, to which palynology, palaeontology, and radioactive dating methods have made significant contribution.

Systems Ecology

It is the modern branch of ecology which is particularly concerned with the analysis and understanding of the function and structure of ecosystem by the use of applied mathematics, such as advanced *statistical techniques*, *mathematical models*, characteristics of computer sciences.

Community Ecology

It deals with the study of the local distribution of animals in various habitats, the recognition and composition of community units, and succession.

Taxonomic Ecology

It is concerned with the ecology of different taxonomic groups of living organisms and. eventually includes following divisions of ecology: *microbial ecology*, *mammalian ecology*, *avian ecology*, *insect ecology*, *parasitology*, *human ecology* and so on.

Population Ecology (Demecology)

It deals with thestudy of the manner of growth, structure and regulation of population of organisms.

Applied Ecology

It deals with the application of ecological concepts to human needs and thus, it includes, following applications of ecology: *wild-life management*, *range management*, *forestry*, *conservation*, *insect control*, *epidemiology*, *animal husbandry*, *aquaculture*, *agriculture*, *horticulture*, *land use* and *pollution ecology*.

Evolutionary Ecology

It deals with the problems of niche segregation and speciation.

Production Ecology

It deals with the gross and net production of different ecosystems like fresh water, sea water agriculture, horticulture, etc., and tries to do proper management of these eco-systems so that maximum yield can be get from them.

Human Ecology

It involves population ecology or man and man's relation to the environment, especially man's effects on the biosphere and the implication of these effects for man.

Geographic Ecology (ecogeography)

It concentrates on the study of geographical distribution of animals (zoogeography) and plants (*phytogeography*), and also of *palaeoecology* and *biomes*.

Radiation Ecology

It deals with the study of gross effects of radiations and radioactive substances over the environment and living organisms.

Ecosystem Dynamics

It deals with the ecological study of the processes of soil formation, nutrient cycling, energy flow, and productivity.

Ecological Genetics

An ecologist recognised kind of genetic plasticity in the case of every organism. In any environment only those organisms that are favoured by 'he environment can survive. Thus, genecology deals with the study of variations of species based upon their genetic potentialities.

Ecological Energetics

It deals with energy conservation and its flow in the organisms within the ecosystem. In it *thermodynamics* has its significant contribution.

Chemical Ecology

It concerns with the adaptations of animals of preferences of particular organism like insects to particular chemical substances.

Pedology

It is a branch of terrestrial ecology and it deals with the study of soils, in particular their acidity, alkalinity, humus contents, mineral contents, soil-types, etc., and their influence on the organisms.

Physiological ecology (ecophysiology)

The factors of environment have a direct bearing on the functional aspects of organisms. The ecophysiology deals with the survival of populations as a result of functional adjustments of organisms with different ecological conditions.

Sociology

It is the study of ecology and ethology of mankind.

Ethology

It is the interpretation of animal behaviour under natural conditions. In it, often, detailed life history studies of particular species are amassed.

SCOPE OF ECOLOGY

Ecology is a *multidisciplinary* science and it includes not only the life sciences but *chemistry*, *physics*, *geology*, *geography meteorology*, *climatology*, *hydrology*, *palaeontology*, *archeology*, *anthropology*, *sociology* and *mathematics* and *statistics* as well.

For explaining the behaviour of an organism or biotic community in a given environment, an ecologist has to integrate the data which is obtained from many sources-*morphology*, *taxonomy*, *genetics*, *physiology*, *soil science*, *climatology*, *geology*, *physics* and *chemistry*.

The scope of ecology is quite vast. The study of ecological principles provides a background for understanding the fundamental relationships of the natural community and also the sciences dealing with particular environment such as forest, soil, ocean and inland waters.

Many practical applications of this subject are found in agriculture, *horticulture*, *forestery*, *limnology oceanography*, *fishery biology*, *biological survey*, *game management*, *pest control*, *public health*, *toxicology*, *pollution control*, *conservation*, etc. Ecological knowledge helps in discovering new sources of food (algae, krill, etc.), new unpolluting sources of energy (i.e., solar energy), and new methods of pest control such as biological control which causes no environmental pollution.

By applying certain ecological techniques, some ecologists have been successful in diagnosing the cause of desertness of certain Australian deserts and they investigated that these deserts lack certain trace elements like *zinc*, *copper* and *molybdenum*, so they called them trace element deserts (Anderson and Underwood, 1959). Now they have cured their ecological diseases and have converted them into new rich agricultural lands.

Approach to the Study of Ecology

The ecology has several methods of approaches which are given below:

(*i*) Zoological approach. In Zoological approach mainly the animals are considered while the habitat and plants are considered as the part of the environment.

(*ii*) Botanical approach. In Botanical approach mainly the plants are considered while the animals and the habitat are considered secondarily.

(*iii*) Biotic approach: Includes the *flora* and *fauna* of a particular region. This approach considers the interrelationship between plants and animals, between the plants themselves, between animals themselves and between living being and environment.

(*iv*) Habitat approach. When the study is focused mainly on the habitat, such as freshwater, marine, estuarine habitat and terrestial habitat etc. It includes forest ecology, grass land ecology, cropland ecology, desert, ecology, fresh water ecology, marine ecology etc.

(*v*) Productivity approach. It considers the yield resulting from the energy relationships between the organisms., and habitat.

(*vi*) Population approach. It includes group relations and deals with population dynamics in pure or mixed strands.

(vii) Ecosystem approach. This approach is not specific, instead it includes habitat, plants and animals together i.e., an ecosystem, like a pond or lake or part of the ground.

(*viii*) Gene-ecology. It is concerned with the genetic make up of a species or population in relation to environment.

(*ix*) Conservation ecology. It deals with the proper management of natural resources for the benefit of human beings.

(*x*) lcological Energetics. It is a recent branch of ecology which deals with the energy conservation and flow in the organisms within the ecosystem.

The ecologist focuses his attention primarily on the inter-relationship between the organism and its environment. The possible scope of ecology becomes wide the due to variable environmental conditions and more abundance of plants and animals.

The main function of ecology, however, is to show the general principle under which the natural community and its component parts operate. Then these may be applied to the interpretation of activities of the particular plants and animals found in a given situation.

The biota (flora and fauna) of an area may be identified and. counted. The physical forces may be recognised at work, yet, neither an account of biota, nor a description of the habitat makes an ecological investigation.

Similarly, if one makes a list of hydrophytes or mesophytes or xerophytes without any consideration of the relation of the occurrence of these species to other environmental factors, he cannot be called an ecologist. Modern ecology is concerned with the functional interdepe-ndence (relationship) between living things and their surroundings and it is a field subject.

The study of ecological principles provides a background for further detailed investigation not only into the fundamental relationship of the natural community but also into sciences dealing with particular environments such as forest, soil, ocean and inland waters.

Many practical applications of this subject are found in agriculture, biological survey, game management, pest control, forestry and fishery biology. An understanding of ecology is more valuable for suitable conservation, whether in relation to soil, forest, wildlife. water supply or fishery resources.

In a wider sense ecology is also significant for us as citizens because man himself is most important element in the environment. Thus the scope of ecology is not narrow but wide.

Factors of the Environment

The environment is of two types physical or non-living or abiotic and living or biotic environment. The abiotic or nonliving environment includes medium in which an organism live and climate which surrounds it. For living organisms, plants as well as animals, four types of media are available soil, water, air and bodies of other organisms.

Soil is the upper most strata of the earth which contains organic matter which is capable of nourishing vegetation. Thus the chemical composition of soil is important in determining the presence of plants and animals.

The texture of the soil has also its own significance because it regulates the moisture conservation. Water forms the important medium for aquatic animals and plants. Water plays an important role in respiration more so because protoplasm is composed of large quantity of water besides other constituents. It also helps the body in metabolism.

Air is present all around the earth in the gaseous form. Although it is a mixture of gases yet oxygen and nitrogen are present in 21 parts and 78 parts respectively. The remaining one part contains carbon-dioxide, ozon, neon, argon etc. Other constituents like organic matter, dust, *micro-organisms*, salt, *sulphates*, *water vapour* etc., are also present.

The percentage of these substances vary very much depending upon time and place and has considerable effect on climate, weather, radiation and comfort.

Bodies of organisms are found in other animals and they, live as parasites. The parasites fullfil their requirements of oxygen from internal environment of the host and protect themselves from digestive or other juices. There are very little *fluctuations* in such *environment*.

The biotic or living environment may be explained by two popular terms the intra-specific and inter-specific. The intra-specific relationship denotes the relationship between the members of the same species while inter-specific-relationship includes the relationship between the members of different species. The intra-specific relationship is governed by reproduction, assistance, competition and definite hostitity.

The reproduction affects the intra-specific-relationship. During sexual or asexual reproduction number of individuals are increased and if the rate of reproduction is high it will result to over production and leads to competition or struggle for food and space.

The assistance means the parental care or protection given; by the parents to their helpless young ones.

The competition results from over production of offspringss and limited food and shelter.

The definite hostility involves struggle over territoral limits and in the selections of mates.

According to Darwin's theory also whenever there is rapid reproduction and limited supply of food there is always struggle for exhistance and then only the fittest survives or the survival of the fittest.

The inter-specific-relationship is governed by competition for food, prey predator relations, host-parasite relations, commensalism symbiosis and slavery.

The competition amongst the members of the same species is very fierce because the needs of the members of the same species are the same as regards to food, shelter, selection of mate etc.

The prey-predator relationship denotes the feeding of one animal over other. The animal which feeds is the predator and 'which is eaten, is called as the prey. The predators can survive ,only when the prey are available or in other words the prey cannot survive if the predators are many in number.

The host-parasite relation may be complete or in part parasite may depend on its host partly or completely. The commensalism is the phenomenon in which two individuals lie in mutual reation with each other but none is dependent on other.

The symbiosis is a close *physiological* relationship that exists between members of different species completely dependent on each other. The slavery includes making of slaves. When certain social animals capture the other animals, make them slaves and utilize their services, the *phenomenon* is called as *slavery*.

2

Soil and its Weathering

Over 3 billion years ago, rain and snow fell upon the earth much as today. *Solid rocks* were reduced to grains of sand by the action of water, ice, and chemically active solutions. We know this from clues left in ancient rocks whose great *antiquity* has been established by *radioactive dating*. The processes by which rocks are broken into smaller particles and chemically decomposed have continued *unabated* down through the eras of *geologic time*.

We term these most enduring of geologic processes *weathering*. Weathering is of *enormous* importance to all of us. It causes *solid rock* to crumble and thereby *facilitates erosion*. Weathering provides much of the sediment for the making of sedimentary rocks.

Without weathering there would be no soil for the growth of plants that are vital to ourselves and all other forms of life. Weathering is a phenomenon that combines two *categories* of processes. On the one hand are those processes that result in the *fragmentation* of once solid rock without *chemical change*, as when water freezes and *expands* in crevices so as to cause the rock to break apart, or when rocks are wedged apart by the growth of roots from *trees* and *shrubs*.

These processes of physical disintegration are designated mechanical weatherinp. In contrast, chemical weathering involves the chemical decomposition of rocks as their minerals react with water and air. Mechanical and chemical weathering work together in the *destruction* of rocks at the earth's surface, although one may *predominate* over the other. In areas of extreme cold or aridity, for example, mechanical weathering may *predominate*, but in warm wet regions, chemical decomposition is the predominant kind of weathering.

Although *mechanical breakup* and *chemical decay* of a rock are partners in weathering, it is advantageous to discuss these two components of weathering separately, because disintegration involves largely mechanical *processes*, whereas decomposition *entails* the chemical interaction of water, gases, and minerals.

MECHANICAL WEATHERING

The chief agents of mechanical weathering, or disintegration, are *frost action*, *temperature changes*, *unloading*, *crystal growth*, and the *wedging action* of plant roots. Many different factors influence the efficiency of these agents in causing *disintegration*.

The composition and texture of the rocks being weathered and the presence of joints, fractures, and voids clearly affect the rate at which solid rock can be reduced to *rubble*. Mechanical weathering is also affected by climate, *opography*, and the length of time over which weathering agents have been operating.

In general mechanical weathering predominates over chemical weathering in regions characterized by extreme cold or in warm arid regions. By definition, mechanical weathering involves the physical disintegration of solid masses of rock into loose *fragments*. There is little chemical change in the rock itself. Thus, a chemical analysis of the *disintegrated* rock would be similar to that of the *parent rock*.

Frost Action

Water expands by about 9 per cent when it freezes. If ther water freezes in a confined space, pressure caused by the expansion may cause rock masses to be pushed apart and *ruptured*. Such *frost*, action has an important effect in mechanical weathering in that the *freezing* water is capable of exerting thousands of pounds of pressure per square inch.

Many of us have become aware of the effects of frost action during-severe winters-when *concrete roads* and side-walks—are cracked by-alternate-freezing and thawig The way freezing water disrupts solid rock is similar to the manner in which it breaks up streets and side-walks. After water has filled a *crack* in the rock, the water at the lip of the crack may freeze.

Once this has occurred, the water deeper in the crack is. sealed off, and as it begins to freeze and expand, it *pushes* against the walls of the fracture, and thereby widens the space between those walls. In a subsequent thaw, fragments of rock may slip down into the crack and act as wedges to hold it open.

These processes are most prevalent in areas where water is abundant and where temperatures drop to below freezing at night and then warm during the day. *Mountainous* regions in temperate zones have this kind of daily temperature change, and in such rugged regions frost action is an important weathering process.

Insolation

Rocks, like many other solids, expand when they are warmed and contract when they are cooled. The heat is provided by the sun and so geologists refer to the weathering that may result as insolation, weathering, It would seem logical that repeated daytime beating and nighttime cooling of rocks (with concurrent *expansion* and *contraction*) would weaken the boundaries between grains and eventually cause them to separate from the rock mass.

Most geologists believe that insolation is only a minor contribulor to mechanical weathering. Its effect is usually obscured by other weathering processes.

Perhaps in desert regions where there are *large-scale* fluctuations in temperature, insolation may have some effect in weathering rocks.

Unloading

Quarrymen and *miners* are well aware that when the heavy weight of rock is removed from a mine with consequent loss of support to the surrounding rock, the outside pressure may sometimes cause 4 veritable explosion of rock fragments into the excavations.

In nature, erosion may similarly remove large volumes of surface rock, thus lightening the load on deeper rock and allowing it to expand. Because the mass of rock is still confined on all sides, it can only respond to the release of pressure by *expanding* upwards. As it expands it will rupture and form joints that are roughly parallel to the surface *topography*.

The process is called *unloading*, and the joint systems are referred to as sheeting. Sheeting is often seen in granite and other massive crystalline rocks that have been laid bare by glaciation or running water. It can also be readily observed along the upper walls of quarries, where it may even facilitate the removal of the stone.

Sheeting provides planar passageways along which solution and frost action may proceed *vigorously*. Half Dome at-Yosemite National

Park and Stone Mountain, Georgia, are examples of mountains whose shape has been controlled, at least partially, by sheeting.

Saline Crystal Growth

The growth of *crystals*, especially crystals of *sodium chloride*, *calcium sulphate*, or *magnesium sulphate* have been found to cause scaling in exposed rock surfaces and to *dislodge grains* and crystals from their parent rock.

The process is particularly effective in porous rocks in which crystals exert large expansive stresses as they grow. Disintegration of building stone because of the growth of crystals in pore spaces has been a vexing problem for *architects* involved in the preservation of historica!ly important buildings.

The Temples at Luxor, Egypt, for example, have been seriously damaged by alternate solution and *crystallization* of salt. During dry spells, magnesium (and calcium) sulphate have been known to crystallize along zones of weakness in the dolomitic building stones of London's Houses of *Parliament*, thereby causing *spalling* and *crumbling* at a rate that has caused considerable anxiety among *restoration* specialists.

The magnesium sulfate is formed as a result of a chemical reaction between coal smoke and the maguesium in the dolomite.

Root Wedging

When one observes the growth of a plant from a seed, it is apparent that even a frail seedling is capable of exerting sufficient force to push aside relatively *firm soil*. As they grow into rock *fractures* and *expand*, the roots of large plants such as trees can exert correspondingly greater forces and are capable of widening cracks and accelerating the rate of disintegration by significant amounts.

When the plant dies and the roots decay, they leave openings in which freezing water may accumulate and further widen the void space. Plants also react with rocks chemically, as will be described in the following section.

CHEMICAL WEATHERING

Chemical weathering refers to the decomposition of rocks at or near the earth's surface and under relatively low temperatures. During chemical weathering, water and chemically active water solutions as well as oxygen and carbon dioxide from the *atmospheieattack* the minerals *comprising* rocks.

The susceptible parent minerals are frequently altered to softer secondary minerals, as when *feldspars* are converted to clay minerals and lose certain ions to solution. Chemical weathering is an exceedingly important process, for it leads to the formation of soils and in some parts of the world has resulted in the *concentration* of *iron*, *aluminum*, *uranium*, *gold*, and *tin*.

Relation of Disintegration to Decomposition

The processes of chemical weathering and mechanical weathering are not truly independent of one another. Because of *climatic factors*, especially the amount and frequency of rainfall, one or the other process may be *dominant* in a particular location.

For the most part, however decomposition and disintegration are interacting processes. For example, disintegration greatly promotes decomposition by reducing large intact rock masses to accumulations of smaller fragments.

This fragmentation provides more total surface area for chemical attack than was originally present in the larger mass of rock. One can see what happens readily by imagining a block of rock measuring 2 meters on each edge. Such a block would have a total of 24 square meters of surface area.

If the block is split once along each of three perpendicular planes, each resulting block would have 6 square meters of surface area or a total of 48 square meters for all eight pieces. Chemically reactive solutions are only able to decompose surfaces they can reach, and so the rate of chemical attack is enhanced by increasing surface area.

One can demonstrate this fact by applying a few drops of dilute hydrochloric acid first to an unfragmented piece of calcite and then to a similar piece of calcite that has been *pulverized*. Because of the greater amount of total surface area, the *pulverized* rock will display the more *vigorous* efferve scence.

Processes of Chemical Weathering

People sometimes are surprised to learn that many rocks. exposed at the earth's surface are really not in chemical *equilibrium* with their environment but rather are unstable and are slowly but continuously reacting with *atmospheric* components, to dissolve or change to new substances that are more nearly stable at the earth's surface.

Geologically, weathering proceeds in accordance with a generalization called the *rule of stability*, which states that a mineral approaches stability most closely in an environment similar to that in which it formed.

Intrusive igneous rocks, of course, are formed under conditions of high temperature, high pressure, and a deficiency of free oxygen and fresh water. When such rocks are *laid bare* on the continents, they find themselves, in an environment of low temperature, *low pressure*, and *abundant* oxygen and water.

Chemical change is *inevitable*, and the minerals most susceptible to change are those that formed under physical and chemical conditions most removed from conditions at the earth's surface. For example, among the common rock-forming *silicate minerals*, olivine forms at high temperatures and pressures early in the *crystallization* of a *magma*.

Consequently, it rapidly weathers in the environments that exist at the earth's surface. *Quartz* forms much later under less extreme conditions of temperature and pressure and is less susceptible to weathering. In reference to the *Browen Reaction Series* it is apparent that minerals nearer the top of the series generally weather more rapidly than those near the base.

We noted how silicon-oxygen tetrahedra are joined together by 'eharing some oxygen ions and that the number of *metallic* ions needed to neutralize the *crystal* is reduced by this sharing. This increased lbxygen sharing by silicon results in a greater number of strong *covalent* like bonds between silicon and oxygen, and this in turn greatly increases the ability of the minetal to resist weathering.

For example, the ratio of oxygen to silicon in olivine is 4, in pryoxene 3, in hornblende 2.7, in biotite 2.5 and in quartz 2. The diminishing ratios correlate nicely with greater resistance to weathering. All of the oxygen atoms are shared by *silicon atoms* in *quartz*, and this *partially* accounts for its great resistance to weathering.

The chemical weathering of rocks involves reactions that are interrelated, that may occur *simultaneously*, and that utilize water, oxygen, carbon dioxide, and *organic acids*. These processes include *hydrolysis*, *oxidation*, *carbonation*, *solution*, *hydration*, and *chemical* changes induced by the growth of plants.

Hydrolysis

Hydrolysis is a chemical reaction between a mineral and water. It involves a reaction between the H^+ or OH^- ions in the water and relatively active *metallic ions* such as *sodium*, *calcium*, *potassium* and *magnesium*. *Hydrolysis* is particularly important in causing the decomposition of *silicate minerals*.

Although it may occur in the presence of pure water, in nature hydrolysis nearly always involves *carbon dioxide*. To illustrate, small. quantities of carbon dioxide from the atmosphere or soil are dissolved in water to form carbonic acid.

$$\underset{\text{water}}{H_2O} + \underset{\text{carbon dioxide}}{CO_2} \rightleftarrows \underset{\text{carbonic acid}}{H_2CO_3}$$

The carbonic acid may then ionize to form hydrogen ions and bicarbonate ions.

$$\underset{\text{carbonic acid}}{H_2CO_3} \rightleftarrows \underset{\text{hydrogen ion}}{H^+} + \underset{\text{bicarbonate ion}}{(HCO_3)^-}$$

Next, the hydrogen ions penetrate into the crystal lattices of silicate minerals such as potassium feldspar. They have little difficulty in gaining admission because of their small size, and once within the lattice, they *disrupt* the charge balance as they displace cations such as potassium.

$$\underset{\text{water}}{H_2O} + \underset{\text{hydrogen ions}}{2H^+} + \underset{\text{potassium feldspar}}{2(K\ Al\ Si_3O_3)} \rightarrow$$

$$\underset{\text{potassium ions}}{2K^+} + \underset{\text{kaolinite clay}}{Al_2Si_2O_6(OH)_4} + \underset{\text{silica}}{4(SiO_2)}$$

The potassium ions released from the feldspar may becarried away in solution, utilized by plants, or become incorporated into clay minerals. A small part of the silica is removed in solution, although the greater part remains in the clay-rich weathered residue.

Carbonation

As implied by the term, carbonation involves the chemical addition of carbon dioxide to earth materials. Carbon dioxide. in the atmosphere (and in the air trapped within soils) is readily absorbed bo water to form carbonic acid.

Although relatively weak, carbonic acid nevertheless has a pervasive cumulative effect in the chemical weathering of a variety of different kinds of rocks. It, is involved in the dissolution of common silicate minerals and is particularly effective in dissolving limestones and dolostones. The reaction for limestone is indicated below.

$$\underset{\text{water}}{H_2O} + \underset{\text{carbon dioxide}}{CO_2} \rightarrow \underset{\text{carbonic acid}}{H_2CO_3}$$

$$\underset{\text{carbonic acid}}{H_2CO_3} + \underset{\text{calcite (in limestone)}}{CaCO_3} \rightarrow \underset{\text{soluble calcium bicarbonate}}{Ca(HCO_3)_2}$$

In older for carbonation to occur, water must be readily available. For this reason carbonation is most vigorous in most. climates. In the weathering of *silicate minerals*, *carbonation* and *hydrolysis* work together as the earth's most important processes for achieving decompo-sition of rocks.

The hydrolysis component provides clay minerals and takes silica into solution, while *simultaneously* carbonation removes metallic elements as ions in solution.

Oxidation

Oxidation, the addition of oxygen to a compound, is one of the main kinds of changes produced in rocks by chemical weathering. Oxygen has a strong affinity for iron, which may be present in such *silicate minerals* as *hornblende*, and *olivine*, as well as *sulphides* such as *pyrite* (FeS,).

The oxidation of the iron (essentially what we call rusting) takes place chiefly in the presence of atmospheric moisture and results in the range, of red and brown colourations we see in soils, and weathered rocks. In the oxidation process, oxygen gas dissolved in water reacts with iron to from *hematite* (Fe_2O_3) or *limonite* ($Fe_2O_3 \cdot H_2O$). The process is illustrated by the following formula:

$$\underset{\text{iron}}{4Fe} + \underset{\text{oxygen}}{3O_2} + \underset{\text{water}}{nH_2O} \rightarrow \underset{\text{"limonite" iron hydroxide or "rust"}}{2(Fe_2O_3) \cdot nH_2O}$$

The oxidation of a common nonsilicate such as pyrite (fool's gold") involves combining oxygen with both and sulphur as follows;

$$\underset{\text{pyrite}}{4FeS_2} + \underset{\text{water}}{nH_2O} + \underset{\text{oxygen}}{15O_2} \rightarrow \underset{\text{"limonite"}}{2Fe_2O_3 \cdot nH_2O} + \underset{\text{sulphuric acid}}{8H_2SO_4}$$

Here, the relatively insoluble iron compounds may remain as a coating on the rock, whereas the *sulphdric acid* is leached away and becomes available for chemical reactions with other minerals.

Hydration is a process whereby water is absorbed by a mineral and incorporated into the weathering product. For example the mineral anhydrite (CaSO,) may take in water to become *alabaster gypsum* ($CaSO_4 \cdot nH_2O$), or hematite (Fe_2O_3) may be converted to *limonite* ($Fe_2O_3 \cdot nH_2O$).

Hydration is an important process in the development of clay and accounts for the presence of water within many *clay minerals*. Another aspect of hydration is that the *hydrated mineral*, because of the water it has taken up, larger than the parent mineral. The increase in volume causes growing hydrated *crystals* to exert pressure on the walls of the spaces they occupy, and such pressure may contribute to rock disintegration.

Solution

We have seen how the dissolving power of water for certain rocks and minerals is increased when carbon dioxide is present. Even without the addition of car bon dioxide, however, water has the ability to dissolve *rocks* and *minerals*. The dissolving away of thick beds of salt and gypsum is an example of simple solution *weathering*.

A quartz sandstone also may weather by solution, although the process is exceedingly slow because of the low *solubility of quartz*. The ability of water to dissolve substances is related to the *configuration* and *electrical properties* of the water *molecule* itself.

A water molecule consists of a large strongly negative oxygen ion and two hydrogen ions. The hydrogen ions have contributed their electrons to the molecule and thus exist as two small positively charged protons. Both of the protons are located on the same side of the molecule, so that it has an *electrically* positive side and an electrically negative side. It is termed a *dipolar molecule*.

The electrical charges at either end of the water rmolecule not only attract their opposites in other water)molecules but also attract compounds in rocks and minerals that likewise have separate centers of positive and negative *electrical* charge. These compounds are taken into solution as weathering proceeds.

Biochemical Weathering

Rooted plants also play a role in the weathering of materials at the surface of the earth. During *photosynthesis*, *plants utilize* the energy of the sun's radiatian to combine water and carbon dioxide and produce tissue necessary for *growth* and *maintinance*.

Part of the hydrogen from *moisture* taken in by the plant is released at the surface of rootlets where it exchanged for ions of *calcium*, *magnesium* and *sodium* from adjacent particles of clay and other minerals. These exchanged ions are required by the plant for nutrition.

The hydrogen ions transferred to the clay particles render the play slightly acidic, and this triggers weathering reactions with neighbouring *feldspars* and other *silicates*. Eventually, some of these minerals also decompose to clay, thus *perpetuating* the weathering process.

RATES OF WEATHERING

The Role of Climate

How rapidly a particular exposure rock will weather is dependent on several different interacting factors in the environment. Climate is important because it controls temperature and rainfall. Warmer temperatures, of course, promote chemical reaction. Even an increase of as little as 10°C can double reaction rates.

Similarly, high rainfall *accelerates* rates of weathering by increasing the possibilities for solution and reaction and by helping to wash away surface debris and expose fresh surfaces for chemical attack. Both higher temperatures and an *abundance* of moisture promote the growth of plants, and *luxuriant* plant growth assists in weathering by extracting ions from minerals and adding chemically reactive compounds.

The importance of temperature and rainfall is at least partly evident in the thickness of loose material or regolith that develops over bedrock under various climatic conditions.

In temperate regions having level topography, the layer of regolith is usually only about a meter deep, whereas in similar *topography* of the *tropics*, the loose material may from a blanket tens of meterss thick. Arctic areas are only thinly covered by regolith.

Parent Rock

Depending on their composition, texture, and such features as fractures and joints, rocks exposed at the earth's surface may exhibit a wide range of resistance to weathering. *Limestones* and *dolostones*, for example, are highly susceptible to solution.

In regions having high rainfall, these rocks weather more rapidly than in arid regions. This observation suggests that it is. difficult to list rocks in the order of their resistance to weathering because a rock might be more *durable* than another under one set of conditions and the same rock less durable under different conditions.

As a general rule, igneous and metamorphic rocks are more resistant to weathering than *sedimentary rocks*. A *silica-cemented* quartz sandstone, however, is among the most *enduring* of rock types.

Statues and other sculptured edifices that have actual dates carved into the stone permit one to assess rates of weathering. In cities, because of the higher levels of carbon and sulphur dioxides, chemical weathering rates are generally higher than in non-industrialized areas. The bust of Beethoven was erected in a St. Louis park in 1884.

In spite of many attempts to treat the Italian Carrara marble from which the bust was carved, it continued to *decompose*. The composer's gruff expression has been so altered that St. Louisans refer to the statue as "poor Beethoven.

The texture of the parent rock will also influence its *susceptibility* to weathering. In general, coarsergrained porous varieties of rocks of the sam e com position tend to w eather m ore rapidly-than dense *finegrained* varieties. Rocks that have a large number of fractures provide a greater amount of surface area for chemical attack and therefore are also more readily weathered.

Acid Rain

Rates of chemical weathering are, to be Tsure, affected by the acidity of the solutions that attack rocks and minerals. As described above even unpolluted rainwater contains *carbon dioxide* and is slightly acidic. In recent years, however, this weak natural carbonic acid has been *augmented* by strong acids formed where rain has fallen through air polluted with oxides of nitrogen and sulphur.

This acidic precipitation includes both nitric and *sulphuric acid*. It is called acid rain. Acid rain commonly exceeds the natural acidity of rainwater by more than 200 times, and in a few instances by over 1000 times. If not neutralized by *alkaline rocks* and *soils*, the acid accumulates in lakes and *streams* where it is often lethal to fish and other forms of aquatic life.

Acid rain also damages the *foliage* of plants and reduces the quality of soil by leaching away nutrients. The acid solutions attack limestone, marble, and *concrete* building materials and damage valuable works of art.

Presently, millions of dollars are being expended in acid rain research in the hope ope that a solution to the problem can be found. Aside from local chemical treatment of particular areas, however, a long-term solution must involve reduction in *atmospheric* pollutants that form acid rain.

SPHEROIDAL WEATHERING

Spheroidal weathering is a term used to describe the spalling away of concentric surphicial shells of the rounded surface of a boulder or rock mass. Such "onion-skin" weathering its believed to result primarily from the mechanical effects of chemical weathering. When *feldspars* decompose the clay product has a greater volume than the parent feldspar.

The increase in volume disrupts the interlocking texture of mineral grains in the rock and causes *breakage* and *separation* of the layer of partially weathered rock near the surface. Corners of *roughly* rectangular blocks broken loose along joints are decomposed along three surfaces *simultaneously* and are progressively rounded by spalling until the rock mass assumes the *spheroidal* form.

Spheroidal weathering operates most effectively on relatively small rock masses such as those of boulder size. The kind of spheroidal weathering involving a larger-scale breaking off of *concentric plates* from bare rock surfaces is referred to as *exfoliation*.

Rocks that have experienced exfoliation may resemble those having sheet structure, but while sheet structure is caused by release of pressure when overlying rock masses are removed by *erosion*, all forms of *spheroidal* weathering result from physical and chemical weathering.

THE DECAY OF GRANITE

The mineral alterations involved in chemical weathering are nicely illustrated by the decay of a granitic parent rock. *Granite* is a common igneous rock composed of about two parts *orthoclase*, one part quartz, one part *plagioclase*, and small amounts of *ferromagnesian minerals*.

Where masses of granite have been exposed for a long period of time, one may find places where the weathered products of the granite have not been washed away but have accumulated as a *clayey granular* residue.

On close examination, this material is, found to consist quartz grains, partly decayed and *clay-coated feldspars*, *rust-coloured particles* of partially decayed ferromagne sian minerals, and clay. The quartz grains in the weathered material are relatively unaltered because of the great resistance quartz has to chemical attack.

As other minerals in the granite decompose around them, quartz grains are freed from the rock matrix, later to be transported and deposited as sand, and perhaps ultimately to become components of *sandstone*.

Granite provides a good example of differential weathering, by which its various components weather at different rates. We have noted that feldspars are aluminosilicates of potassium, sodium and calcium. In the *weathering process*, *potassium*, *sodium*, and *calcium* are largely dissolved and carried away in solution.

Subsequently they may be combined with other elements and incorporated into sedimentary rocks. At least some of the potassium is retained in newly forming clay minerals. The remaining *aluminum* and *silicon* in the feldspars become the chief *ingredients* of clay and this accounts for the coating of clay frequently found around *feldspar* grains and the clay residue found adjacent to bodies of weathering. granite. Later, this same clay may find its way into the making of sedimentary rocks like shale and claystone.

During the decomposition of the ferron)agnesian minerals present in the granite source rock, potassium, sodium, and calcium are dissolved in the same way as inthe *fieldspars*. Again, *aluminum* and *silicon* go into the construction of clay minerals. The ions that remain are iron and magnesium.

The iron combines readily with oxygen to form iron oxide minerals such as hsmatite (Fe_2O_3) and hydrous iron oxide minerals like goethite, FeO(OH). These iron *minerals* colour sediment and rocks in tints of yellow, orange, and brown. Finally, the magnesium that is derived from parent *ferromagnesian* minerals may find its way into limey sediments or become a component of certain clay minerals.

SOIL

In terms of importance to human populations, the most significant aspect of weathering is in the development of soil. Soil can be defined as weathered material that will support the growth of rooted plants. A heap of quartz sand is not soil according to this definition, for it will not support *vegetation*. Nor is the so-called "*lunar soil*" of the moon a true soil.

It is merely disintegrated mineral matter and should more properly be termed regolith. *Regolith* refers to the debris of rock and mineral matter that rests on solid bedrock. It includes *soil*, *alluvium*, and *weathered fragments* of the *bedrock*. Soil is not a mere accumulation of particles derived from *mechanical* and *chemical* weathering.

It is a vital natural material that would not develop were it not for the activities of a myriad of bacteria, fungi, worms, and insects. Actually, soil can be considered an *intricate mixture* of *mineral solids*, *water*, *gases*, *dissolved substances*, remains of dead organisms, and multitudes of *thriving organisms*. Why is a certain amount of organic material necessary in order for weathered material to support the growth of *rooted plants*?

One reason is that the organic material supplies nutrients required for vigorous plant growth. Plants need nitrogen in order to synthesize protein, but they are unable to take free nitrogen (N_2) from the air. Certain soil *bacteria*, however, are able to use this free nitrogen and convert it into usable fixed nitrogen compounds (nitrates).

Also, the decaying vegetation and animal waste contain ammonia (NH_3) the nitrogen of which can be utilized by most plants. The material that colours the upper parts of many soils gray or black is called humus. Humus is organic material that is so thoroughly decayed that one cannot discern the nature of the parent organisms.

This essential organic mixture increases the prorosity and water-holding capacity of the soil, provides a buffer against rapid changes in acidity, and assists in the retention of chemicals needed as plant nutrients.

Carbon dioxide liberated by *humus* will, as we have noted, combine with water to form a weak acid *capable* of dissolving calcium carbonate. Once the calcium is separated from the *carbonate* part of a compound, chemicals in humus known as *chelating agents*, bond to the calcium and prevent it from again forming $CaCO_3$.

Most plants are unable to extract the calcium they need directly from $CaCO_3$, but they have evolved mechanisms for releasing the chelated calcium that exists in humus.

Factors Governing Soil Development

Five factors are involved in soil formation. These are climate, parent material, topography, time, and biologic activity. Of these factors, climate is of greatest importance. Indeed, soil types and climate are so closely related that maps showing *global* distribution of climates resemble maps showing the occurence of different soil types.

Temperature and *rainfall*, of course, influence not only rates of weathering but the nature of vegetation. Given enough time, soil-informing *processes* operating within a given climate will prevail over differences in parent material and provide a basically climate-controlled soil type. The reserve is also true.

Identical rocks in temperate high-rainfall regions and in semitropical arid regions will produce quite different soils. The influence of parent material on the formation of soils is of secondary importance but can be observed in soils that have recently developed from *unaltered bedrock*. Such soils stills retain *textural* and *mineral* components that are derived from the parent *rock* but which may become obscured after the soil has evolved to a further stage.

In some cases, various influences of parent material will persist in the developing soil. Soils develaped above quartz sandstones may tend to be more acidic than soils formed on *limestones*, and these differences will be reflected by the natural vegetation living on each soil type. Soils forming on rocks that are deficient in certain elements such as *magnesium* or *boron* will ordinarily also lack these constituents.

Not all soils are developed from underlying *consolidated bedrock*. Many fine *agricultural* soils are formed on loosely consolidated sediment laid down by streams, winis, glaciers, or the waters of lakes. Topography also influences the ultimate nature of soils.

On steep slopes, for example, erosion is usually more vigorous and the soil layer *generally thinner*. Also, water falling on slopes is partially lost to runoff, and therefore there is less water available for *percolation* into deeper layers of soil. Even the direction of slope may have a bearing on soil development.

In the northern *hemisphere*, *slopes* facing toward the south tend to be warmer and dryer and therefore support quite different kinds of plants than do the *northern slopes*. The factor of time in soil formation is often not fully appreciated by those who clear away soil for construction or mining and expect nature to *quickly* restore this important resource.

The development of soil is an exceedingly slow process. Depending on climatic conditions, several hundred to several thousands of years are required to produce a fertile soil. *Agricultural* soils formed during this lengthy natural process may be lost to erosion in only a few years, particularly in areas where soil conservation measures are not followed.

The problem is not trivial, for an estimated 3 billion metric tons of good agricultural soil is lost each year from agricultural fields in the United States alone.

Soil Horizons

Soils are not uniform in texture and *composition* from bedrock to the surface but rather consist of a number of *fairly distinct* ayers or soil horizons, which differ in composition and physical characteristics. The stack of *soil horizons* is called a *soil profile*.

A simple profile, such as might develop in a humid region on granitic rock, has three distinct divisions. Soil scientists have named these layers the A, B, and C horizons. The A horizon, also known as "top soil," which lies immediately *beneath* the *surface*, is characterized by a high content of organic matter.

It is also a zone in which soluble compounds are dissolved and, along with fine clay particles, carried downward to be deposited in the underlying B horizon. Becauses of these losses, the A horizon is referred to as leached or eluviated, whereas the B layer is sometimes called the washed in or illuviated zone.

Iron and clay minerals tend to accumulate in the B layer. In humid regions one can often recognize the B horizon by its more brownish colour and clayey texture. The C horizon of the soil' profile consists of partially altered parent material. In it one finds evidence of chemical weathering, but soil development has not progressed to the level at which the original characteristics of the bedrock are unrecognizable. Beneath the C horizon lies unaltered parent material.

Soils developed on *limestones* in humid regions often do not exhibit a clear division between the B and C horizons. In such soils, the A horizon consists of dark humus-rich material that changes downward into relatively light coloured clay and then stained and *partly* dissolved limestone.

The clays in these soils are residues of clay impurities left when the limestone was. dissolved. How does the sequence of soil horizons develop in a humid region underlain by granitic rock? Imagine that glacination has recently stripped away all loose sediment over a granite outcrop. Initially, *disintegration* and *decomposition* of the granite will produce a sandy layer composed mostly of grains of quartz the feldspar along with clay *derived* from the weathering of silicate minerals.

As the layer of granular material thickens, plants establish themselves, and organic material from a variety of sources becomes incorporated into the surface layer. Meanwhile, with each rainfall, soluble ions and *clay particles* are flushed downward from the surface layer into a lower level.

This lower level soon takes on the clayey character of the B horizon. While these events are taking place, solutions reaching still deeper continue the chemical attack on the parent material, thus perpetuating the C horizon.

MAJOR KINDS OF SOILS

Soil scientists employ a rather complex nomenclature for thee great variety of soil types present at one place or another around the globe. Fortunately, most of the names in these lengthy classifications can be avoided if one desires only a general understanding of a few major kinds of soils.

For example, the soils that *predominate* in the eastern United States and southeastern Canada are called predalfers. The name was fabricated to emphasize the fact that in such soils aluminium (al) and iron (fer) have been leached from the A horizon and deposited in the underlying B horizon.

Pedalfers are *clayey soils* that develop in regions having an abundance of rainfall: As this water percolates through the humus, it becomes acid, and this accounts for its ability to leach *aluminium* and iron from the topsoil. It is also effective in dissolving *carbanates*, which are then carried away by ground water. The acidity of some pedalfers may diminish their fertility, and so farmers often spread finely ground limestone (*agricultural lime*) on their fields to *combat* the actidity.

As a consequence of the fact that the top soil or A horizon in *pedalfers* is *leached*, it is usually a lighter colour than the underlying subsoil where iron has *accumulated*. *Pedalfers* include several lesser categories of soils, which differ in their profiles.

Most important among these are podzols, which typically have an ashy gray A horizon. In the more arid regions of the world, less humus develops in soils, and there is less opportunity for solution and leaching. In the absence of *water*, *chemical*, *weathering* is slower, and less clay is produced.

Usually, there is insufficient ground water to flush soluble materials such as calcite out of the B horizon, so it accumulates there as soil moisture is lost by evaporation. Because of the persistence of calcite in these soils, they are called pedocals (*pedon*, *soil*, and call for *calcium carbonate*).

Frequently in dry areas, there is not only insufficient water to cause downward leaching, but there is an upward movement of water because of the high rate of evaporation at the surface. Mineral matter dissolved in the diminishing soil water is precipitated at the surface as a hardpan or caliche layer.

In the hot and humid regions of the tropics, the characteristic soils are laterites. The term "laterite" is derived from the Latin word latere or brick, and originally referred to the use of this material to make bricks in India and Cambodia.

Laterites have a telatively thin organic layer covering a reddish leached layer, which is often underlain by a still darker red layer. In laterites, oxidation and hydrolysis have been so intense that feldspars and ferromagnesian minerals are completely decayed. Not only is calcium carbonate removed, but also silica. Only the most *insoluble* compounds, mainly aluminium and iron oxides, accumulate in these soils.

Although laterites may support a lush growth of natural tropical vegetation, they are not good agricultural soils. When forested areas with *lateritic soils* are cleared and *plowed*, the thin organic cover tends to be rapidly oxidized in the *prevailing* warm climates.

A thick accumulation of organic matter such as that found in rich black soils of more temperate regions cannot develop. After a few years of tilling and *planting*, the organic component of the soil is so depleted that fields must be *abandoned*.

In some *laterites*, the concentration of either iron or aluminium may reach levels that permit the deposits to be profitably mined. The iron-rich laterites originate from the weathering of parent materials that also contained iron, although not concentrated into ore bodies. Extensive lateritic ores of iron occur in *Cuba*, *Columbia*, *Venezuela*, and the *Philippines*.

If there is little iron in the parent material and an abundance of aluminium, then laterites rich in hydrated aluminium oxides map form. Such *materials* are called *bauxites*. *Ancient* bauxite deposits are mined in *Guyana*, *Ghana*, *northern Queensland*, and *Arkansas*.

Concentration of bauxite takes place in tropical areas of low relief where temperatures exceed 25°C most of the time and where there is an abundance of water for leaching and chemical reactions. At the present time, bauxite is the only are from which it is economically practical to extract aluminium.

Soil Erosion

It takes nature thousands of years to produce a fertile soil. That same soil can be lost to erosion in only a few decades. Clearly, as we attempt to feed our expanding world population, care must be taken to prevent unnecessary erosional losses of this vital resource.

Soil erosion results primarily from uncontrolled runoff of surface water. In areas that have never been tilled, soil is protected by a cover of plants, and there is an approximate balance between the slow loss of soil by *erosion* and the development of new soil from underlying *parent material*.

Whenever the protective shield of vegetation is, broken, however, erosion will follow. There, are, of course, natural events that can destroy the vegetative cover. These include droughts, plagues of insects, epidemics of *plant disease*, and fires caused by lightning.

Agriculture, however, has been a far more potent factor in causing erosional loss of soils. Some of the erosion resulting, from farming is unavoidable. We must have food, and so we must break into the natural *vegetative cover*.

There are, however, farming methods that reduce the loss of valuable topsoil to erosion, and these methods are practiced widely. For, example, farmers now plow and plant their crops in rows that follow contours so that rainwater is retained rather than allowed to run off.

Efforts are made to reduce the amount of timebetween preparation of the soil for planting and planting itself so that the bare soil will not remain exposed to erosion for long periods. Strip-cropping is also practiced. This technique involves planting alternate bands of erosion-resistant crops such as clover and alfalfa with open-spaced crops like corn.

Soil losses in the erosion-susceptible corn strip are trapped in the .adjacent strip of denser crops. Where fields are *temporarily* not utilized, soil-holding "*cover*" crops are planted, not only to retard *erosion* but to improve the soil by adding nitrogen.

Because ordinary grass in an effective retardant for erosion, overgrazing by cattle and sheep must be prevented. One of the most troublesome erosional problems faced by farmers is the control of gullies. Gullies start in either natural depressions or plow furrows and generally extend themselves toward higher ground by a process called *headward* erosion.

The gully head receives rainwash from a wide area. This water converges so as to(flow rapidly into the steep depression at the upper end of)the gully, eroding vigorously as it enters the channel. It is this rapid erosion that causes the gully to cut ever farther in the headward or upslope *direction*.

To halt this destructive process, steps can be taken that prevent water from entering the gully. Normally this is done by *excavating* a shallow diversion ditch around the gully head to trap its potential water supply and "*starve*" the gully. Because gullies grow by headward erosion, disposing of old *refrigerators* and *automobiles* in these ditches has no effect at all in retarding their growth.

3

UTILIZATION OF WATER

An ecosystem is a basic functional unit of nature comprising ·both organisms and their nonliving environment, intimately linked by a variety of *biological*, *chemical* and *physical processes*. The living and nonliving components interact among themselves and with each other; they influence each other's properties, and both, are essential for the *maintenance*, and development of the system.

An ecosystem, then, can be visualized as a grouping of components-living organisms, organic debris, available nutrients, primary and secondary minerals and atmospheric gases-linked by food webs, flows of nutrients and flows of energy.

A typical forest ecosystem might be visualized as a 1,000hectare stand of mature deciduous forest. (A hectare is 2.47 acres.) The lateral boundaries of the system can be either an -edge of the stand or an arbitrarily determined line. The upper boundary is the treetop level, and the lower one is the *deepest level* of soil where significant biological activity takes place. *Nutrients* are found in four basic compartments of the *ecosystem* that are intimately linked by an array of natural processes.

The organic compartment consists of the living organisms and their debris. (There are probably more than 2,500 species of plants and animals in a 1,000-hectare system.) The available-*nutrient compartment* is composed of nutrients held on the surface of particles of the clay-*humus complex* of the soil or in solution in the soil.

Roots as they grow produce positively charged hydrogen ions that exchange with the nutrient ions (of *calcium*, *magnesium* and so on) held on the negatively charged particles, and the nutrients are then taken up by the roots. The third compartment consists of soil and rocks containing nutrients in forms temporarily unavailable to living organisms. The atmospheric *compartment* is made up of gases, which can be found on only in the air but also in the ground. *Nutrients* can flow between these compartments along a variety of *pathways*.

In most cases the flow is powered directly or indirectly by solar energy. Available nutrients are taken up and assimilated by vegetation and *microorganisms*. They also -*circulate* in complex food webs within the organic compartment, subsequently being made available again through decomposition or leaching.

Minerals in soil and rock are decomposed by weathering, so that nutrients are made available to organisms. Sometimes available nutrients are returned to the soil-and-rock compartment through the formation of new minerals such as clay. Nutrients tend to cycle between the organic, *available nutrient* and soil-and-rock compartments, forming an *intra-system cycle*.

Nutrients in gaseous form are continually being transferred to and form other compartments by inorganic chemical reactions such as oxidation and reduction and by organic reactions related to such processes as *photosynthesis*, *respiration* and the *fixation* and *volatilization* of nitrogen. As ecosystem is connected to the surrounding *biosphere* by its system\of inputs and outputs.

They arrive or leave in such forms as radiant energy, gases, inorganic chemicals and organic substances. Inputs apd outputs can be transported across ecosystem boundaries by *iueteorologica* forces such as precipitation and wind, *geological forces* as running water and gravity and *biological* vectors involving the movement of animals in and out of the system.

The nutrient cycle is closely connected to the water cycle: precipitation brings nutrients in, water leaches them from rocks and soil and stream flow carries them away. Hence one cannot measure the input and output of nutrients without *simultaneously* measuring the input and output of water.

The problem usually is that subsurface flows of water, which can be a significant fraction of the *hydrologic cycle*, are almost impossible to, measure. Several years ago it occurred to us that under certain; circumstances the interaction of the *nutrient cycle* and the *hydrologic cycle* could be turned to good advantage in the study of an *ecosystem*.

The requirements are that the ecosystem be a watershed underlain by tight bedrock or some other *impermeable base*. In that case the only inputs would be *meteorological* and *biological*, *geological* input need not be considered because there would be no transfer between adjacent water, sheds. In humid areas where surface wind is a minor factor losses from the system would be only geological and biological.

Given an *impermeable* base, all the geological output would inevitably turn up in the streams draining the watershed. If the watershed is part of a larger and fairly homogeneous biotic unit, the *biological* output tends to balance the *biological* input because animals move randomly in and out of the *watershed, randomly* acquiring or *discharging nutrients.*

Thus one need measure only the meteorological input and the geological output of nutrients in order to arrive at the net gain or loss of a given nutrient in the ecosystem. We measure the *meteorological* inputs to these *watersheds* by means of a network of *gauging stations.*

We measure the geological outputs by means of a weir built at the foot of each watershed, that is, at the point where the principal stream leaves the *watershed.* With the weir, which also includes a ponding basin, one scan both measure the water that is leaving the watershed and, by combining these data with frequent chemical measurements, ascertain the quantities of chemical substances that are leaving the watershed.

Inasmuch as the impermeable base prohibits deep seepage in these watersheds, the loss of water by evaporation and by transpiration through leaves is calculated by subtracting the hydrologic output from the hydrologic input. Water budgets for the six watersheds from 1955 to 1968 indicate an average annual precipitation of 123 centimetres and a runoff of 72 centimetres, with *evapotranspiration* therefore averaging 51 centimetres.

Precipitation is distributed rather evenly throughout the year, but runoff is uneven. Most of the runoff (57%) occurs during the snow-melt period of March, April and May; indeed, 35 per cent of the total runoff occurs in April. In contrast, only 7 per cent of the yearly runoff takes place in August.

We accomplish chemical measurements by taking weekly samples of the water output (stream water at the weir) and collecting the total weekly water input (rain and snow) and analyzing them for *calcium, magnesium, potassium, sodium, aluminium, ammonium, nitrate, sulphate, chloride, bicarbonate, hydrogen ion* and *silicate.*

The concentrations of these elements in precipitation and in stream water are entered in a computing system, where weekly *concentrations* are *multiplied* by the weekly volume of water entering and leaving the ecosystem.

In this way the input and output of *chemicals* is computed in terms of kilograms of an element per hectare of watershed. Knowing the input and output of chemicals, we have made *nutrient budgets* for nine elements. Considering four of the major ones, we find the following annual averages in kilograms per hectare entering the system and being *flushed out* of it: calcium, 2.6 and 11.8; sodium, 1.5 and 6.9; magnesium, .7 and 2.9, and potassium, 1.1 and 1.7.

These inputs and outputs represent connections of the undistributed forest ecosystem with worldwide *biogeochemical systems*. The data also provide a comparative basis for judging the effects of *managerial practiceson biogeochemical cycles*. Net losses of calcium, sodium and magnesium were recorded each year even though the period of measurement included wet and dry years as well as years of average precipitation.

Potassium, a major component of the bedrock, showed net gains in two years and a smaller average net loss than wasrecorded for the other elements. Evidently *potassium* is accumulating in the ecosystem with respect to other elements. One reason may be that it is retained in the structure of *illitic clays* developing in the ecosystem.

Perhaps also potassium is retained in proportionately larger amounts than other elements are in the slowly increasing biomass of the system. Highly predictable relations appear between the concentrations of dissolved chemicals in stream water and the discharge rates of the stream. For example, the concentrations of sodium and silica are inversely related to discharge rates, whereas the *concentrations* of *aluminium*, *hydrogen ion* and *nitrate* increase as discharge rates increase.

Magnesium, calcium, sulphate, chloride and potassium are relatively independent of discharge' rate. The magnitudes of change of concentration, however, are *fairly small*. The concentrations of potassium, calcium and magnesium hardly change at all, and the concentration of sodium decreases by only three times as the discharge rate increases by four orders of *magnitude*.

These results wereunexpected: we had thought that during the spring melt period there would be considerable dilution, making the concentrations of elements in stream water relatively low. All these relations show how strongly stream-water chemistry is under the control of processes inherent in the forest ecosystem.

Because of the comparative constancy of chemical *concentrations*, the total output of elements is strongly dependent on the volume of *stream flow*. Hence it is not possible, knowing, only the *hydrologic* output, to predict with fair *accuracy* both the output and the concentration of chemicals in the stream water draining from our mature, forested ecosystem.

This relation would seem to have considerable value for regional planners concerned with water quality. A particularly interesting finding is that almost the entire loss of *cations* (positively charged nutrient ions) from the *undisturbed* forest ecosystem is balanced by the input of positively charged hydrogen ions in precipitation.

The proportion of hydrogen ions is related to the amount of sulphate in precipitation. It is estimated that 50 per cent of the sulphate in precipitation results from industrial activities that put sulphur dioxide and other sulphur products into the air. These sulphur compounds may ultimately from *ionized sulphuric acid*, which consists of *hydrogen ions* and *sulphate ions*.

When the precipitation enters the ecosystem, the hydrogen ions replace the nutrient cations on the negatively charged exchange sites in the soil, and the cations are washed out of the system in stream water. Thus air pollution is directly related to a small but continuous loss of *fertility* from the land area of the ecosystem and a small but *continuous* chemical *enrichment* of streams, and lakes.

The relation appears to represent an important hidden cost of air pollution, made apparent through the analysis of ecosystems. So far we have mentioned only chemical losses appearing as dissolved substances. Losses also arise when chemicals locked up in *particulate matter* such as rock or *soil particles* and in organic matter such as leaves and twigs are washed out of the ecosystem by the stream.

We have measured these outputs and developed equations expressing the loss of particulate matter as a function of the discharge rate of the stream. The loss is highly dependent on the discharge rate. Losses of dissolved substances account for the great bulk of the chemical loss from our *undisturbed ecosytem*.

Whereas they are largely independent of the discharge rate, losses of particulate matter are highly dependent on it. This point is of particular interest since forest management practices can either increase or decrease stream-discharge rates and thereby shift the balance between the loss of dissolved substances and the loss of particulate matter.

Weathering, or the release of elements bound in primary minerals, is another factor that must be considered in an *ecosystem*, since the elements thus released are made available as nutrients to the *vegetation* and animals. Based on net losses of elements from our ecosystem, a *relatively* uniform *geology* in the region and a knowledge of the bulk chemistry of the rock and soil, we estimate that the nutrients contained in some 800 kilograms per hectare of rock and soil are made available each year by weathering.

We now have for the undisturbed Northern hardwood ecosystem of Hubbard Brook estimates of chemical input in precipitation and output in stream water and the rates of generation of ions by the weathering of minerals within the system.

To complete the picture of nutrient cycling it is necessary to measures the nutrient content of the four compartments and the flow rates among them arising from uptake, decomposition and leaching and the formation of new *minerals*. The annual net loss of calcium from the ecosystem is 9.2 kilograms *per hectare*. This loss represents only about .3 per cent of the calcium in the available nutrient and organic compartments of the system and only 1.3 per cent of what is in the available-*nutrient compartment* alone.

The data suggest that Northern hardwood forests have a remarkable ability to hold and circulate nutrients. It was against this background that we and the Forest Service embarked on the experiment of cutting down everything that was growing in one *watershed*. One of the objectives of this severe treatment was to block a major pathway of the ecosystem-the uptake of nutrients by higher plants-while the pathway of ultimate decomposition continued to function.

We questioned whether or not the ecosystem had the capacity under these circumstances to hold the nutrients accumulating in the available-nutrient compartment. We also wanted to determine the effect of deforestation on stream flow, to examine some of the *fundamental* chemical relations of the forest ecosystem and to evaluate the effects of forest *manipulation* on nutrient relations and the *eutrophication* of stream water.

The experiment was begun in the winter of 1965-1966 when the forest of Watershed No. 2, covering 15.6 hectares, was completely levelled by the Forest Service. All trees, saplings and shrubs were cut and dropped in place; their limbs were removed so that no slash was more than 1.5 metres above the ground.

No products were removed from the forest, and great care was taken to prevent disturbance of the surface of the soil that might promote erosion. The following summer *regrowth* of *vegetation* was inhibited by an aerial application of the *herbicide Bromacil* at a rate of 28 kilograms per hectare.

Deforestation had a pronounced effect on *runoff*. Beginning in May,

1966, runoff from the cut watershed began to increase over the levels that would have been expected if there had been no cutting. The *cumulative runoff* for 1966 exceeded the expected amount by 40 per cent. The largest difference was recorded during the four months from June through September, when the runoff was 418 per cent higher than the expected amount.

This difference is directly attributable to changes in the hydrologic cycle resulting from the removal of the transpiring surface. Accelerated runoff has continued through the succeeding summers. Our treatment also resulted in a fundamental *alteration* of the *nitrogen cycle*, which in turn caused *extraordinary* losses of soil fertility.

In an undisturbed ecosystem nitrogen incorporated in organic compounds is ultimately decomposed in a number of steps to ammonium nitrogen (NH_4^+), a positively charged ion that can be held fairly tightly in the soil on the negatively charged exchange sites. *Ammonium ions* can be taken up directly by green plants and used in the fabrication of nitrogen-containing organic compounds.

Ammonium ions can also be used as the substrate for the process of nitrification. In this process two genera of soil bacteria, Nitrosomonas and Nitrobacter, oxidize ammonium to nitrate (NO_3^-). Two hydrogen ions are produced for every ion of *ammonium oxidized* to nitrate. As we have already mentioned, hydrogen ions can play a key role in the release of *nutrient cations* from the soil.

Nitrate, being negatively charged, is highly *leachable*. If it is not taken up by higher plants, if can easily be removed from the ecosystem in *drainage water*. The available evidence indicates that nitrification is of minor importance in *undisturbed forests* such as ours, underlain by *acid podzol soil*.

The nitrate drained by our streams (*invariably* in low concentration) can be largely accounted for by its input in precipitation. In fact, our budgetary *analyses* show that undisturbed ecosystems are accumulating nitrogen at a rate of about two kilograms per hectare per year. The concentration of nitrate in *stream water* from undisturbed forests shows a seasonal cycle, being higher from November through April than it is from May through October.

The decline in May and the low concentration in the summer are correlated with heavy demand for nutrients by the vegetation and generally increased *biological activity* associated with warming of the soil. Beginning in June, 1966, the concentration of nitrate in the *deforested watershed rose* sharply.

At the same time the undisturbed ecosystem showed the normal spring decline. The high concentration has continued in the *deforested* watershed during the *succeeding* years. Average net losses of nitrate nitrogen were 120 kilograms per hectar per year from 1966 through 1968. We estimate that the annual turnover of nitrogen in our *undisturbed* forests is about 60 kilograms per hectare.

Therefore an amount of elemental nitrogen equivalent to double the amount normally taken up by the forest has been lost from the deforested watershed each year since *cutting*. The *magnitude* of nitrate loss is a clear indication of the *acceleration* of *nitrification* in the watershed.

There is no doubt that the cutting drastically altered the conditions controlling the nitrification process. Another factor of interest about nitrification is the body of evidence from other regions that certain types of vegetation can *inhibit nitrification chemically*. Presumably the effect is to inhibit production of the highly leachable nitrate ion.

At the same time the positively charged ammonium ions may be held within the system on the negatively charged exchange sites in the soil. If this inhibition process goes on at *Hubbard Book*, cutting the vegetation would promote nitrification.

The effect may account for much of the nitrate loss from the deforested ecosystem. The export of nitrate to the small stream draining the cut watershed has resulted in nitrate concentrations exceeding the levels established by the U.S. Public Health Service for drinking water. In general the *deforestation* has led to *eutrophication* of the stream and to the development of algal "*blooms*."

This finding indicates that in some circumstances forest-management practices can contribute significantly to the eutrophication of streams. Since nitrification produces hydrogen ions that replace metallic cations on the exchange surfaces in the soil, one would expect a loss of metallic nutrients from the deforested watershed. We have recorded substantial losses of this kind.

The *concentrations* of calcium, magnesium, sodium and potassium in the stream water increased almost simultaneously with the increase in nitrate. About a month later the concentration of aluminium rose sharply. Net losses of potassium were 21 times higher than those in an undisturbed watershed of calcium, 10 times; of aluminium, nine; of magnesium, seven, and of sodium, three.

These figures represent a substantial loss of nutrients from the ecosystem. The finding suggests that *commercial forestry* should focus more on the effect of *harvesting* practices on the loss of *nutrients*, giving more consideration to such corrective procedures as selective cutting and the promotion of regrowth on cut areas.

Our results indicate that the capacity of the ecosystem to retain nutrients is dependent on the maintenance of nutrient cycling within the system. When the cycle is broken, as by the destruction of vegetation, the loss of nutrients is greatly accelerated. This effect is related both to the cessation of nutrient uptake by plants and to the larger quantities of drainage water passing through the system.

The loss may also be related to increased rates of decomposition resulting from such changes in the *physical environment* as higher soil temperature and moister soil. We also found a basic change in the pattern of loss of particulate matter in the *deforested* watershed. The data for three years indicate an increase of some ninefold over a *comparable* undisturbed ecosystem.

After an initial surge the loss—of particulate organic matter has declined as a result of the virtual *elimination* of the production of primary organic matter in the ecosystem. In contrast, the loss of *inorganic* material from the stream bed has accelerated because of the greater erosive *capacity* of the *augmented* stream flow and also because several biological barriers to the *erosion* of surface soil and stream banks have been *greatly* diminished.

The continuous layer of litter that once protected the soil surface is now discontinuous. The *extensive network* of fine roots that tended to stabilize the stream bank is now dead, and the dead leaves that tended to plaster over exposed *banks* are gone.

The erosive trend can be expected to rise exponentially as long as regrowth of vegetation is inhibited in the watershed. Our study clearly shows that the *stability* of an ecosystem is linked to the orderly flow of nutrients between the living and the nonliving components of the system and the production and decomposition of biomass.

These processes, integrated with the seasonal changes in climate, result in relatively tight *nutrient cycles* within the system, a minimum output of nutrients and water and good resistance to erosion. *Destruction* of the vegetation sets off a chain of *interactions*.

Their net effect is an, increase in the amount and flow rate of water and the breakdown of biological barriers to erosion and transpo-rtation, coupled with an increase in the export of nutrient capital and inorganic particulate matter. Three points, which are inherent in the ecosystem concept and are emphasized by the Hubbard Brook study, should be recognized as being basic to any wise scheme for managing the use of land. First, the ecosystem is a highly complex natural unit composed of organisms (plants and animals, including man) and their inorganic environment (air, water, soil and rock).

Second, all parts of an ecosystem are *intimately* linked by natural processes that are part of the ecosystem, such as the uptake of nutrients, the fixation of energy, the movement of nutrients and energy through food webs, the release of nutrients by the decomposition of *organic matter*, the weathering of rock and *soil minerals* to release nutrients and the formation of new minerals.

Third, individual ecosystems are linked to surrounding land and water ecosystems and to the biosphere in general by connections with food webs and the worldwide circulation of air and water. Failures in *environmental* management often result from such factors as failure to appreciate the complexity of nature, the assumption that it is possible to manage one part of nature alone and the belief that somehow nature will absorb all types of *manipulation*.

Good management of the use of land-good from the viewpoint of society at large-requires that managerial practices be imposed only after a careful analysis, and evaluation of all the ramifications. A focus for this type of analysis and *evaluation* is the ecosystem concept.

NUTRIENT CYCELS

Nutrient Pools and Exchanges

Nutrients can be used as an organizing focus in ecosystem studies. We can view the biological community as a complex processor in which individuals more nutrients from one site to another within the ecosystem. These biological exchanges of nutrients interact with physical and chemical exchanges, and for this reason, nutrient cycles are also called biogeochemical cycles.

All nutrients reside in *compartments*, which represent .a defined space in nature. Compartments can be defined very broadly or very specifically. It includes all of the plants in the ecosystem as one compartment, but we could recognize each species of plant as a separate compartment or even the leaves and the stem of a single plant as separate compartments.

A compartment contains a certain quantity, or pool, of nutrients. The phosphorus dissolved in the water is *one pool*, and the *phosphorus* contained in the herbivores is another pool. *Compartments* exchange *nutrients*, and thus we must measure the uptake and outflow of nutrients for each compartment.

The rate of movement of nutrients between two compartments is called the flux rate and is measured as the .quantity of nutrient passing from one pool to another per unit of time. The *flux rates* and *pool sizes* together define the nutrient cycle within any particular ecosystem. Ecosystems are not isolated from one another, and nutrients come into an ecosystem through meteorological, geological, or *biological, transport mechanisms* and leave an *ecosystem* via the same routes.

Meteorological inputs include dissolved matter in rain and snow, atmospheric gases, and dust blown by the wind; geological inputs include elements transported by surface and subsurface drainage; and biological inputs include movements of animals between *ecosystems*. Nutrient cycles can be studied by the introduction of radioactive tracers into *laboratory* or *natural ecosystems*.

Studies on the movement of radioactive *phosphorus* in small *aquariums* illustrate this approach. There are changes that followed the introduction of 100 microcuries (μc) of ^{32}P-labelled phosphoric acid in a 200-litre aquarium. There is a very rapid initial uptake of ^{32}P by the *phytoplankton*. One-half of the ^{32}P had been taken up by the phytoplankton within 2 hours, and within 12 hours there was an *equilibrium* of uptake and excretion of 32P between the *phytoplankton* and the water.

Filamentous algae attached to the sides and bottom of the aquarium slowly picked up ^{23}P, and crustaceans *grazing* on *phytoplankton* began to accumulate ^{32}P even more slowly. As the experiment progressed, an increasing fraction of the radioactive tracer began to accumulate in the bottom mud and was tried up in less active or bound form in the *sediments*.

Some ^{32}P does move from the sediment back into the water column, but more moves down into the sediment and thus accumulates. The nutrient cycle of phosphorus in aquariums is broadly similar to that in natural lakes. Phosphorus and other nutrients tend to accumulate in the sediment of lakes so that continual nutrient inputs are required to maintain high productivity.

The pattern of movement of phosphorus helps to explain the design of the lake-fertilization experiments described. A continued input of phosphate is needed to sustain high availability for *phytoplankton*. These results are also critical for understanding how lakes can recover from the effects of nutrient additions from pollution.

Thus the sediments of lakes become nutrient-rich deposits. Nutrient cycles may be subdivided into two broad types. The *phosphorus cycle* we have just described is an example of a sedimentary or local cycle, which operates within an ecosystem. Local cycles involve the less mobile elements that have no mechanism for long-distance transfer. By contrast, the *gaseous cycles* of *nitrogen*, *carbon*, *oxygen*, and *water* are called global cycles because they involve exchanges between the *atmosphere* and *ecosystem*.

Global nutrient cycles link together all of the world's living organisms in one giant ecosystem called the biosphere, the whole earth ecosystem. The nitrogen cycle is a good example of a *gaseous global* cycle and is illustrated in.

Gaseous nitrogen is the most abundant element in the atmosphere, and the atmospheric N_2 provides a large reservoir for nitrogen-fixing organisms. The quantity of nitrogen tried up in living organisms is very small compared with the total capacity of the atmosphere.

Almost all nitrogen available for plants comes from nitrogen-fixing

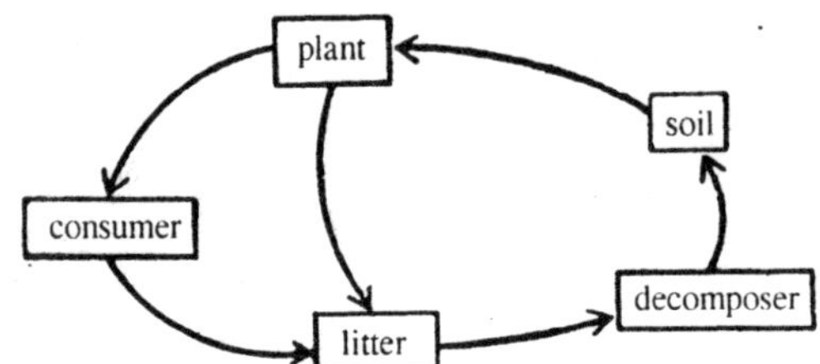

(a) Local cycles of P, K, Ca, Mg, Cu, Zn, B, Cl, Mo, Mn, and Fe.

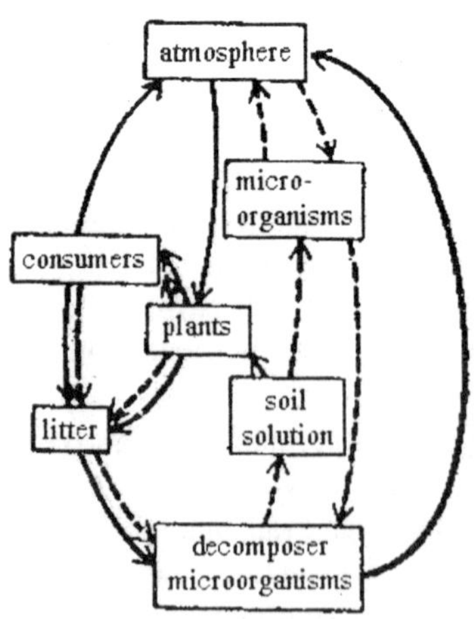

(b) Global cycles of C, N, O and H.

Figure 3.1: Generalized diagrams of two types of nutrient cycles. The dashed lines in the global cycles refer to nitrogen only.

bacteria or algae. In many *tertestrial* ecosystems, the fixation of nitrogen may limit plant growth, and there can be intense competition for soil nitrogen.

Nutrient Cycles in Forests

The harvesting of forest trees removes nutrients from a forest site, and this continued nutrient removal could result in a long-term decline in forest productivity unless nutrients are somehow returned to the system. Because of the economic question of forest productivity, an increasing amount of work is being directed toward the analysis of nutrient cycles in forests.

Figure elsewhere in this chapter shows the factors that must be quantified in order to describe the nutrient cycle in a forest. Some examples of nutrient cycles in forest stands will illustrate these concepts.

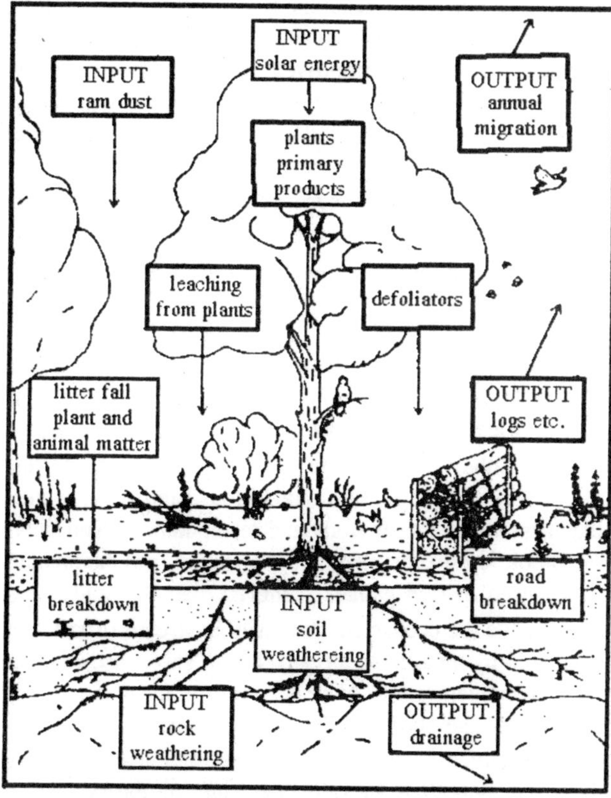

Figure 3.2: Forest ecosystem dynamics.
Arrows indicate the flows of matter and energy.

Figure elsewhere in this chapter shows the potassium cycle in two adjacent woodlands in Great Britain. In the oak woodland, the potassium flow is largely through the oak trees and is returned to the soil as leaf litter every year.

In the pine woodland, the bulk of the potassium flows through the ground flora (particularly bracken fern), and the pines take up relatively little potassium. Thus different species of trees have different nutrient demands, in the same way that different agricultural crops have different J nutrient requirements.

Fertilization experiments in forests have provided additional data on nutrient cycling within forest sites. Some forest sites respond to artificial fertilization by increasing production, but other sites do not. Tamm (1975) describes a 14-year fertilization experiment on a Norway spruce stand in Sweden.

The addition of nitrogen caused the trees to build a crown of green needless more rapidly, so that during the first few years of the experiment, tree growth was improved, but the effects of nitrogen addition were nullified as time went on. Stem growth was reduced at high nitrogen levels, and total primary production differed little among treatments.

In this forest stand, the nitrogen cycle was operating efficiently, and thus nitrogen was not limiting primary production of the trees. One of the most extensive studies of nutrient cycling in forests has been carried out at the Hubbard Brook Experimental Forest in New Hampshire.

The Hubbard Brook forest is a nearly mature, second-growth hardwood ecosystem. The area is underlain by rocks that are relatively impermeable to water, so all runoff occurs in small streams.

The area is subdivided into several small watersheds that are distinct yet support similar forest communities, and these watersheds are good experimental units for study and manipulation. Nutrients enter the Hubbard Brook forest ecosystem in precipitation, and the precipitation input was measured in rain gauges scattered over the study area.

Nutrients 'leave the ecosystem primarily in stream runoff, and this loss was estimated by measuring stream flows. Table elsewhere in this chapter gives the concentrations of dissolved substances in precipitation and streamwater for the Hubbard Brook wntersheds.

For Most dissolved nutrients, the streamwater leaving the system contains more nutrients than the rainwater entering the system. About 60 per cent of the water that enters as precipitation turns up as stream

Table 3.1: Biomass of Trees.

		Fertilizer Treatment							
		Control	*PK*	*1*	*N_2PK*	*N_s^3*	*N2PK*	*N_4*	*N4PK*
Mean height (cm)	1956	186	163	158	181	167	172	165	172
Stem volume (o.b.m^3)	1960	27	20	26	35	31	33	31	33
	1970	143	125	130	171	145	160	137	152
Dry weight (kg/ha)									
Stem wood	1960	8,520	6,920	8,740	10,530	9,680	10,760	10,340	10,700
	1970	40,060	35,380	38,490	49,090	43,520	47,570	41,860	45,740
Stem bark	1960	1,720	1,400	1,760	2,120	1,960	2,170	2,100	2,160
	1970	6,400	5,720	6,260	7,760	6,970	7,560	6,770	7,260
Branches	1960	7,510	6,570	9.200	10,480	9,920	10,880	10,610	10,680
	1970	12,860	11,190	11,020	15,190	12,470	14,490	12,110	13,980
Needles	1960	8,680	7,560	10,840	12,310	11,670	12,790	12,480	12,540
	1970	13,400	11,770	11,580	15,530	12,940	14,900	12,680	14,360
Total above stumps	1960	26,430	22,450	30,540	35,440	33,230	36,600	35.530	36,096
	1970	72,720	64,060	67,350	87,570	75,900	84,520	73,420	81,340

(Table 3.1 Contd.)

(Table 3.1 Contd.)

		Fertilizer Treatment							
		Control	*PK*	*1*	N_2PK	N_s^3	*N2PK*	N_4	*N4PK*
Stumps	1970	2,390	2,160	2,380	2,880	2,610	2,820	2,570	2,700
Roots > 5 mm diam.	1970	11,070	9,180	9,850	13,150	10,910	12,130	10,780	12,170
Roots < 5 mm diam.	1970	4,740	4,740	4,740	4,740	4,740	4,740	4,740	4,740
Total biomass	**1970**	**90,920**	**81,140**	**84,320**	**108,340**	**94,160**	**104,210**	**91,510**	**100,950**

***Note:* Plots were fertilized annually with nitrogen alone or with mixtures of nitrogen, phosphorus, and potassium starting in 1957.**

flow most of the remaining 40 per cent is transpired by plants or evaporated.

The chemical composition of the precipitation and the stream discharges changed very little from year to year. Table elsewhere in this chapter gives the annual nutrient budgets for watersheds in the Hubbard Brook system, based on the difference between. precipitation input and stream outflow.

Eight elements show net losses from the ecosystem: calcium, magnesium potassium, sodium, aluminium, surphate, silica, and bicarbonate. Three elements showed an average net gain: nitrate, ammonium, and chloride. If we assume that these nutrient budgets should be in equilibrium in this undisturbed ecosystem, the net losses must be made up by chemical decomposition of the bedrock and soil.

With this background, Bormann *et al.*, (1974) studied the effect of logging on the nutrient budget of a small watershed at Hubbard Brook. One 15.6-hectare watershed was logged in 1966, and the logs and branches were left on the ground so that nothing was removed from the area.

Table 3.2: Average Concentrations of Various Dissolved Substances in Bulk Precipitation and Streamwater for Undisturbed Watersheds.

	Precipitation (mg/L)	*Stream water (mg/L)*
Calcium	0.21	1.58
Magnesium	0.06	0.39
Potassium	0.09	0.23
Sodium	0.12	0.92
Aluminium	([a])	0.24
Ammonium	0.22	0.05
Sulphate	3.10	6.40
Nitrate	1.31	1.14
Chloride	0.42	0.64
Bicarbonate	([a])	1.90[b]
Dissolved silica	([a])	4.61

[a] *Not determined, but very low.*

[b] *Watershed 4 only.*

Great care was taken to prevent disturbance of the soil surface to minimize erosion. For the first three years after logging the area was treated with a herbicide to prevent any regrowth of vegetation. This deforested watershed was then compared with an adjacent intact watershed. Runoff in the small streams increased immediatedly after the logging, and annual runoff in the deforested watershed was, respectively, 41, 28, and 26 per cent above the control in the 3 years after treatment.

Detritus and debris in the stream outflow increased greatly after deforestation, particularly 2 to 3 years after logging. Correlated with this was a large increase in streamwater concentrations' of all major ions in the deforested watershed. Nitrate concentrations in particular increased 40-to 60-fold over the control values.

For 2 years the nitrate concentration in the streamwater of the deforested site exceeded the health levels recommended for drinking water. Average streamwater concentrations increased 417 per cent for calcium, 408 per cent for magnesium, 1558 per cent for potassium, and 177 per cent for sodium in the 2 years after deforestation.

The net result of deforestation in the Hubbard Brook forest is that the ecosystem is simultaneously irrigated and fertilized, so that for a short time after logging, primary production could be stimulated. An array of species has evolved to exploit these transient nutrient-rich situations following a disturbance by fire or logging.

These transients help to prevent further nutrient loeses and to restore some of the nutrient capital lost by logging or fire. The Hubbard Brook experiment was repeated by Kimmins and Feller (1976) in the coastal coniferous forest of British Columbia.

The experimental conditions were more realistic because the experimental areas were commercially logged by clearcutting, and one area was later slash-burned to reduce the amount of branches and small stems lying on the ground. The results were similar to those observed at Hubbard Brook. Losses of potassium were increased 10-fold, and net losses of nitrate occurred.

The losses of nutrients after logging could be severe on forest sites that have poor soil, and special efforts should be taken to protect these sites. The work on nutrient cycling in forests has shown the need for guidelines to specify sound management procedure in forestry.

For example, bark is relatively rich in nutrients, and hence lumbering operations ought to be designed to strip the .bark from the trees at the field site and not at some distant processing plant. The conservation of nutrients in forest ecosystems can be done intelligently only when we understand how nutrient cycles operate in these systems.

Table 3.3: Annual Nutrient Budgets (kg/ha) for Watersheds

	1963-1964	*1964-1965*	*1965-1966*	*1966-1967*	*1967-1968*	*1968-1969 1963-1969*	*Mean*
1	**2**	**3**	**4**	**5**	**6**	**7**	**8**
Calcium							
Input	3.0	2.8	2.7±0.07	2.7±0.03	2.8±0.05	1.6±0.02	2.6
Output	12.8±0.8	6.3±0.4	11.5±0.6	12.3±0.7	14.2±0.7	13.8±1	11.8
Net	–9.8	–3.5	–8.8	–9.6	–11.4	–12.2	–9.2
Magnesium							
Input	0.7	1.1	0.7±0.02	0.5±0.005	0.7±0.013	0.3±0.004	0.7
Output	2.5±0.06	1.8±0.09	2.9±0.07	3.1±0.08	3.7±0.08	3.3±0.12	2.9
Net	–1.8	–0.7	–2.2	–2.6	–3.0	–3.0	–2.2
Potassium							
Input	2.5	1.8	0.6±0.02	0.6±0.008	0.7±0.01	0.6±0.009	1.1
Output	1.8±0.1	1.1±0.08	1.4±0.09	1.7±0.1	2.2±0.15	2.2±0.16	1.7
Net	+0.7	+0.7	–0.8	–1.1	–1.5	–1.6	–0.6
Sodium							
Input	1.0	2.1	2.0±0.04	1.3±0.01	1.7±0.03	1.1±0.02	1.5
Output	5.9±0.3	4.5±0.3	6.9±0.5	7.3±0.6	9.14-0.3	7.6±0.6	6.9

(Table 3.3 Contd.)

(Table 3.3 Contd.)

	1963-1964	*1964-1965*	*1965-1966*	*1966-1967*	*1967-1968*	*1968-1969 1963-1969*	*Mean*
1	**2**	**3**	**4**	**5**	**6**	**7**	**8**
Net	-4.9	–2.4	–4.9	–6.0	–7.4	–6.5	–5.4
Aluminium							
Input	—	(*)	(*)	(*)	(*)	(*)	(*)
Output	—	1.2±0.18	1.7±0.75	1.9±0.87	2.1±1.00	2.2±1.04	1.8
Net	—	—	–1.7	–1.9	–2.1	–2.2	–1.8
Ammonium							
Indut	—	2.1	2.6±0.06	2.4±0.04	3.2±0.06	3.1±0.07	2.7
Output	—	0.27±0.03	0.92±0.03	0.45±0.07	0.24±0.02	0.16±0.06	0.4
Net	—	+1.83	+1.7	+2.0	+3.0	+2.9	+2.3
Nitrate							
Input	—	6.7	17.4±0.3	19.9±0.2	22.3±0.3	15.3:1:0.3	16.3
Output	—	5.6±0.4	6.5±0.02	6.6±0.4	12.7±0 3	12.2±04	8.7
Net	—	+1.1	+10.9	+13.3	+9.6	+3.1	+7.6
Sulphate							
Input	—	30.0	41.6±0.3	42.0±0.3	46.7±0.3	31.2±0.3	38.3

(Table 3.3 Contd.)

(Table 3.3 Contd.)

	1963-1964	*1964-1965*	*1965-1966*	*1966-1967*	*1967-1968*	*1968-1969 1963-1969*	*Mean*
1	**2**	**3**	**4**	**5**	**6**	**7**	**8**
Output	—	30.8±0.4	47.8±0.4	52.5±0.4	58.5±0.4	53.3±0.3	48.6
Net	—	–0.8	–6.2	–10.5	–11.8	–22.1	–10.3
Dissolved Silica							
Input	—	(*)	(*)	(*)	(*)	(*)	(*)
Output	—	20.8±0.1	36.1±4.8	41.6±4.8	42.1±5.7	55.0±6.0	35.1
Net	—	—	–36	–42	–42	–35	–35
Bicarbonate							
Input	—	—	(*)	(*)	(*)	(*)	(*)
Output	—	—	12.0	16.8	16.5*	13.1*	14.6
Net	—	—	–12	–17	–17	–13	–14.6
Chloride							
Input	—	—	2.6±0.04	6.7_+_0.12	5.0±0.09	6.4±0.05	5.2
Output	—	—	4.3±0.05	4.8±0.1	5.3±0.01	5.2±0.08	4.9
Net	—	—	–1.7	–1.9	–0.3	+1.2	+0.3

Note: *Error limits are 1 standard deviation of the mean.*

** Not measured, but very small.*

Table 3.4: Annual Losses of Particulate Matter in Streams on Watershed 6 (Control and Watershed 2 (Deforested) at Hubbard Brook, New Hampshire

Source of Output	*Watershed 6 (Undisturbed Forest)*			*Watershed 2 (Deforested)*		
	Organic	*Inorganic*	*Total*	*Organic*	*Inorganic*	*Total*
1	**2**	**3**	**4**	**5**	**6**	**7**
1965-1966						
Ponding basin	2.12	1.77	3.89	5.97	7.16	13.13
Net	0.34	0.01	0.35	0.19	0.00	0.19
Filter	1.37	1.28	2.65	1.44	1.44	2.88
Total	**3.83**	**3.06**	**6.89**	**7.60**	**8.60**	**16.20**
1966-1967						
Ponding basin	13.41	17.07	30.48	24.96	41.83	66.79
Net	0.39	0.01	0.40	0.27	0.01	0.28
Filter	2.72	2.95	5.67	4.81	5.49	10.30
Total	**1-6.52**	**20.03**	**36.55**	**30.04**	**47.33**	**77.37**
1967-1968						
Ponding basin	3.83	5.93	9.76	28.56	63.38	91.94

(Table 3.4 Contd.)

(Table 3.4 Contd.)

Source of Output	*Watershed 6 (Undisturbed Forest)* Organic	Inorganic	Total	*Watershed 2 (Deforested)* Organic	Inorganic	Total
1	2	3	4	5	6	7
Net	0.43	0.01	0.44	0.28	0.01	0.29
Filter	2.61	2.82	5.43	4.59	5.12	9.71
Total	**6.87**	**8.76**	**15.63**	**33.43**	**68.51**	**101.94**
1968-1969						
Ponding basin	4.61	8.31	12.92	36.31	158.34	194.65
Net	0.42	0.01	0.43	0.26	0.01	0.27
Filter	2.57	2.81	5.38	4.21	4.74	8.95
Total	**7.60**	**11.13**	**18.73**	**40.78**	**164.09**	**203.87**
1969-1970						
Ponding basin	11.28	30.67	41.90	45.16	320.15	365.31
Net	0.40	0.01	0.41	0.25	0.01	0.26
Filter	3.30	3.69	6.99	6.16	7.07	13.23

(Table 3.4 Contd.)

(Table 3.4 Contd.)

Source of Output	*Watershed 6 (Undisturbed Forest)*			*Watershed 2 (Deforested)*		
	Organic	*Inorganic*	*Total*	*Organic*	*Inorganic*	*Total*
1	2	3	4	5	6	7
Total	**14.98**	**34.37**	**49.30**	**51.57**	**327.23**	**378.80**
Average per Year Based on 5 Years						
Ponding basin	7.05	12.75	19.79	28.19	118.17	146.36
Net	0.40	0.01	0.41	0.25	0.01	0.26
Filter	2.51	2.71	5.22	4.24	4.77	9.01
Total	**9.96**	**15.47**	**25.42**	**32.68**	**122.95**	**155.63**

Notes: Data are kilograms of oven-dry weight of materials per hectare of watershed. Losses are separated by size as ponding basin (coarse maferials), net (finer materials), and filter (very fine materials)

Nutrient Cycles in Tundra Ponds

We discussed the role of nutrients in limiting phytoplankton production in freshwater lakes. We will now describe the carbon cycle of a tundra pond ecosystem to illustrate how nutrient cycling can be described in detail for an aquatic system.

We will also use this example to illustrate the steps involved in the construction of a systems model for part of the tundra pond ecosystem. The arctic coastal plain of northern Alaska contains thousands of small ponds, typically about 50 metres in diameter and 20 cm deep.

They are frozen for 9 months of the year and contain no fish or other vertebrates. These ponds have been studied intensively as part of the International Biological Programme's tundra biome study. The major compartments and carbon-flow pathways for the ponds are shown in Figure elsewhere in this chapter.

We will discuss here only one part of this whole tundra pond ecosystem, the epipelic algae. The epipelic algae are algae living in and on the sediments and are treated here as a unit, not as individual species.

The carbon-flow pathways for the epipelic algae are shown in Figure elsewhere in this chapter. Live epipelic algal cells are distributed

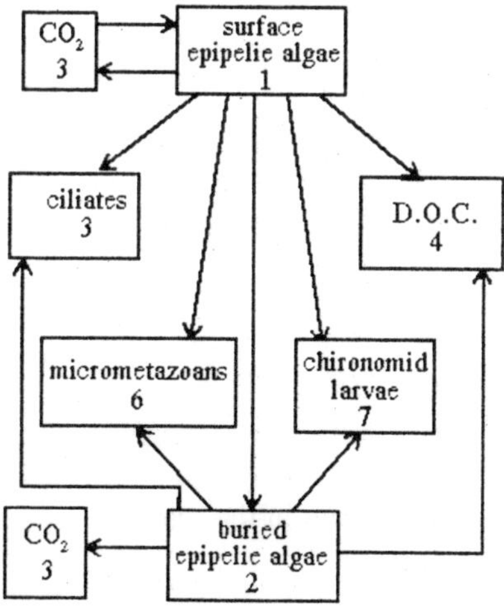

Figure 3.3: Compartment representation of the epipelic algae submodef of the tundra pond ecosystem model shown in Figure elsewhere in this chapter. Each compartment is given a number code to identify it in the equations described in the text. Equations describing the flux rates for all the arrows shown in this submodel are given in Table elsewhere in this chapter.

throughout the upper 5 cm of sediments in the ponds, but photosynthesis is limited to the top few millimetres because of light extinction in the sediment.

For this reason, the epipelic algae have been divided into two compartments in the system model-surface algae and buried algae. Once we have identified trhe compartments in our model, the next step is to qualtifyu the arrows (transfers) shown in figure elsewhere in this chapter.

To do this, we need the physical and biological factors that affect carbon flow. We will describe these relationships first in simple words and then provide a detailed mathematical statement of these relationships.

Consider first the uptake of carbon in CO_2 by the surfacealgae. The rate of photosynthesis depends on temperature and solar radiation:

$$1.\quad \begin{pmatrix}\text{Rate of } CO_2 \text{ uptake by}\\ \text{surface algae}\end{pmatrix} = f\begin{pmatrix}\text{algae biomass, rate}\\ \text{of photosynthesis per}\\ \text{mg of algal carbon,}\\ \text{temperature, solar}\\ \text{radiation}\end{pmatrix}$$

The respiration rate of the surface algae is described as

$$2.\quad \begin{pmatrix}\text{Rate of } CO_2 \text{ release by}\\ \text{surface algae}\end{pmatrix} = f\begin{pmatrix}\text{algae biomass, respiration}\\ \text{rate per mg of algal carbon,}\\ \text{temperature}\end{pmatrix}$$

Excretion of organic compounds represents another loss from the algae and a gain for thedis solved organic carbon (DOC) .compartment. This process can be described by the equation

$$3.\quad \begin{pmatrix}\text{Rate of release of dissolved}\\ \text{organic carbon by surface}\\ \text{algae}\end{pmatrix} = f\begin{pmatrix}\text{rate of photsynthesis,}\\ \text{algal biomass}\end{pmatrix}$$

Algae at the sediment surface are continually transported downward into the sediment by a variety of physical disturbances, primarily from aquatic invertebrates burrowing in the mud:

$$4.\quad \begin{pmatrix}\text{Rate of burial of}\\ \text{surface algae}\end{pmatrix} = f\begin{pmatrix}\text{algal biomass, density of}\\ \text{aquatic invertebrates,}\\ \text{activity of benthic invertebrates}\end{pmatrix}$$

Grazing by benthic invertebrates removes some of the epipelic algae and can be described by the general equation

5. $\begin{pmatrix}\text{Rate of grazing of} \\ \text{epipelic algae}\end{pmatrix} = f\begin{pmatrix}\text{invertebrate biomass,} \\ \text{algal biomass, temperature}\end{pmatrix}$

This rate of grazing has to be applied for each of the three ain classes of invertebrate grazers shown in figure elsewhere in this chapter. Finally, we can calculate the rate of change in biomass of the surface and the buried algae as follows:

6. $\begin{pmatrix}\text{Rate of change in} \\ \text{surface algal carbon}\end{pmatrix} = \begin{pmatrix}\text{(gross photosynthesis)} - \text{(respi} \\ \text{tion)} - \text{(raexcretion)} - \text{(burial)} \\ -\text{(grazing losses)}\end{pmatrix}$

These questions are given in more precise mathematical form in Table elsewhere in this chapter. The main point to note is that in this systems model, we have achieved a mathematical description of each of the arrows shown in Figure elsewhere in this chapter.

We can now put all these equations together and see if they provide an accurate description of the system. The field observation on three tundra ponds, the model's predictions based on the equations in Table elsewhere in this chapter, and the temperature and solar radiation data measured in the field.

It is clear that the model does provide an accurate description of carbon flow into the epipelic algae compartment of these tundra ponds. Two steps need to be taken next. First, this model is only part of a larger model, which needs to be integrated together. Second, the model is presently not capable of dealing with the effects of increased nutrient-loading on the tundra ponds.

Because this model has been constructed for carbon flow, we do not know how to translate increased loadings of phosphorus or nitrogen into the carbon cycle. Note that in its present form, this model does not contain any explicit reference to phosphorus, nitrogen, or any other nutrient. The interrelationships of nutrient cycles are poorly understood, and more experimental studies on controlling nutrients must be done..

Nutrient-Recovery Hypothesis

One of the most striking biological events on tundra areas of North America and Eurasia is the lemming, cycle. Every 3 to 4 years these small rodents build up to high densities, only to decline and become rare again in a never-ending cycle.

This biological rhythm has been studied in detail on the arctic coastal-plain tundra near Point Barrow, Alaska. Lemmings exert a dominant effect on the tundra ecosystem at Point Barrow and cause striking yearly changes in primary production, nutrient concentrations in plants, decomposition rates, and abundances of vertebrate predators. From early observation on the effects of lemmings on the tundra ecosystem of arctic Alaska, Pitelka and Schultz proposed the nutrient-recovery hypothesis to explain the lemming cycle.

This hypothesis linked together in an ingenious fashion the entire tundra ecosystem and has performed the basis of an extensive analysis of the Alaskan tundra as part of the International Biological Programme. The arctic tundra ecosystem can be described as a set of interlocking gears, or feedback loops, in which each compartanent either counteracts or amplifies the change of state of the -next compartment.

Thus, for example, high nutritional quality of forage may help the lemming population to increase, but by grazing, a high-density lemming population will reduce theplant biomass. The feedback-loop model of the arctic tundra is oversimplified but makes an important point-ecosystem compartments are usually part of several interlocking feedback loops.

Many different casual pathways can be traced, and no ,one factor governs the system. The ecosystem of the arctic coast of Alaska is simple compared with more temperate or tropical ecosystem. There are about 100 species of vascular plants, but 10 species comprise 90 per cent of the plant biomass. There is only one major herbivore, the brown lemming, whose diet is largely comprised of three species of vascular plants.

There are two major bird predators and six minor mammal and bird predators that eat lemmings. The tundra ecosystem is underlain by perennially frozen soil, or permafrost, and only the top 25 to 40 cm of soil thaws during the short summer. The permafrost stops water movement down into the soil, and the surface layers of the tundra are often saturated with water during the summer.

Nutrient cycles in the tundra ecosystem contrast sharply with those in temperate and tropical habitats. The total amount of carbon in the tundra ecosystem of northern Alaska is about the same as that in a tropical rain forest But only about 2 per cent of the carbon is held in living materials in the tundra, compared with 64 per cent in living organisms in a tropical rain forest.

The same conclusion seems to hold for nitrogen and phosphorus. In the northern Alaska tundra, 96 per cent of the carbon is bound up in peat, and the activity of decomposers seems to limit the rate of nutrient cycling in xundra ecosystems. Of the nutrients held in living tissue in the tundra ecosystem, the majority is held underground. About 75 per cent of the carbon in living plants is tied up in roots, rhizomes, and stem bases. Nutrient cycles in the arctic coastal tundra are not in a steady state because organic matter is slowly accumulating as peat.

Little nutrient input occurs through precipitation at Point Barrow since precipitation averages only 110 mm per year. Because of the flat terrain, there is little runoff, and most of the precipitation evaporates. Thus the tundra ecosystem shows extreme conservation of nutrients, in contrast to temperate forest ecosystems such as Hubbard Brook.

Primary, production in the arctic coastal tundra near Barrow is restricted to the short summer season by temperature, but within the growing season, production is limited by nutrients (SS hultz 1969). Fertilization of 6 acres of tundra with nitrogen, phosphorus, potassium, and calcium increased primary production to three to four times that of control plots.

The calcium and phosphorus levels of green plants increased dramatically and remained high on the fertilized plot. The fertilization experiment clearly demonstrated that in spite of the high nutrient capital in the tundra ecosystem little is directly available to plants.

Lemmings have an important effect on nutrient cycles in the Barrow tundra ecosystem, and this has been the basis of the nutrient-recovery hypothesis. The interactions proposed by Schultz (1969) between the lemming, vegetation, and soil compartments of the ecosystem are as follows:

1. Intensive grazing occurs during the winter buildup of lemming numbers, and this releases a pulse of nutrients on the tundra surface by decomposition of litter, urine, and feces.
2. These nutrients are rapidly leached and absorbed by plants after snow melts and cause high nutrient concentrations early in the growing season.
3. Grazing removes plant materials, and thus, reduces insulation of the soil, allowing more radiation to warm the soil so that the depth of soil thaw increases.
4. Plant roots are allowed to penetrate lower in the soil, where roots are allowed to penetrate lower in the soil, they are exposed to lower concentrations of nutrients, and this results in lower nutrient uptake by plants in late summer,
5. Low nutrient uptake by plants results in poor-quality forage in the sumrner after a lemming density peak.
6. Lemming density declines for reasons unrelated to strife no cycling perhaps because of predation social Or some other factors).

7. Brae in by lemmings is inhibited in the year following peak density because of low nutrient supplies, parti phosphorus, in the forage.
8. During the next 2 to 3 years the process is reversed: Vegetation slowly recovers, and the standing crop of to a ncre after increases. Depth of thaw decreases due to the asing Insulation, and active roots are confined surface soil. Nutrient quality of the forage increases, and lemming breeding improves.

A considerable amount of evidence supports some of the now seem doubtful the nutrient-recovery hypothesis, but others Phosphorus changes in the forage at Barrow do, indeed, rise and fall with lemming densities. Heavy grazing by lemmings in the grazing grasses and peak year reduces the standing crop the lansedges about 50 per cent, and this decrease in the plant canopy does increase the depth of thaw in the soil by approximately to 30 per cent.

But the increased depth of thaw by itself does not seem to reduce nutrient content of the forage as suggested in points 4 and 5 in the list, and this part of the nutrient recovery hypothesis seems to be in error. Nevertheless, nutrients in vegetation in the coastal tundra are often possibility reduced tin the years after a lemming peak, and the that these nutrient levels affect lemming reproduction during the winter.

In summer, primary prodution exceeds the lemmings requirements, and lack of food cannot explain the continued population decline. The value of the nutrient-recovery hypothesis is that it has focused on the entire ecosystem and has attempted to integrate the complex interchanges that occur through the compartments. of this ecosystem.

The arctic coastal tundra is a relatively simple ecosystem, but its nutrient cycles are still difficult to disassociate and measure. The dominant dynamic feature of the tundra system is its low energy input, and this affects the biological community mostly through the physical effects of permafrost. Permafrost affects the availability of nutrients, which in turn affect primary and secondary production and thus ultimately the rates of nutrient cycling.

Efficiency of Nutrient Use

Large areas of the Northern Hemisphere have been glaciated, and the soils, derived from till in which the bedrock has been pulverized, are very fertile, with a high availability of nutrients. Areas of volcanic activity can also have rich soils. But in much of the world, soils are very old, highly weathered, and basically infertile. For example, the continents derivedfrom Gondwanaland-Australia, South America, and

India-have large areas covered with very old, poor soils. The vegetation supported on these soils has adapted remarkably well to efficient nutrient use by recycling within the plant and by leaf fall and reabsorption.

Australian soils are typical of very old, highly weathered soils and contain almost no phosphorus. Eucalyptus are adapted to grow on soils of low phosphorus content. Table elsewhere in this chpater gives the biomass and nutrient content of forest ecosystems from temperate areas growing on good soils and from Australian sites on poor soils.

There is no suggestion from Table elsewhere in this chapter that eucalyptus growing on poor soils have lower amounts of nutrients than forests in other countries, with the single exception of phosphorus. Eucalyptus have only onehalf to one-fifth the amount of phosphorus in their tissues as do Northern Hemisphere forests.

Plants growing in nutrient-poor soils, one would think, ought to use nutrients more efficiently and contain less nutrients than plants in fertile soils. In fact, the opposite is true. Plants from infertile habitats consistently have higher mutrient concentrations than plants from fertile habitats when grown, under the same controlled conditions.

Plants from nutrient-poor habitats may achieve this by being more efficient than plants from nutrient-rich habitats. An abundance of data is available from forests to investigate nutrient use efficiency. For a forest we can define:

Nutrient use efficiency

$$= \frac{\text{grams of organic matter lost from plants}}{\text{grams of nutrient lost}}$$

These are two measures for a variety of forests from tropical a o and temperate areas. Two extreme hypotheses are the line of equal of nutrient-use efficiency and constantly decaying nutrient use efficiency. The data fit neither extreme hypothesis but fall closer to line Nutrient-use efficiency is clearly above expectations in habitats with low nitrogen levels and below expectations in habitats rich in nitrogen.

One consequence of this is that forest productivity may be high on soils with low nutrient levels. A classic example is the tropical rain forest of the Amazon Basin, which; represents one type of nutrient cycling strategy.

The oligotrophic strategy occurs on nutrient-poor soils, like the Amazon Basin, and the eutrophic strategy occurs on nutrient-rich soils. In the temperate zone, where most forest research has been done, forests are usually of the eutrophic type.

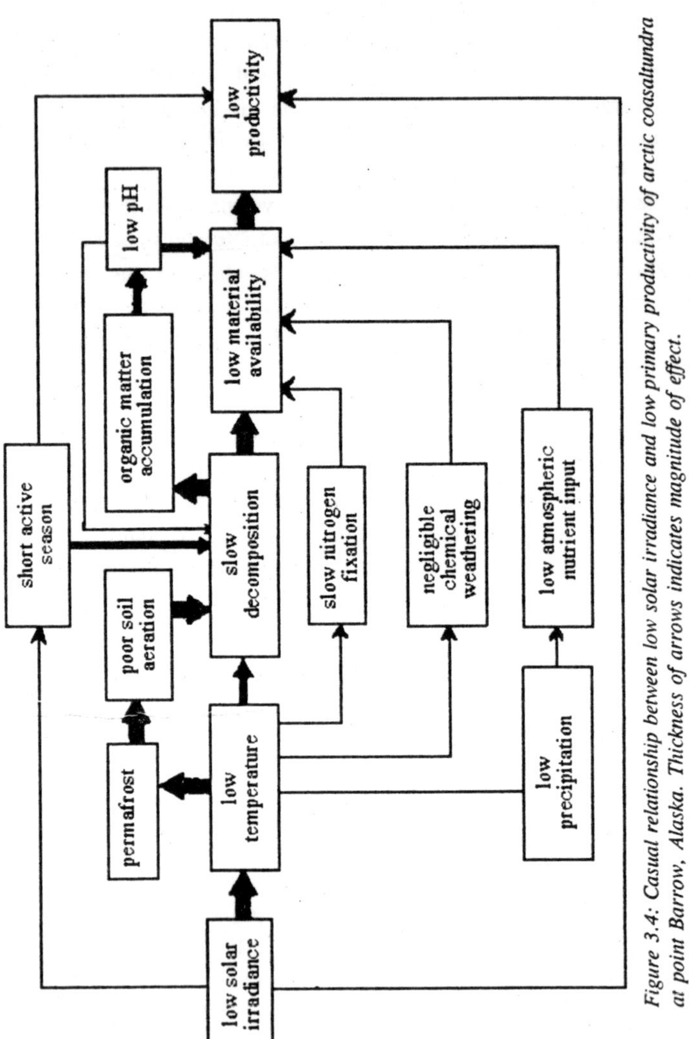

Figure 3.4: Casual relationship between low solar irradiance and low primary productivity of arctic coasaltundra at point Barrow, Alaska. Thickness of arrows indicates magnitude of effect.

Oligotrophic ecosystems constitute a much greater proportion of the tropics. But exceptions occur, and not all tropical forests are oligotrophic nor all temperate forests . eutrophic. Table elsewhere in this chapter compares two eutrophic and two oligotrophic forest ecosystems.

There are some striking differences between these forest types. Oligotrophic systems have a large biomass in the humus layer of the soil, and this layer of fine roots and humus is critical for nutrient cycling and nutrient conservation in these systems.

Productivity and nutrient cycling do not differ significantly in oligotrophic and eutrophic forests, as long as these ecosystems are not disturbed. But when the forest is cleared for agriculture, the nutrient-poor systems quickly lose their productive potential, while the nutrient-rich ones do not.

Once the humus and root layer on top of the mineral soil is disturbed in oligotrophic systems, the mechanism of efficient nutrient recycling is lost, and nutrients are leached out of the system. Oligotrophic ecosystems cannot be used for crop production unless critical nutrients are supplied in fertilizers.

Acid Rain: The Sulphur Cycle

Human activity through the combustion of fossil fuels has altered the sulphur cycle more than any of the other nutrient cycles. While human-produced emissions of carbon dioxide and nitrogen are only about 5 to 10 per cent of the level of naturalemissions, for sulphur we produce about 160 per cent of the level of natural emissions.

One clear manifestation of this alteration of \the sulphur cycle is the widespread problem of acid rain in Europe and North America. Acid precipitation is defined as rain or snow that has a pH of less than 5.6. Low pH values are caused by strong acids (sulphuric acid, nitric acid) that originate as combustion products from fossil fuels.

Over large areas of Western Europe and eastern North America, annual pH values of precipitation average between 4.0 and 4.5, and individual storms may produce acid rain of pH 2 to 3. Ore smelters and electrical generating plants have increased emissions during the past 50 years. To offset local pollution problems, smelters and generating plants have built taller. stacks, which reduce pollution at ground level.

Tall stacks (over 300 m) now are the standard, and they have exported thepollution problem downwind. The effects of acid rain on the environment are the subject of much current research. Some effects are very clear already. Freshwater ecosystems seem to be particularly sensitive.

In areas underlain by granite and granitoid rocks, which are highly resistant to weathering, the acid rain is not neutralized in the soil, so lakes and streams become acidified. Lakes in thess, bedrock areas typically contain soft water of low buffering capacity. Thus bedrock can be an initial guide to sensitive areas.

The Precambrian Fennoscandian Shield in Scandinavia, the Canadian Shield, all of New England, the Rocky Mountains,, and other areas are thus potential trouble spots. The clearest effects of acid precipitation

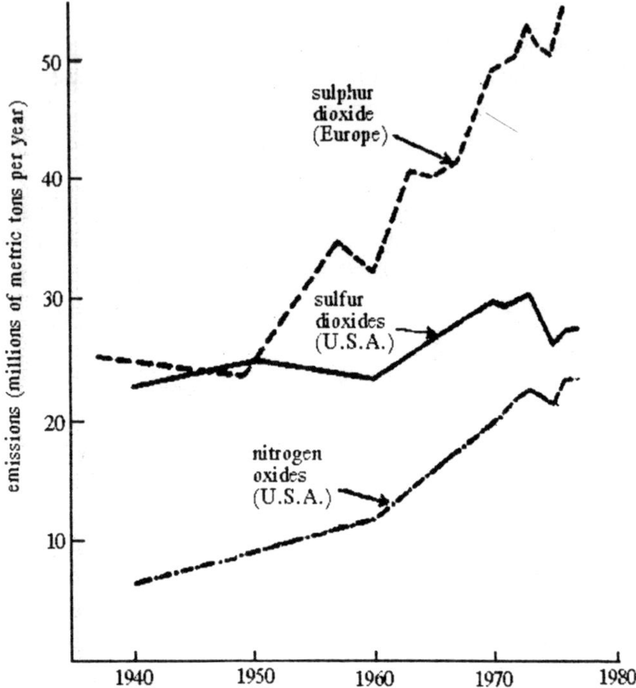

Figure 3.5: Rise in the emissions of sulphur and nitrogen oxides in the United States and Europe, 1937-1977. The curves reflect increases in the burning of fossil fuels and the smelting of ores. Sulphur and nitrogen, may be converted into strong acids in precipitation.

have been on fishpopulations in Scandinavia and eastern Canada.

Fish populations have been reduced or eliminated in many thousands of takes in southern Norway and Sweden once the pH in these *waters* has fallen below pH 5. The effect on terrestrial ecosystems is more complex and difficult to unravel.

Highly acidic precipitation can reduce primary production in terrestrial plants by direct toxicity or leaching of nutrients from the foliage. The rate of decomposition in the soil may be slowed by lower pH, and this could interfere with nutrient cycling of other ehemical elements.

In some cases, productivity of terrestrial systems might increase if a limiting nutrient like nitrogen or phosphorus is added in the :precipitation. The main point is that acidic precipitation has the potential to change nutrient, cycling in 'natural ecosystems in a great variety of ways we cannot yet understand, much less predict.

We cannot continue this aerial bombardment of ecosystems in the naive belief that nutrient cycles have infinite resilience to human inputs.

UTILIZATION OF WATER

In many parts of the world an inadequate supply of water is the most conspicuous and continuing limitation to crop growth. Water relations thus occupy a central place in any survey of developmental physiology. But much of this subject lies outside the scope of a discussion of root function in the soil.

Meteorological factors and the characteritics of plant shoots can greatly influence the effects on crops of variations in water supply. These are referred to only briefly in this chapter and attention is directed mainly to the absorption of water by root systems, to the effects of variations in water supply on their growth and function and to their morphological features which contribute to the survival of plants when the supply of water is limiting.

The discussion of a number of aspects which require the joint consideration of characteristics of the soil and of the plant is deferred to Part II of this book, for example the effects of waterlogging and the transfer of water across the root/soil interface.

THE DRIVING FORCE FOR THE MOVEMENT OF WATER

If the water economy of plants is to be seen in perspective, account must be taken of their evolutionary history. They originated in an aquatic environment and photosynthesis, the unique metabolic process on which plant growth depends, requires the absorption of carbon dioxide from the environment with the simultaneous release of oxygen.

In submerged plants this exchange occurs in solution but when terrestrial plants evolved, the site of photosynthesis being necessarily in the above-ground parts, the exchange of carbon dioxide and oxygen with an unsaturated atmosphere had the inescapable consequence that water vapour was simultaneously lost.

No membrane system was evolved-nor has synthetic chemistry yet produced one which permits the free exchanges of oxygen and carbon dioxide between an aqueous phase in plant cells and an unsaturated atmosphere without the loss of water. Transpiration is thus an inescapable physical consequence of the development of terrestrial vegetation,

Studies of the utilization of water by crops entered a new phase with the work of Penman (1948). Earlier discussions had frequently been concerned with the transpiration coefficient; that is to say the quantity of water used per unit of dry matter produced, a physiological relationship between growth and, water loss often being implied. Penman, however, showed that, during summer in temperatre regions, the quantity of water lost from, a complete ground cover of short grass, which was well supplied with water, is about 0.8 of the water loss from the same area of a free water surface; in spring or autumn the corresponding figure was somewhat lower, c. 0.7.

Somewhat different values, apply to other types of ground cover and Penwan's work provided a valuable and widely used basin fog estimating the water requirements of growing crops.

Transpiration by leaves in thus the driving force for the mo· cnlcat of water through plants. The simplicity of this relationship should not however, obscure the complexity of processes which can regulate the movement of water within plants, especially when they are subject to a degree of water-stress.

This ma‥er can be meaningfully discussed only with a thermodynamic background which is here considered only briefly; Slatyer: Kramer; Kozlowski and Weatherley are among the standard sources from which fuller information can be obtained.

WATER POTENTIAL

The movement of water depends on the existence of gradients of decreasing water potential-that is to say its free energywhich bears no direct relationship to the total quantity of water present. The transfer of water from the soil through plants to the atmosphere is thus appropriately considered in terms of potential gradients.

None the less the quantity of water present -exerts an important indirect effect; it largely determines how the potential changes when water is introduced into the system or withdrawn. The same basic thermodynamic principles apply to the movement of nutrient ions into plants.

However, in the majority of circumstances it is adequate to consider only their concentration in the solution with which roots arc in contact, since it is usually sufficiently dilute for the chemical. activity of an ion to vary closely with its concentration.

PASSAGE OF WATER THROUGH THE PLANT

Resistances to Flow

The smaller loss of water from a complete vegetation cover than from a free water surface, as shown by Penman reflects resistances to the flow of water along its' pathway from the soil to the transpring leaves. Ohm's law provides 'a ' convenient analogy which has been widely used since van den Honert (1948) drew attention to its usefulness; if water moves at a constant rate through a system, the ratio of the drop in water potential to the resistance to water flow at each step in the transfer process will be constant.

Thus, the relative magnitudes of the resistances to water movement along the soil-plant atmosphere pathway, under constant conditions, can be derived from the change in potential. To describe the passage of water realistically the simple Ohm's law analogy must, however, be amplified in two respects.

First, the major resistances to water flow in the plant can vary in a complex manner. *Second* account must be taken of the capacity of the system, to use another electrical analogy; if increased transpiration leads to a lowering of the water potential in any part of the transpiration stream, water will be withdrawn from the surrounding cells with a corresponding drop in their water potential.

It does not, however, indicate all processes which cause water to move in plants. Although transpiration is dominant under normal circumstances it is not the sole cause of water movement. If plants are maintained in a humid atmosphere the flow of water through them does not usually cease completely; in some species droplets of water may be released by guttation through hydathodes at leaf tips.

This process is attributed to gradients in water potential created by osmotic forces; the bleeding sap which can pass out of cut stems or roots, which is sometimes regarded as evidence of the 'active' uptake of water is similarly explained. These processes are not considered further as they account for only a very small fraction- of the total water which moves through transpiring plants.

Movement of Water Through Plant Shoots to the Atmosphere

When plants are transpiring in a relatively dry atmosphere the decrease in water, potential between the interior of the leaf and air exceeds by a considerable factor that in any other part of the system.

Between the soil and the transpiring leaf the decrease in water potential is unlikely to exceed about 50 bar in an unwilted plant and is often very considerably less, but the drop is water potential from the interior of the leaf to the atmosphere may approach 1000 bar.

It follows, therefore, that the highest resistance to water movement in a plant system can occur in the leaf. The movement of water across the cuticle on the leaf surface is small except in plants habituated to constantly humid environments and the major gas exchange occurs through the stomata. 'The finely balanced mechanisms which control the movement of the guard cells have been the subject of considerable research.

The two main circumstances which usually lead to stomatal closure are an increase in the concentration of carbon dioxide in the gaseous phase within leaves and a decrease in water potential of leaf cells; these two responses are believed to be linked by a hormonal process in which abscisic acid is involved.

The role of stomata in water conservation is thus evident; when decreasing leaf water potential causes stomatal closure, the loss of water can be much less than that which the prevailing meteorological factors would permit. However, the efficiency of the control mechanism varies widely between species and it reduces water loss to a negligible level only in xerophytes.

The spraying of plants with artificial 'anti trans pirant's' can restrict water loss, the action of some such substances being to modify stomatal action. The resistance to the upward movement of water through the xylem of the stem and leaf traces is small beside that across the leaf surface.

This is well illustrated by the fact that the raterate of transpiration is little affected when an appreciable port of the xylem in the stem has been severed by transverse cuts. It is often assumed that thee resistance to the passage of water across the leaf varies only because of stomatal movement but there is some evidence that the resistance in the mesophyll may also decrease' if the rate of transpiration rises.

Transfer of Water Across Roots

The main resistance in roots to the movement of water is is its. radial :passage across the cortex to the xylem. Next to the resistance in leaves it is the principal barrier to water movement throughout the plant; by comparison resistance in the xylem of the root is usually small.

This can be easily demonstrated by cutting off roots of plants which are immersed in a solution; transpiration may then increase because water can move directly into the cut ends of the conducting tissue.. None the less the resistance in the xylem of the root is not necessarily negligible.

Passioura (1972) has suggested that, when grasses are absorbing water mainly from deep in the sub-soil, viscous resistance of water flow in the conducting tissues of their thin roots can he important. Newman

(1974) cites evidence which points to the. same conclusion of roots exceed c. 1 m in length.

It is usually considered that water crosses the cortex of roots to the endodermis mainly, if not entirely, in the free space, but some workers consider that cytoplasmic movement, or transfer between vacuoles in cortical cells, may make some contribution.

When plants of different species are grown in the same environment considerable contrasts in the permeability of roots to water have been detected (Newman, 1973) and there is much evidence that the resistance to the radial transfer of water across a root can vary with environmental factors.

Decreased transpiration caused by anaerobiosis, or unfavourable temperature in the rooting medium, has been attributed to the reduction in the permeability of membranes; the application of respiratory inhibitors can have a similar effect. A review of the effects of temperature by Kramer (1969) indicates that the restriction of absorption caused by low root temperatures is greatest in plants adapted to warm habitats.

Variations in the rate of transpiration may also modify the resistance to the radial transfer of water across roots. Weatherley and his co-workers found in several species that if transpiration is increased by a reduction in the humidity of the atmosphere, the resistance to the movement of water across the root decreased.

This effect has not, however, been found by all investigators and some observations suggest that it may occur only at a limited range of transpiration rates. Differences in experimental methods may perhaps help to explain discrepancies between investigations.

Comparative studies of the entry of water into different parts of root systems provide additional evidence that the radial movement of water across roots is influenced by the rate of transpiration. When the supply of water is ample it enters more rapidly into the apical zones of roots where the endodermis is not suberized.

However, experiments by Brouwer (1953) indicate that changes in the rate at which water is absorbed can modify the extent to -which it enters different parts of young roots. The uptake of water by a single root of broad bean *(Vicia faba)* was enhanced either by transferring the plant from dark to light or by placing the other roots in an osmolyte of osmotic potential c.-2.0 bar.

Both treatments led to considerably more rapid uptake of water, especially 7.6-12.5 cm from the apex; absorption by theni then exceeded that in the special 2.5 cm in which the rate of uptake had been greater when transpiration was low. Newman (1974) has reviewed other evidence that the entry of water into diffe rent parts of young roots can be varied by external factors but this subject is still very incompletely understood even when the entire root system experiences the same water potential.

When plants receive a restricted water supply in soil, further complications may be introduced as a result of discontinuous contact between roots and the soil. None the less, all investigations of the uptake of water by different parts of the root system indicate that water can enter most readily into the young unsuberized zones of roots, but absorption is not confined to them.

In woody perennial plants, of which over 99 per cent of the root system may be suberi slow abrorption through the order tissues is likely to make a major contribution to the total water up-take (Kramer and Bullock, 1966) Sources or more detailed information on the water relations of plants include Kramer (1969); Hsiao (1973); Newman, (1975) and Monteith and Weatherley (1976).

EFFECTS OF THE EXTERNAL SUPPLY OF WATER ON THE FUNCTION AND GROWTH OF ROOT SYSTEMS

In the preceding chapter the effects of the supply of nutrient's on absorption by roots and on the form of root systems was discussed primarily on the basis of observations when roots were grown in solution culture and no other factors were varied.

There is no corresponding simple and direct way for studying the effects of differenes in the external water potential; it cannot be varied in controlled artifical systems with the same facility as the concentration of nutrients. Evidence on the effects ow water potential on root function comes mainly from experiments in soil.

Thus there is some overlap between this chapter and those in Part II of this book, which are more directly concerned with soil conditions.

GENERAL RELATIONSHIPS BETWEEN WATER POTENTIAL AND ROOT FUNCTION

The terms permanent wilting point 'and' wilting percentege are used to decribe the maximum water potential, or water content, in soil which causes plants to wilt. Slatyer (1967) has pointed out that the permanent wilting point should not be regarded as a soil constant since wilting depends on the loss of turgor from leaves and it is influenced by the rate of transpiration as well as by the osmotic pressure of the vacuolar sap of cells.

Beyond this the practical usefulness of the wilting point concept in field. situations is often limited because ample water in part of the rooting zone may permit growth to continue although the soil adjacent to much of the root system is close to the wilting point.

It is generally considered that a water potential of 15 bar throughout the rooting zone would lead to the permanent wilting of the majority of crop plants but the rate of root extension starts to decrease at much higher water potential e.g., often about c-0.5 bar though root extension may continue slowly until the water potential falls to-10 bar or lower.

Some experiments with maize (com, Zea mays) and tomatoes (Lycopersicon esculentum) indeed indicate that if part of a root system is well supplied with water, some growth can still occur in roots which are surrounded by soil in which the water potential is less than. -40 bar; they may remain alive at appreciably lower water potentials.

When osmotic forces contribute appreciably to the water potential, for example in saline soils, or after large addition of fertilizer, the restriction of growth may be greater than if low soil water potential arises from matric forces alone Osmotic. potentials c-2 to —4 bar can be injuriour to many plants, but halophyles are more tolerant.

The injury caused by low osmotic potential may be associated with inter-ference with hormonal processes. Because of the experimental problems of varying the water potential uniformly through the rooting zone, other factors, being maintained constant, the effects of water potential on nutrient uptake have been little studied independently of those, on growth.

However, if low water potential reduces root growth a restriction of nutrient uptake is to be expected because of the reduced metabolic activity of the roots, moreover the metabolic demand of the whole plant for nutrients can be reduced.

If osmotic as opposed to matric forces are responsible for low water potential, nutrient uptake may also be affected by competitive processes for example, in saline soils a high concentration of sodium can depress the absorption ofother cations.

Effects of Gradients in Water Potential Within the Rooting Zone

Except when the soil is close to or above field capacity appreciable gradients in water potential usually occur. When water is lost in dry weather its potential usually decreasesmore rapidly near the surface than in the deeper soil layers. This is due pot only to the downward movement of water, but also to its evaporation into the atmosphere

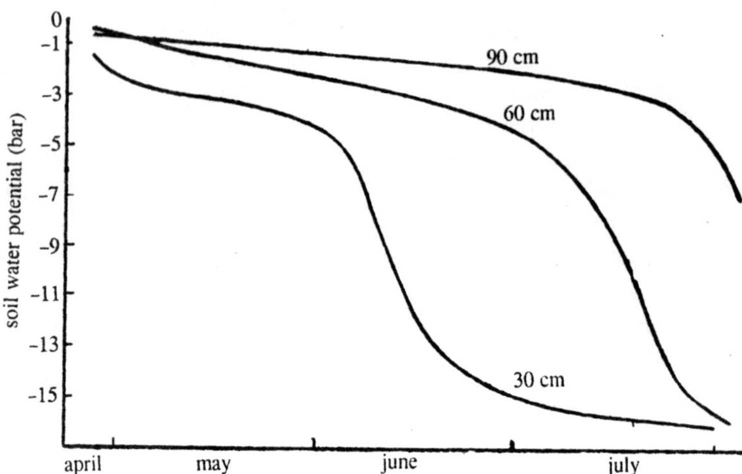

Figure 3.6: Changes in water potential at three depths in a light alluvial soil underlying an established pasture during three summer months in which the pasture ?was sheltered from rain. The water potential at 15 cm different little from that at 30 cm during the major part of the period.

and absorption by roots which are often more abundant near the surface. The gradient can be enhanced if gravitational drainage is is slower in the deeper layers and sometimes also because their capacity for water retention is higher.

Climate, the distribution of roots and soil characteristics -all interact in determining the magnitude of gradients of water potential in the soil under growing plants. Thus, the relationship observed in any set of circumstances cannot be regarded as widely representative.

None the less Fig. elsewhere in this chapter, constructed from the work of Garwood and Williams (1967a), illustrates the types of situation which can develop in dry summer weather in a temperate locality; during three summer months a sward of perennial ryegrass (Lolium perenne) in, southern England was protected from rain by a transparent cover at sufficient height to allow free air circulation.

A period of drought was thus reasonably simulated. The water potential fell considerably more rapidly at and above 30 cm than at greater depth, and as time passed the uptake of water became increasingly dependent of roots which had penetrated deeply. The general manner in which these conditions affect the distribution of roots and the absorption of nutrients will now be considered.

Root distribution. Under field conditions variations in water Supply are frequently the major: cause of differences in the distributed of

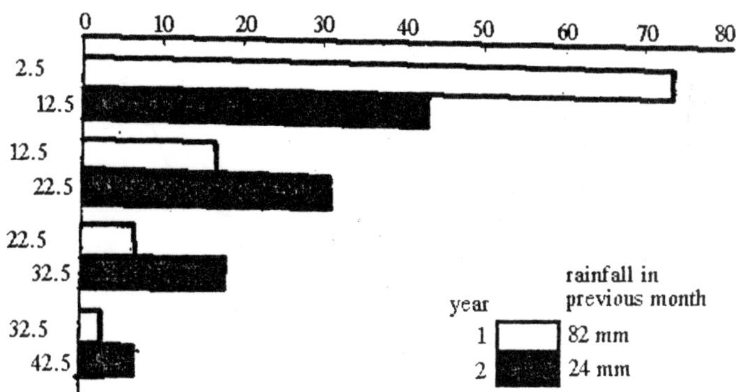

Figure 3.7: Constrasting distribution of living roots of spring burley" grown in the same field in successive years: measurements two months after planting. In Year 2 driver conditions in thesurfce soil much reduced the fraction of roots in that zone.

roots, particularly the depth they attain in soil. It illustrates contrasing rooting patterns in comparable soils due to climatic differences while Figure elsewhere in this chapter shows variations caused by differences in rainfall on the same field in two successive years. This variability is another example of the capacity of roots of 'compensatory growth' a restriction of growth in part of the root system may lead to increased growth of more favourably placed root members.

The analyse adequately the effects of water supply on root growth in the soil, account must be taken not only of the water potential at different depths but also of the rate at which water moves through the roil towards roots; the determines the extent to which water potential is maintained adjacent to the root as absorption proceeds.

The difficulty of measuring the potential and the quantity of water in soils simultaneously with root distribution has restricted detailed studies of this subject. The Rhizotron at Auburn.

Alabama, in which the growth of roots observed in large volumes of soil against glass windows has, however, provided interesting information Figure elsewhere in this chapter shows the distribution of the roots of cotton (Gossypium hirsutum) grown in a uniform fine, loamy send of relatively low water retention at the beginning and the end of a twenty-one day period in which no water was added to the soil.

Initially when the water potential throughout the rooting depth was c.—0.1 bar the density of roots decreased from the surface downwards. However, during the during cycle when water was lost considerably more rapidly from the surface layers, the pattern of root distribution was reversed. The density of roots in the dry surface soil decreased due

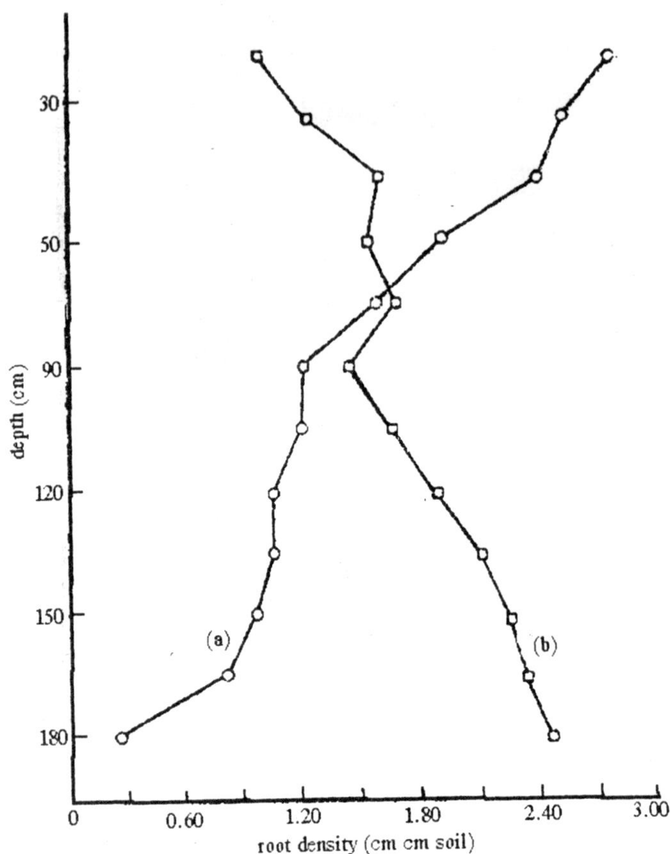

Figure 3.8: Effect of decreasing water potential for three weeks specilly in the appear soil on root distribution in cotton plants (Gossypium hirsutum), (a) at beginning of experiment; (b) at end, changes in soil water content and potential are shown in figure elsewhere in this chapter.

to death by desiccation, while a considerable proliferation occurred in the deeper layers in which the soil water potential fell little until late in the experiment. When plants were grown simultaneously in indentical conditions, except that an ample water supply was maintained throughout the rooting zone, there was little change in distribution of roots during the three week periods.

The effects of the desiccation of the upper part of the root system shown in Fig elsewhere in this chapter are basically similar to those which can be induced by lowering the solution level when plants are grown in solution culture The continuing-often enhanced-growth of the lower parts of a root system when water shortage inhibits growth nearer the soil surface has also been demonstrated by Newman (1966); however a response as great as that shown in Figure elsewhere in this chapter seldom occurs under field conditions.

Nutrient Uptake

Quite short periods of warm, dry weather can cause large variations in the absorption of nutrients from near the soil surface. This is conveniently illustrated by experiments in which soil at different depths has been labelled with radioactive tracers; they enable uptake from different depths to be compared.

Figure elsewhere in this chapter gives the results of an experiment conducted in this way; variations in the moisture content at the depth of 5 cm in soil under a sward of perennial ryegrass (Lolium perenne) led to corresponding variations in the absorption of calcium from that depth relative to the deeper soil layers, phosphate showed a similar response.

In dry conditions the restriction of nutrient uptake from near the soil surface can impose a particular restraint on plant growth because, when the water supplys is ample, the surface layers of soil are not infrequently the major source of nutrients for many annual crops as well as perennial grasses; not only is the density of roots greatest in this zone but also nutrients are usually most aundant.

Thus, if the water potential of the surface soil decreases, but ample water remains accessible to the deeper roots, the restriction of plant growth may be largely due to the limited ability of plants to absorb nutrients in this zone; improved plant growth would thus be expected if nutrients were located at a greater depth in the soil even if water supply remained the same.

Garwood and Williams (1967b) illustrated this effect. Swards of Lolium perenne were subjected to drought regimes similar to those used to obtain the water potential profiles illustrated in Figure elsewhere in this chapter; the plants absorbed nitrogen from a fertilizer source considerably more readily when it was placed some depth below the soil surface, whereas when the supply of water was abundant superficial applications were effective

It has sometimes been suggested that if a root experiences a gradient of soil water potential it is able to transfer water from the soil of higher to lower potential. Klute and Peters, (1069) have suggested that this does not occur to an important extent. The results in Figure elsewhere in this chapter and Table elsewhere in this chapter accord with this, view.

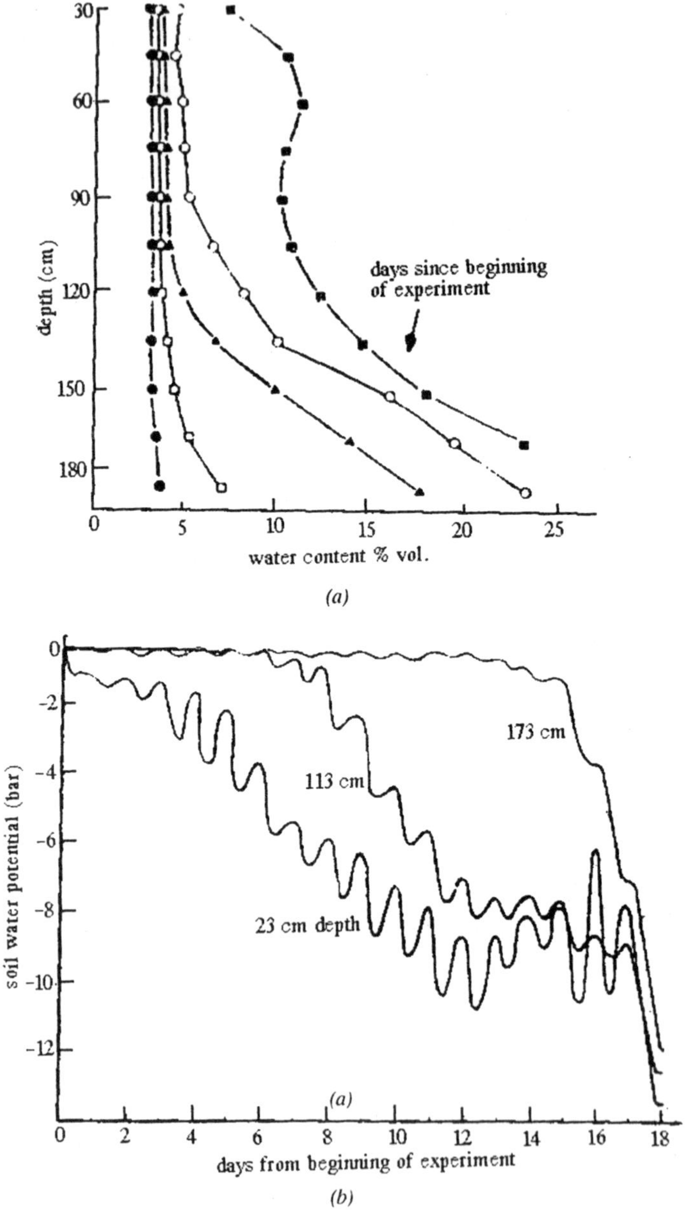

Figure 3.9: Changes in soil water content (a) and soil water potential (b) at different depths in the soil during the experiment in which root distribution. Diurnal variations in soil water potential maximum at 06.00 hours are evident.

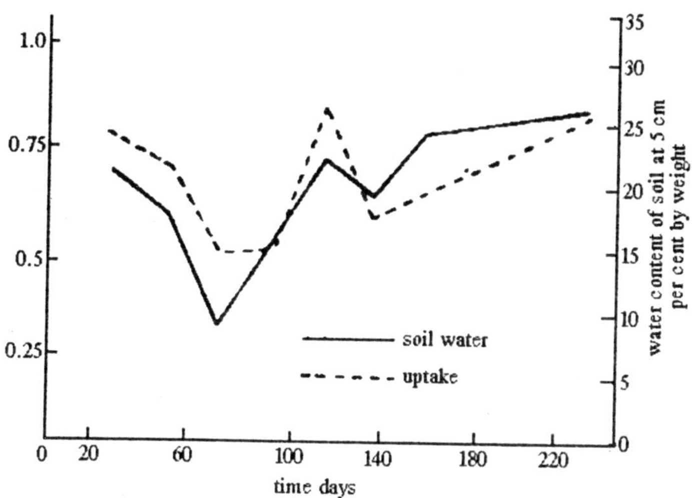

Figure 3.10: Effect of variations in water content of the surface soil (percentage by weight) during summer on the uptake by perennial ryegrass (Lodium perenne) of calcium from the depth of 5 cm, relative to that from deeper soil layers (10, 20 and 40 cm).

Table 3.5: Effect of the Depth at which Ammonium Nitrate is Placed in the Soil on the Growth of Perennial Ryegrass (Lolium Perenne) Under drought Conditions.

	Ammoniun nitrate equivalent to 112 kgN ha^{-1} Applied to all treatments		
Depth of placement of fertilizer (cm beneath *soil* surface)	0	46	76
Increase in Yield of herbage due to fertilizer: per cents	57	82	102
Apparent recovery of fertilizer nitrogen : *pet* cent**	35	75	80

* *Man yield in absence of fertilizer was 2.2 tonne dry matter ha^{-1}.*

***Apparent recovery of fertilizer nitrogen taken as increase in nitrogen content of herbage due fertilzer.*

THE SURVIVAL OF WATER STRESS

Definition of Water Stress

The term 'water' can convey different meanings depending -on whether interest centres mainly on physiological, ecological or agronomic aspects. In the strict physiological sense plants can be regarded as suffering a degree of water stress when cells are not fully turgid—that is to say when their water potential falls below zero.

Mild water stress as thus defined occurs whenever plants are transpiring at an appreciable rate; this is implicit in the fact that the flow of water through plants depends on a gradient of decreasing water potential from the roots to the mesophyll of the leaves.

However, in envirnoments favourable for plant growth the continued upward movement of water during the hours of darkness, when transpiration has ceased, largely or completely restores the turgor of leaves. Such situations, which are represented diagrammatically in Figure elsewhere in this chapter, are thus normal; none the less, measurements of leaf' water potential during daylight hours indicate an appreciable loss of turgor.

From the ecological or agronomic viewpoint water stress becomes of concern when it imposes a conspicuous restraint on plant growth. In dry weather, when evaportranspiration exceeds ' precipitation and soil water potential becomes progressively lower, the decrease in the water potential' in the plant during the hours of daylight may not be offset by the continuing absorption of water at night.

This situation, which is usually accompanied by an appreciable restriction of growth, is illustrated in simplified from in Figure elsewhere in this chapter. Eventually. if the water potential throughout all or at least the major part of the rooting zone falls to the wilting point growth cases. usually with irreversible injury to foliage. However; regeneration may still be possible.

Characteristics of Shoots which Influence Survival

This discussion is concerned primarily with root growth in· relation to the survival of water stress but if this subject is to be seen in perspective the role of the above-ground tissue must be borne in mind. The shoots of no important crop plants possess to a marked degree the characteristics which enable xerophytic. plants to withstand considerable periods of desiccation.

Note the less, there can be wide differences between species in the extent to which water loss is restricted by stomatal movement in periods of dry weather, In addition, morphological characteristics can greatly influence the ability of plants to recover after relatively severe desiccation.

The regeneration of many pasture grasses after summer drought is, for example, due to the presence of well protected buds near the base

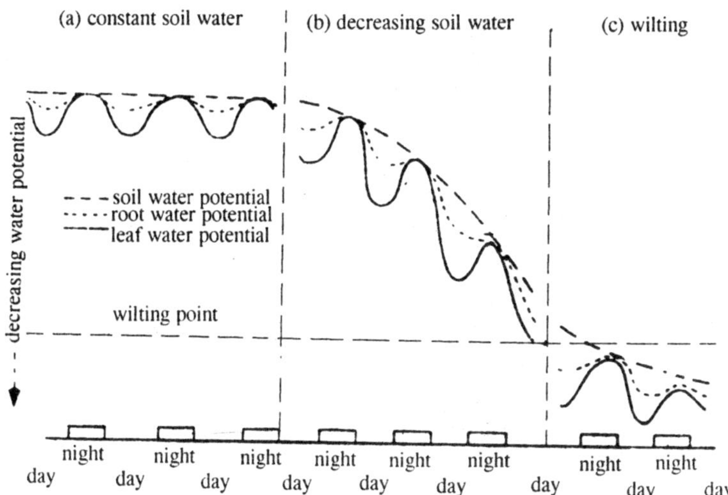

Figure 3.11: Possible relationships between water potential in soil, root and leaf under conditions of appreciable transpiration when the soil water potential remains high and constant (a), is decreasing (b) and when the wilting point is reached (e).

of shoots. Even when the water potential in the greater part of the rooting zone has been close to wilting point for many weeks in summer, so that growth ceases, a considerable development of foliage can occur in a few weeks after the soil is returned to field capacity. This is well illustrated by the experiments of

Garwood and Williams (1967) with perennial ryegrass (Lolium perenne): growth had ceased before the water potential of the soil was reduced to the low values indicated in the right hand side of Fig. 5.1, but rapid growth was resumed within a few weeks of ample water being again provided.

Characteristics of Roots which Influence Survival

The most important characteristic of the root systems of many crop plants, which contributes toltheir survival in dry conditions, is the ability of root axes to extend sufficiently rapidly that they maintain continuing contact with zones of soil in which the water potential remains adequate under dry conditions.

This is a characteristic which causes lucerne (alfalfa, Medicago sativa) to be among the most drought resistant to crop plants. The importance of root depth in determining water uptake under dry conditions is well from the work of Long and French (1967) who compared water withdrawal from the soil in a period of dry summer weather by meadow fescue (Festuca prantensis), a relatively deep rooted grass, and the more shallow rooted timothy (Phleum pratense). Meadow fescue absorbed considerably more water from below 35 cm, and also a greater total .quantity, than the shallow rooted species.

The difference in water extraction between the two species makes it evident that the resistance to the movement of water through the soil to the root zone (sometimes called the *pararhizal* resistance) can be much greater than the resistance to its movement through the vascular tissue of roots.

Next to root depth, extensive root branching is often the most important characteristic of root systems which favours the uptake of water. If there is an ample supply of water throughout the rooting zone the size of root systems may be more than ample to supply the needs of the plant and the removal of an appreciable part of the root system can have little effect on the total water uptake.

But the situation is very different in dry conditions when steep gradients of water potential make it possible for water to be absorbed by only a small part of the root system. When water stress occurs for only a limited period a further *characteristic* of the root system can be of considerable importance; namely the rapidity with which new roots develop after the water potential in the *soil*-especially often the surface layers-again becomes favourable.

Many gramineae can rapidly develop new nodal or crown roots in these circumstances and this can contribute to their recovery after periods of drought; but it is not necessarily the only reason. Evidence that the older parts of cereal roots, in which a considerable part of the cortex has collapsed, can absorb nutrients from solutions, makes it seem probable that after a root has been surrounded by dry soil for an extended period the absorption of water, as well as nutrients, can be resumed when the water supply again becomes ample provided that the vascular tissue remains intact. This question does not, however, appear to have been studied detail.

To sum up, the combined effect of the depth to which roots penetrate, the extent to which they ramify in zones where water is constantly available and their *ability* to regenerate when the water supply becomes favourable appear to be the most important *morphological* characteristics of root systems which enable plants to withstand water stress. But this may not always be so.

Passioura (1974) has described laboratory experiments, with simulated drought conditions, in which plants depend on water stored in the soil throughout their entire period of growth. He found that the yield of grain of wheat (*Triticum aestivum*) could be enhanced when only a single seminal axis was allowed to penetrate the soil.

The benefit of this treatment was attributed to a more economical use of water during the earlier phases of growth which resulted from the higher hydraulic resistance of the restricted root system.

VARIABILITY—THE DIFFICULTY OF PREDICTION

The response of root systems to variations in water supply under natural conditions is perhaps the most difficult aspect of the *behaviour* of plants to predict or to describe in quantitative terms. Uncertainty is caused both by the rapid, and largely unpredictable, changes in water supply which *seasonal weather* can bring about and the equally rapid response of plants to these changed conditions-including sometimes injury due to anaerobiosis caused by waterlogging.

Moreover, it is possible that the closeness of contact between roots and the soil, and hence the resistance to the transfer of water, can be affected. Figure elsewhere in this chapter illustrates the impacticability of even describing the form of the root system of a single species in a single soil in a truly representative manner.

Because root density normally decreases with depth it is not surprising that an exponential relationship can often account for a large part of the variation in root distribution with depth in soil. But this is not a constant *relationship*, it happened in this first (wetter) year illustrated in Figure elsewhere in this chapter but in the se: and (dry)- year the relationship was closely linear.

In both years, however, there were considerable discrepancies between the density of root observed at each depth and that calculated from the exponential or linear equations which *fitted* the observations most closely. *Mathematical* relationships to describe the growth of plant roots in uniform environments have been developed.

However, these models can at present help little in the study of field problems since an understanding of root function is of the greatest interest when they are subject to stresses-often transient and unpredictable ones. The *recognition* of this in no way disputes the *desirability* of seeking as fully as possible to derive quantitative relationships which may assist in describing the response of plants to their environment.

4

ABIOTIC ECOSYSTEM

The environmental factors may be defined as the whole complex of *climatic*, *edaphic*, and *biotic factors* that act upon an organism or an ecological community and ultimately determine its form and *survival*. On the other hand organisms, react to differences or changes in their environment in several characteristic ways, either by trying to avoid harmful situations or by being able to adjust *physiologically*, within their genetic limits, to *adverse factors*.

In ecological studies the total environment is said to be made of some nonliving components as well as some biotic or living components, thus making the nonliving environment and living environment respectively. The nonliving environment includes the nonliving factors both physical and chemical, which influence the life of organisms.

They are *temperature*, *light energy*, *water*, *atmosphere*, including *atmospheric gases* and air current etc., fire, gravity, topography, (the configuration of the earth's surface), soil, pH, and nutrients, etc. The living environment includes the living or biotic factors, i.e., animals and plants.

How organisms are influenced by their environment is determined largely by the following principles:

1. *Shelford's Law of Tolerance:* According to the law of tolerance, organisms have an ecological minimum and maximum, with a range in between which represents the limits of tolerance. Some subsidiary principles to the law of tolerance may be stated as follows:

(a) Organisms may have a wide range of tolerance for one factor and a narrow range for another.

(b) Organisms with wide ranges of tolerance for all factors are likely to be most widely distributed.

(c) When conditions are not optimum for a species with respect to a particular environmental factor, the limits of tolerance may be reduced with respect to other factors. For example, according to Penman (1950), when soil nitrogen is limiting, the resistance of grass to drought is reduced.

(d) The limits of tolerance for reproductive individuals, seeds, eggs, embryos, and larvae are usually narrower than non-reproductive adult plants or animals. For example, adult blue crabs and many other marine animals can *tolerate brackish water*, or fresh water with a high chloride content, but their larvae cannot live in such waters and hence they cannot reproduce in rivers and are not established there *permanently*.

To describe a species with a narrow range of. tolerance for a particular factor, we use the prefix steno-, for those with a wide range we use the prefix eury—he terms stenothermal and eurythermal refer to temperature tolerance. Similarly, *stenohaline* and *euryhaline*, *stenophagic* and *euryphagic*; *stenoecious* and *euryecious* are a few other pairs of words used in respect to salinity, food, and habitat respectively.

2. *Liebig's Law of the Minimum:* This law states that the growth of a plant is dependent on the amount. of food stuff which is presented to ĭt in minimum quantity. This law has been extended by Taylor (1934). According to him, the functioning of an organism is controlled or limited by that essential environmental factor of combination of factors present in the least favourable amount.

But according to Odum, it seams best to restrict the concept of the minimum to chemical materials (*oxygen*, *phosphorus*, etc.) necessary for physiological growth and reproduction, and to include other factors and the limiting effect of the *maximum* in the law of tolerance. However, two subsidiary principles must be added.

The first is a constraint that Liebig's law is strictly applicable only under steady-state conditions, i.e., when inflow of energy and materials balances the outflow. The second important consideration is factor interaction. Thus, high concentration of some substance, or the action of some factor other than the minimum one, may modify the rate of utilization of the latter.

Sometimes organisms are able to substitute partly a chemically closely related substance for one that is deficient in the environment.

Thus, where strontium is abundant, molluscs are able to substitute it for calcium to a partial extent in their shells.

3. *Combined Concept of Limiting Factors:* According to Odum, the presence and success of an organism or a group of organisms depends upon a complex of conditions. Any condition that exceeds the limits of tolerance is said to be a limiting condition or a limiting factor. Among others, temperature is very often a limiting factor.

Thus, organisms are controlled in nature by (i) the quantity :and variability of materials for which there is a minimum requirement, and physical factors which are critical, and (ii) the limits of tolerance of organisms themselves to these and other components of the environment.

Salinity and Osmotic Pressure

The most deterring ecological barrier we know is the salt content of sea water. Only very few plant and animal species can thrive in a range of salinity extending from sea water to fresh water. Moreover, within this continuum of salinity, a particular degree of change is not

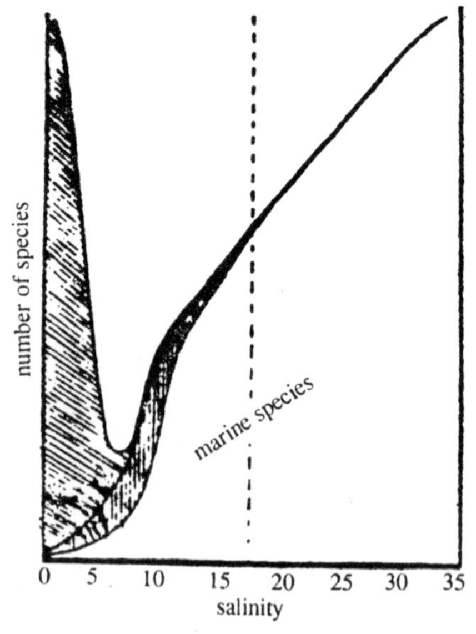

Figure 4.1: The number of species of organisms present in waters of different salinity, reconstructed from many reports. Diagonal hatching: fresh-water species; vertical hatching: specific brackish-water species; unshaded: marine species; black (bottom of graph): species that live in both fresh and salt water. In each case the number of species is represented by the vertical extent of the surface.

necessarily accompanied by a corresponding change in the organisms. In a certain range a relatively pronounced difference in salinity (for example, 25% vs 15%) produces only a slight difference in number of species, whereas in the vicinity of 8 per cent and at the boundary between fresh and brackish water there is a sudden dramatic effect.

These effects of water salinity and the associated osmotic pressure deserve closer attention. We shall take animals as an example. All the animals and plants alive today originated in the ocean. In order for them to invade and conquer terrestrial and fresh-water habitats, they had to undergo adaptive modifications of their original states-at a price, of course.

We must keep this fact in mind whenever we are discussing plants and animals of freshwater and land. To begin, Jet us consider the primary marine animalsspecies which throughout their phylogenesis have occupied no environment other than the ocean. The osmotic pressure of their intercellular fluid is very slightly higher than that of the open sea; it corresponds to 35 per cent total salinity.

The fluid in the cells has the same *osmotic* potential, and differs from that outside the cells only in ionic composition. Whereas inter cellular fluid-in the water-vascular system of echinoderms, for instance, or in the blood vessels of annelids-closely resembles sea water, the cells contain considerably higher amounts of potassium ions.

Even in these animals, then, *ionic* regulation occurs; it leads to the well-known electrical phenomena at cell surfaces. Moreover, the cells also contain organic substances (in particular amino acids, and sugar in many plant cells) which contribute to maintenance of osmotic pressure.

Animals of this type can endure only minimal *fluctuations* in the osmotic pressure (that is, the salinity) of their environment. Their distribution is thus restricted to the *oceanic* plankton or to deep regions of the sea.

The majority of benthonic animals—echinoderms, tunicates, crustaceans, annelids, molluscs, and cnidarians—are in this category. Animals living in shallow water, tidal zones and estuaries must be able to tolerate fluctuations in salinity. *Changes* in the *osmotic* pressure of the milieu, which have an immediate effect on the *intercellular fluid* and thence on the cells, must be compensated.

Without such compensation, reduction of environmental *salinity* would cause water to flow into the animal and its cells, which would swell and burst. Conversely, increase in salinity results in *shrinking* of the cells.

These processes can be counteracted only by active alterationof the osmotic pressure in the cells and in the intercellular fluid. Water is expelled and ions are actively taken up.

Within the cells osmotically effective amino acids are synthesized and broken down. "*Poikilosmotic*" behaviour of this sort, effective over a wide range, is thus by no means a passive phenomenon; it requires energy-consuming activity of single cells and of the entire body.

Animals in this category are characteristic of regions with moderate salinity fluctuations; they invade the tidal zone, the mouths of rivers, and bodies of brackish water. This type represents the point of origin of land and fresh-water animals. But purely *poikilosmotic* behaviour is *potentially* lethal for both lines of development.

No animal can exist with the low osmotic pressure of fresh water in its cells or blood. In addition to the ionic regulation we have just discussed, then, a further mechanisms is necessary—osmoregulation. First let us consider the evolution of the terrestrial habit.

Animals living in an air *milieu* are less exposed to the osmotic pressure of the substrate fluid, because only small areas of the body contact the ground. In the long term, though, they are of course, affected in the same way as water animals, by way of the water they drink and osmotic processes in the parts of, the body exposed to the water in the soil.

The results we shall now consider are based entirely on prolonged culture *experiments*. When, during the course of evolution, many groups of animals migrated from the sea to the land, they moved from a milieu in which the salinity varied hardly at all through one with highly unconstant conditions-the *marine supralittoral* before they again reached a stable, though quite different, situation inland.

Most crustaceans initially protect themselves from the: wide fluctuations in the coastal region by retaining an osmotic pressure higher than that of the external medium (*hypetonicity regulation*). Then the beach forms acquire an additional capacity for hypotonicity regulation; they are able to keep the *internal milieu* at an osmotic pressure lower than that of the environment.

Such constancy of the internal milieu is typical of most of the coastal crustaceans living above the water line (*Uca*, *Ocypode*, *Carcinus*, *Talitrus*, *Orchestia*, *Ligia*). The terrestrial hermit crabs (Coenobita) and some brachyurans also appear to keep their internal milieu constant. In this case, however, another method is used. Evidently these animals require both fresh and sea water; if only one kind is available, the internal osmotic pressure rises or falls and the animals. eventually die. The time of death depends on many other factors (molting is particularly-*hazardous*).

When land hermit crabs drink, then, they sometimes choose fresh water and sometimes sea water. Their internal pressure can vary over a wide range, but can be continually readjusted if water of the appropriate salinity is consumed in time. An entirely different approach enabled gastropods to conquer the *supralittoral zone*.

On flat soft beaches they too develop *hypertonicity* regulation; its acquisition can be followed within genera. For example, Limapontia capitata exhibits no osmoregulation at all, whereas a species living higher up the *beach*, *Limapontia depressa*, can regulate its osmotic pressure.

Gastropods have responded to high salinity by developing a poikilosmotic mechanism effective over a wide range; in this case there is no hypotonicity regulation. By these means, gastropods of the ocean beaches can tolerate extremely wide *fluctuations* of the pressure in the *internal medium* and in the *cell fluid*.

In Ovatella and Assiminea, pressures corresponding to a salinity between 6 per cent and 90 per cent (sometimes up to 100 per cent) have been measured. This situation requires highly specific adaptation of the enzymes, which must remain functional despite great differences in their intracellular milieu. By contrast, *gastropods* on rocky coasts apparently never perform *osmoregulation*.

When conditions are unfavourable they shut themselves off from the outside world by closing the operculum. Of course, adaptation to changing salinity conditions cannot be obtained free of cost. In the case of *homoiosmotic* animals such as Ligia or *Orchestia platensis* the price is obvious.

In both low- and high-salinity water they must perform hard osmotic work, so that it comes as no surprise that with respect to growth and rate of reproduction they exhibit a distinct optimum in the approximately isotonic range. The same is true of poikilosmotic species. *Synthesis* and *breakdown* of the *osmotically* effective substances costs energy.

Even the presence of enzymes that operate with a wide osmotic range evidently represents a drain on energy. *Poikilosmotic* species, then, also pay for their ability to tolerate a wide range of salinity with very different rates of development and *reproduction*. It seems clear that when *organisms* are under such stress the strategy adopted is not to increase energy consumption (which would mean eating greater amounts of food, and this is normally not available) but to cover the cost by slower growth, a lower rate of reproduction, and less resistance to' generally harmful environmental factors.

The poikilosmotic mussels in the inner Baltic Sea, for example, are considerably' less able to tolerate cold than those in the North Sea-although in the Baltic selection for high cold tolerance would be expected. Desert plants and lichens are particularly sensitive to chemicals in their environment.

Only two of the four types were able to evolve further, into true land animals. Terrestrial hermit crabs and snails on rocky coasts need at least occasional access to water of marine salinity. Their evolution therefore ends in the supralittoral. Once the other terrestrial crustaceans and gastropods had evolved into genuine land animals, the salinity at which body fluids could be maintained by maximum regulation fell significantly.

For terrestriall arthropods it corresponds to about 10 per cent, and for soft-skinned land animals to about 6 per cent. At the same time, the ability of arthropods to tolerate high salinity was greatly restricted by loss of hypotonicity regulation. Phylogenetically young land animals (isopods) can still exhibit such regulation, and can thus tolerate high environmental osmotic pressure.

This physiological feature is useless in the present habitat of these animals, and can only be understood in the historical context. In the evolutionary tree of soft-bodied land animals, the poikilosmotic branch is reduced: salinity tolerance is strictly limited.

The pattern that thus developed-in arthropods and land vertebrates (which originated in fresh water), a fixed limit for regulation corresponding to 10 per cent with no hypotonicity regulation, and in soft-bodied land animals (gastropods and annelids) a 6 per cent limit with poikilosmotic behaviour limited to a very small branch-gives the starting point for the recolonization of the ocean by land animals.

Certain animals were predisposed for this return to the sea-desert animals that drink from salt lakes and must excrete salt, and animals from environments with aberrant chemistry such as liquid-manure pits). Another predisposing property, evidently, is alteration in the set level of tonicity during the course of the year, as a protection against cold.

The comparalively massive advance of terrestrial animals (insects, mites) into .arctic oceans argues for this interpretation. In the transition from land to sea arthropods redevelop hypotonicity regulation. Only the Collembola appear to extend the poikilosmotic branch of evolution, which otherwise includes soft-skinned formsamphibians, gastropods (Succinea), and enchytraeids.

The increase of osmotic pressure in the blood of the only truly marine frog (Rana cancrivora, eastern Asia) is brought about not by salts but by dissolved urea. By such modifications secondary marine animals are initially capable of living in either sea or fresh water. They need no salt: they can either tolerate or excrete it.

A real dependence on marine salinity arises by loss of hypertonicity regulation, as has happened in the beach fly 'Coelopa. Once this has occurred, the animal is cut off from both land and fresh water; examples in this category include marine nematocerans (most species of Clunio) and mites (Halacaridae).

These arthropods, which returned to the sea very long ago, exhibit hardly any trace of their old homoiosmotic characteristics; they have secondarily become almost poikilosmotic. Moreover, they have secondarily raised the regulated internal tonicity to such a level that they are isoosmotic in the water of the open ocean, and thus are exposed to only slight physiological stress.

Another route away from the ocean, simpler to understand and not associated with such a diversity of types, is that leading to fresh water by way of brackish water. Salinity does fluctuate in brackish-water regions, but these fluctuations.

Are much smaller than those in the supralittoral. No species travelling this route has developed hypotonicity regulation. Again, a typical feature is lowering of the internal tonicity; in fact, this is much more pronounced than in terrestrial animals. This progression can be readily followed in species of Gammarus from the ocean, brackish water and fresh water.

Soft-skinned fresh-water animals (clams and snails) have the lowest internal osmotic pressures of all animals. Because of this low set tonicity level remigration into the ocean presents difficulties. Bony fish (Teleostei) in the ocean must continually excrete salt: they have developed hypotonicity regulation as an adaptation to marine salinity.

They have also raised their regulated tonicity as compared with bony fish in fresh water, but not enough to make salt excretion unnecessary. And this regulation uses up energy, with severe consequences. Fish in the arctic freeze at higher temperatures than does the medium surrounding them. Selachians (sharks and rays)—like Rana cancrivora and Latimeria—have followed the poikilosmotic route.

They raise their internal pressure to levels equivalent to those of the environment by retaining urea. This feature is an extremely strong indication of the fresh-water origin of selachians-if, indeed, the high urea production does not actually imply a semiterrestrial ancestry. Fresh-water arthropods adapted to marine life by hypotonicity regulation, acquired in a stepwise manner.

A good example of a typical brackish-water arthropod on its way back to the sea is the caddis fly Limnophilus affinis. But only relatively few species returned from fresh water to the open ocean; examples include the bug Halobates and the nematoceran *Cricotopus*. No arthropod that originated in fresh water has been found to have secondarily raised its regulated tonicity level.

The internal osmotic pressure of Clunio, high in comparison to that of other chironomids such as Chironomus and Cricotopus, may well be associated with the terrestrial origin of this genus. *Soft-skinned* fresh-water animals have achieved this return journey only to a slight extent; the chief examples to mention are the *marine rotifers*. Nothing is known about how they maintain water balance.

The river gastropod Theodoxus has advanced. into brackish water up to fairly high salinities; it exhibits a slight increase in poikilosmotic capacity as compared with its *limnetic* relatives. The routes of migration, then, can lead from sea to land, land to sea, sea to fresh water and the reverse-and there are many others.

We shall mention only one, which involves salt lakes and deserts. Salt lakes and highly saline lagoons in arid maritime regions are colonized from the land, from the ocean and from *fresh water*. It is not difficult to distinguish animals of marine and limnetic origin on the basis of differences in internal *osmotic* pressure.

Insects that came from land or fresh water develop a marked *hypotonicity* regulation, though the maintained tonicity is significantly increased. This process can readily be followed within the genus *Chironomus*, which has progressively invaded small bodies of water of increasing salinity.

There are many ways by which animals can migrate from these saline environments to brackish-water regions, where the inventory of species is very similar. We have seen that a given environmental factor can elicit quite different *physiological* responses among animals coexisting in a particular *habitat*.

These responses can be understood only in relation to the ecological history of the animals. The same considerations hold true for ecological factors other than salinity. There is evidently little *connection* between the development of physiological functions and the phylogenesis of the animals in the sense of evolution of higher forms of life. Rather, physiological functions appear to arise chiefly in relation to the changes of habitat that occur during *phylogenesis*.

This interpretation is generally accepted in the case of excretion of nitrogenous metabolic waste. The complicated processes by which ammonia is converted to larger *molecules* inland animals are determined by the *animals* ecological history.

And the same is true of sensory functions. Dolphins evolved the capacity to orient by ultrasound, and it may be that this new adaptation, "*economical*" in terms of the price paid, made possible their great success as inhabitants of the sea-a habitat where other animals in a more favourable osmotic situation and/ or with gill *respiration* are much better off energetically.

One could say that the dolphins can "*afford*" higher energy consumption because of a "newly invented technological trick. In this discussion we have emphasized the costs incurred by animals that avoid intra-specific *competition* by moving to different *habitats*.

The uptake of dissolved organic matter, which plays a decisive role in the nutrition of a great number of marine invertebrates, is much more difficult under the *osmotic* conditions in fresh water indeed, it is impossible. In migrating to fresh water, marine animals gave up an extremely abundant source of energy-rich and qualitatively valuable food, leaving it to the microorganisms.

Furthermore, *hypertonicity* regulation requires that the water drawn in by osmosis be continually pumped out, and that there be continual active uptake of salts: against a concentration gradient. *Special* organs for salt uptake and water elimination are necessary for existence on land and in fresh water. Energy is expended for the construction and operation of these organs.

And there are still other problems. The organs for salt uptake are evidently not so specific that they can recognize precisely the correct ions in the water. They "*confuse*" heavy metals with sodium and potassium ions, and if uptake of the latter is blocked by heavy metals the animal dies. The same problem arises when animals return to the ocean.

Fish and birds and mammals in the ocean must *continually* excrete salt; they must develop snecilic organs for the purpose, as well as others to take in water to replace that lost by osmosis. From the viewpoint of energy *consumption*, fish and birds are inferior to the primary marine animals.

As Dollo's Law of the irreversibility of evolution states, animals returning to this *intrinsically "economically favourable"* environment do not re-evolve the original physiological constitution. It is worth making a cost-benefit analysis to learn how warm *blooded animals* have managed, despite these difficulties, to be so successful in the ocean: but no such analysis has as yet been carefully done.

The best solution to the problem of minimizing costs on the land has been developed by the vascular plants. Their roots extend into the moist and mineral-rich soil, their leaves into the *dry air*. Water evaporates continually from the leaves, generating a flow of sap through the plant, initially always from the roots to the leaves.

Sap flow in this direction makes it possible to maintain, without cost, an osmotic pressure within the plant that is relatively high in comparison with the soil, as well as a cost-free influx of water against the prevailing *osmotic gradient*.

Both the movement of materials from the roots to the leaves and osmoregulation, then, are initially brought about in a purely physical way, by means of the differences in the vapour 'pressures of soil and air and in the structures of the plant below and above ground-all at no cost to the plant. Of course, water consumption is very high. Unlike animals, plants have no internal circulation of water.

In all our discussions of the effects of seawater salinity and osmotic pressure we have been thinking in terms of the normal composition of sea water. The proportions of the different salts are in fact uniform throughout the oceans and in all waters directly connected with the ocean. Saline habitats inland, by contrast, have an entirely different ionic composition.

Thus they can usually not be colonized by primary marine forms, which are really dependent on salt and have *correspondingly* high concentrations of salt in their cells and *body fluids*. Only secondary marine organisms, not actually dependent on salt but simply capable of excreting it efficiently, can colonize such *sites*. This fact explains the great differences between the *fauna* and *flora* of inland saline habitats and those of marine habitats.

A particularly striking characteristic is the absence of most of the true marine algae (only very *pollution-tolerant* forms can .survive in some inland saline sites) and sensitive ocean animals such as all of the *marine Cnidaria*, *echinoderms* and *molluscs*.

The same considerations apply to plants. The primary marine species have tissue osmotic pressures identical to that of the surounding medium.

Plants in fresh water and on land .must actively take in salts and protect themselves from the osmotic influx of water. Land plants have exploited this *situation* as described above, the water simply evaporates, and in the process sets up a current that *simultaneously* carries nutrients through the plant.

If vascular plants return to saline habitats they are in the same predicament as animals, and must eliminate the excess salt. Salt glands develop in such plants, just as in animals. Land and fresh-water plants are thus from the outset in a less *favourable energetic* position than marine plants.

Adaptation to the new habitat exacts a price. Should these terrestrial plants return to the, marine environment, they cannot simply realize the old advantages of life in the sea-they must now bear *additional costs.* If they are to maintain themselves in *competition* with marine plants they must become or remain competitive in a different manner.

This sort of *optimization* in a new habitat can occur in *surprising*

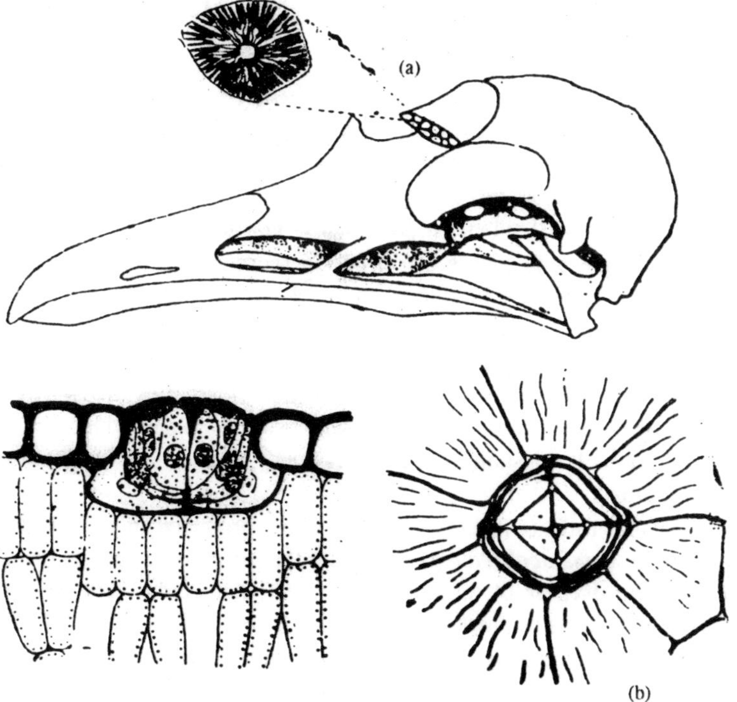

Figure 4.2: a, b,: Salt glands for the excretion of salt from secondary marine organisms. (a) Salt gland of a gull (Larus), (b) Salt gland of sea-lavender Statice gmclini.

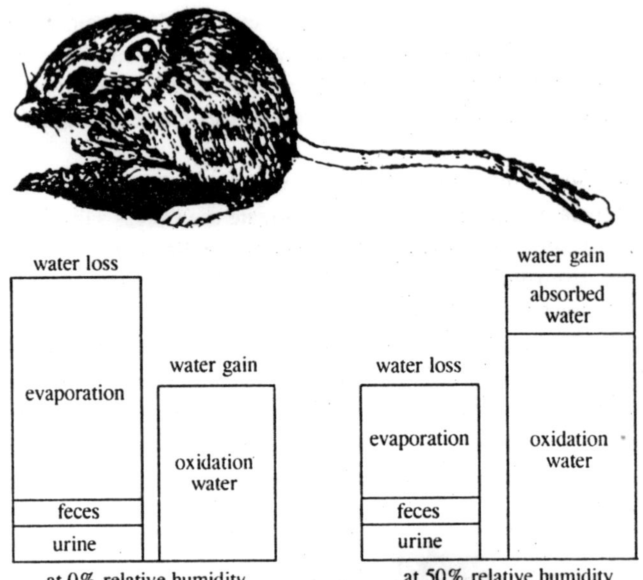

Figure 4.3: Water balance in the kangaroo rat Dipodomys spectabilis at different relative humidities.

ways. A secondary marine animal which relies on the continual excretion of salt can reduce the amount that must be excreted by selective feeding; when marine fish or birds re-taken as food (as they are by many *seals* and *dolphins*) relatively little salt is *consumed*.

An animal with such a diet need not secrete salt as vigorously as one that eats primary marine animals. A desert animal that selects, from the very salty plants available to it, the parts containing little salt, is in a *favourable energetic* position.

For example, the kangaroo rat *Dipodomys microps* of the North American deserts scrapes off the less salty tissues of plants with specially shaped teeth. It consumes only as much salt as a normal *herbivorous* land' animal.

Related rodents make use of the water produced in their bodies when food is *metabolized*—so efficiently that they never need to drink, despite the dryness of their food (they eat mainly the very dry but energy-rich seeds of plants).

Land-dwelling plants and animals face special problems with, regard to water balance. Because of the evaporation of water into the air, their milieu in some respects corresponds to a highly saline environment in which water is lost due to *osmotic effects*.

We shall now discuss the methods by which water is conserved under these conditions, and consider the question whether it is possible to make use of the moisture in the air by taking it in directly. It will become apparent that in the last analysis water balance is merely a special case of salt balance and osmoregulation.

The problem of *moisture*, which occupies a central place in textbooks on terrestrial ecology, must be given less emphasis in a general presentation that includes *marine ecology*. It is therefore treated as a subtopic in this chapter.

First let us consider the strategies by which animals adapt to differences in relative *humidity*. Simple model experiments and theoretical considerations show that a small sphere of *gelatine* loses more moisture per unit time than a larger sphere under the same conditions.

The small *sphere* soon dries up; the larger one retains moisture for a longer time. As a strategy of adaptation to low-humidity regions, then, we would expect to find increase in the size of animals. But this increase brings a *disadvantage*, in that larger animals take longer to reach *sexual maturity*.

Their reproductive rate is fundamentally lower than that of a small animal. Thus in regions where there is little or no danger of desiccation, smaller animals have a selective advantage over larger ones. From the cold deserts of the *arctic* to the arid deserts of the *tropics*, there is a distinct increase in mean body size of the insects sampled (small insects, if present, are active only at night, when *humidity* is high).

On the other hand, the number of individuals per unit area is greater in cold deserts than in hot deserts. What has been said of deserts applies similarly to other habitats. *Humid-cool* regions are occupied, on the *average*, by smaller insects than dry slopes; maritime regions, such as the North Sea coast and 'the British Isles, on the average have smaller insects than continental regions like eastern Prusia or *Hungary*.

But there is a catch in this arrangement-larger insects must pass through juvenile stages small enough to be in danger of desication. The danger is particularly great in *arid regions*. Many of the animals living here provide protection for their young or, by actual brood-care behaviour, shift the emergence of the youngest stages to a time when the humidity is *relatively high*.

They actively select particularly *favourable* (i.e., moist), elements in the habitat. The *youngest* and thus smallest stages of crickets stay in the more *moist places*, near the bases of the plants; mature crickets prefer the open areas between the plants. A similar shift of locale occurs during the bug life cycle; from their original post at the bases of plants, the young stages migrate to the exposed tips. Another way to escape desiccation is to adopt the nocturnal habit.

Mammals lose more water by evaporation when the air temperature is higher than that of their bodies. Under such conditions, they must allow water to evaporate in order to keep the body cool. Some desert mammals save water by doing without such cooling; they are able to tolerate an increase in body temperature when the 'air temperature is very high.

The same species preserve the water ordinarily lost in respiration, by retaining it in the nose with a specific cooling mechanism. On the other hand, remarkably few organisms have developed the ability to withdraw water vapour from the air. Such behaviour is know cnly among a very small number of animals (book lice) and lower plants.

No vascular plants can do it, but many of them can utilize water suspended in the air as droplets-fog, for example. The occurs in the high deserts of the Andes. Very high humidity is unfavourable to terrestrial organismss in all temperature zones. It is obvious that plants should suffer, for they depend on transpiration.

But we still do not know why grasshoppers, crickets, butterflies, beetles, and their larvae show practically no growth or development at relative humidities. above 80 per cent.

Temperature

No environmental factor seems so easily measurable, and there: is no factor of which we are so readily aware, as temperature. Because of its accessibility, a chaotic mass of temperature data has accumulated, most of which is unrelated to the ecological context within which it was published.

In fact, it is difficult to measure temperature at the site of importance to the organismin the organism itself; the temperature here (in the case of land organisms) bears little relationship to the meteorological temperature. The latter can serve only as a rough estimate.

Accordingly, it is considerably harder to establish a relationship between the distribution of an animal or plant and the temperature than, for example, to learn how distribution depend-on the salinity of the available water. As an illustration of the difficulty o, such judgements, consider the following example.

In Bavaria, the part of west Germany with the most continental climate, the nightingale is found in only a very few places where the climate is especially mild. It is of common occurrence in many other parts of Germany. About April 20 nightingale return from its wintering grounds; it cannot tolerate/nighttime frost, and hard frosts are generally to be expected in Bavaria until the beginning of May.

By contrast, the hoopoe is a regular inhabitant of many lacations in Bavaria. It requires considerably higher temperatures than does the nightingale. It arrives later (not before the beginning of May), when the night frosts in general have stopped and the' approaching continental summer brings very warm days and very small amounts of rain.

In most other parts of Germany (apart from Baden-Wurttemberg) the hoopoe is considerably less common, because the summer temperatures are lower and the precipitation greater. It is not clear whether the infuence of temperature here is direct or is exerted by wayof another factor such as food supply.

Temperature affects all chemical processes as formulated in Vant'Hoffs Law: a 10°C increase in temperature accelerates a chemical reaction by a factor of 2-4. We say that this chemical reaction has a Q_{10} of 2-4. The biochemical reactions, of organisms are naturally subject to this law.

Given that the temperature can fluctuate over a wide range during the course of a day, it is understandable that during evolution all organisms have developed mechanisms that liberate them, to a greater or lesser extent, from this temperature dependence. The warm-blooded animals have gone furthest in this respect, and will be discussed separately.

The ectothermic organisms, w'th body temperatures that can change over a wider range (microorgadisms, plants, and poikilothermic animals), seem at first glance to be obliged to follow even the most erratic changes in environmental temperature. But in fact they too *have* developed a lavish array of regulatory mechanisms, and in many respects even these organisms are evidently unaffected by temperature.

The most illustrative example is the physiological clock of plants and 'animals, which runs with period of about 24 h at low temperatures, but their development occurs no more rapidly than would that of tropical organism if it were able to develop at that temperature.

That is, adaptation to permanently low temperatures is bought at the cost of extending the period of development. The stoneflies and mayflies that live in mountain brooks need a whole year to grow to the size of a housefly; but a housefly could not grow at all at such temperatures.

The antarctic fish Trematomus lives in an environment with a constant temperature of -1.6°C and requires about 10 years to reach the size of a small trout. And there are still other costs involved. An animal that has adapted to low temperature and is paying for this *adaptation* with a *prolonged* period of development at the same time loses the ability to exist at higher temperatures.

All the mayfly larvae, stoneflies, and amphipods indigenous to mountain brooks die if exposed to the temperature that any pond will reach during the summer, about 25°C. Typical winter animals such as the snow scorpionfly Boreus cannot *tolerate* temperatures around 20°C for very long.

The price for this adaptation, then, is high. The best proof is given by the fact that we find *refrigerators* useful. If during their millions of years of evolution microorganisms had developed vital functions that could proceed as rapidly at low as at high temperatures, we would not be able to keep food in slmple *refrigerators*. From the outset, then, we would hardly -expect to find truly temperature-coin pen sated processes of development in *ectothermic* organisms.

It is still not entirely clear why organisms were able to achieve independence of temperature in many functions, but never in those of growth and development. Comparative biochemical analyses have led to a current *hypothesis* that can be expressed in *simplified* form as follows:

The normal enzymes of an organism, are adjusted to operate best at temperatures in the range from 28°C to just over 30°C; here they are most effective and last for a long time. There are enzymes that can operate just as effectively at higher or lower temperatures as the "*normal*" enzymes do at 28°-30°C.

However, these enzymes survive only briefly; they soon break down and must continually be resynthesized. The possession of such enzymes costs energy. Functions *involving* these special enzymes can proceed at *temperatures* higher or lower than normal at the same rate as in the normal *temperature* range.

However, because of the high energy requirement, it is not possible to provide all functions with such enzymes; there must be a system of priorities. In' general, rise organs and organs necessary for flight reactions (muscles) end to take *precedence* over organs subserving *metabolism* (an hence growth).

This fundamental hypothesis has found wide acceptance, but cannot as yet be considered sufficiently well documented to be given the status of a theory.

Finally, by Vant'Hoff's Law, the curves we find for temperature dependence are exponential. That is, very slight temperature differences can have very large or small effects. We can imagine a species of which most individuals cannot reach maturity during a normal year; their number decreases from year to year, until eventually one of the rare very warm summmers makes it possible for all the individuals to complete development.

Now the size of the population leaps suddenly from ve small to very large, so that the species can persist during e following normal years. Of course, one must bear in mind that it is not the *temperature* of the air but that of the organism itself that determines. the rate of development.

Body temperature can depart considerably from air temperature. In flight, the temperature of all the larger insects rises to more than 35°C because of the activity of the flight *musculature*. Bees can warm up their hive in this way; *bumble-bees*, by beating their wings, keep their brood warm so effectively that the species can invade even arctic regions.

Furthermore, a great many animals can heat themselves in the sun. Grasshoppers, in the cool of the morning, position themselves broadside to the sun's rays and as a result quickly become very warm. During the midday heat they turn their heads to the sun so as to present the smallest possible surface, and absorb relatively *little heat*: This sunbathing behaviour may well be an absolute necessity for the survival of many insects in temperate and cool regions.

It is characteristic of red ants when they first leave the nest in. spring, of many lepidopterans in arctic and subarctic regions, and probably of a number of insect larvae. Redbugs (*Pyrrhocoridae*) in spring, and later their larvae, use the sun's radiation to regulate their body temperature. Usually they take up a position at the foot of a tree to sun themselves.

But if forced to stay there *permanently*, so that their body temperature is always relatively high, they develop too rapidly; the synchronization between stage of development and time of year is lost, and the animals die. Under natural conditions the bugs move back and forth between sunny and *shady places*, adjusting their movements to the changing conditions through: the year.

On the forest floor in Denmark, the development of thelarge brown weevil Hylobius a reties generally takes three years. But in clearing, where the ground is heated by the *sunshine*, development is complete in two years. As a consequence, the damage this beetled is to *coniferous* forests is considerably greater where clear-cutting is practised.

The difference in duration of development corresponds to a southward shift of about 1,500 km. It appears that all ectothermic land animals begin to lose water when their body temperatures reach 34-35°C, and water loss increases sharply as the temperature continues to rise. This is probably a cooling mechanism.

In experiments on Mediterranean crickets the body temperature could not be raised above this level even by irradiation, whereas similarly irradiated dead animals reached a temperature of about 45°C within two minutes.

Many of thephysiological parameters that have been measured (transpiration, respiration the enzyme activity of various organs) indicate that in terms of the *biochemistry* of their enzyme complement all the eurythermic animals are adapted to an optimal temperature of around 27°C.

In many cases reptiles, too, can invade cold regions only because they use the sun's radiation to accelerate development. The adder and the lizard Lacerta vivipara have advanced further north than any other reptiles. Neither lays eggs; they bear living young. During the day they let their bodies get very hot in the sunshine, and the *unborn* young are heated as well.

Plants can be injured if they are overheated by the sun. Under intense irradiation the dark bark of a tree can become very warm-a danger both in winter, when a sharp temperature gradient is produced between the lighted and shaded sides of the tree, and in summer, when the heating can be sufficient to interrupt sap flow.

Injury so caused is evident at the edges of clearings and alone roads, especially in beeches. Green leaves are not heated very much by radiation; furthermore, their temperature can be brought appreciably below that of their surroundings by *transpiration*. The same is, of course, true of animals; by high transpiration rates and specific behavioural mechanisms *ectothermic* animals can also become cooler than their surroundings.

When desert. birds bury their eggs in sand, in many cases it is done to protect them from heat. For the same reason—*insects*, *spiders*, and *lizards* seek out *shady places*. It is evident, then, that the temperature of an organism can fluctuate even more widely than the meteorological temperature. On a *sunny day* it can mount very *rapidly*, to *plunge* within minutes when a cloud passes.

Even on cool spring days sunbath.ing butterflies and lizards can achieve body temperatures above 35°C, whereas at night they are chilled by frost. Can we make direct comparisons between such changing temperatures and what we know about the effects of constant temperatures?

If we know the time (in hours or minutes) during which an organism is exposed to a particular temperature; and its rate of development under constant temperatures, we should be able to calculate how long it would need for development under a particular changing-temperature regime.

As early as 1928 Kaufmann made such calculations. His conclusions have been confirmed recently by a large number of experiments. The calculations are complicated by the exponential relationship between growth had temperature, and by the existence of a threshold-a null point for development.

Because of these features, growth and development in general proceed more rapidly under fluctuating temperatures than in a constant temperature equal to the mean, and the difference is most *pronounced* at low temperatures. However, there are a few notable *phenomena* that have

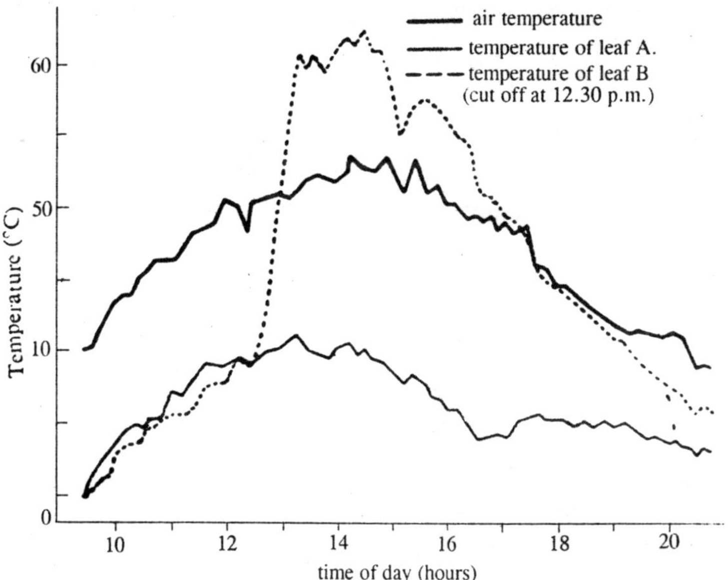

Figure 4.4; The temperature of a leaf can be well below that of the air, as a result of transpiration and the associated cooling. A cut off leaf is, rapidly heated by sunlight, because of lack of water.

not yet been satisfactorily explained.

1. The productivity of many plants is increased when the temperature fluctuates. Perhaps low nighttime temperatures act to prevent high respiratory losses. Such an explanation could also apply to the diurnal vertical migrations of plank tonic animals, which when they are not feeding sink to the colder levels in the water.
2. In many, of the ectothermic animals that have been studied the rate of reproduction is greatly increased in fluctuating temperatures. Parasitic wasps of the genus Trichogramma raised under fluctuating-temperature conditions have appreciably greater effects, when they are set free for the control of the host insects, than those raised in constant temperature.

So far it has not been possible to decide whether such examples represent a general rule, nor do we know enough about their physiological bases. In view of the ecological significance of such an increase in the production of organic matter or of eggs, this phenomenon definitely deserves further study.

Finally, temperature almost always acts in concert with wind and moisture (rain). Their effects are practically inseparable. Indeed, it seems almost miraculous that we are able to say anything at all about the influence of temperature on animal distribution.

In the area of forest entomology it has proved useful to construct climate curves based on both precipitation and temperature. Merkel (1977), for example, used such climate curves to study 'a bark beetle. Temperature was automatically recorded on an hourly basis; the times when it -exceeded 7° C, the null point for movement and feeding by the -beetle, were added and the effective temperature sum per day and month was calculated.

Plotting these sums on the x axis of a coordinate system and the sums for precipitation on the y axis gives the climate curve. When there is heavy rainfall the curve rises steeply, and when the weather is dry it is nearly parallel to the x axis.

By entering observations of stages in the life of the beetle in this graph, one obtains data specific to the measurement site which can be compared with results similarly obtained at other locations or in other years.

Using this method, researchers have developed considerable insight into the dependence of insects on the climate in their habitats. But even this procedure is not entirely satisfactory, because depending on the general state of the weather the beetles can require different integrated temperatures.

For example, the large bark beetle fps typographus does not appear until the temperature at the site where it has spent the winter rises above 7° C. By this time the surface of the soil has reached 10-20° C. The beetles then begin feeding under the bark; to do so, they require temperatures between 12° and 19° C.

The temperature sums necessary for maturation of the gonads vary depending on the weather. The breeding flight of the mature beetle can occur only if the air temperature is at least 20° C. The body of the animal must have reached at least 23° C, which can happen at an air temperature of 20° C if the weather is sunny but requires 23° C air temperature under overcast skies.

Another approach to the difficult problem of temperature in terrestrial habitats is to determine the effective mean temperature (eT) by the method of Pallmann et al.. This procedure is based on the fact that sucrose in- aqueous solution is broken down by hydrogen ions to form glucose and+ fructose. In a buffered solution, with constant hydrogen-ion concentration, the reaction is temperature-dependent.

The degree of sucrose inversion can readily be monitored polarimetrically, providing a convenient measure of the temperature situation in a particular period of time. The advantage of thee method lies in the fact that the reaction rate, like the growth processes of ectotherms, rises exponentially with temperature.

Sucrose inversion ought therefore to give a very -precise measure of temperature-dependent biological processes. But in spite of this obvious advantage the method has not been widely adopted, no doubt for fear of overgeneralization. That is, there are no really well documented relationships between organic life and the temperatures recorded in this way. Exemplary studies in which this method is compared with others would be most informative

In water things are simpler. A general heating by the sun's radiatio i is impossie because infrared light does not penetrate the wate far enoughal It is almost completely absorbed is the upper millimeters, which may become distinctly warmer than the rest of the body of water' If black bodies (heat-absorbing objects) are present in this uppermost layer they become quite warm. By this means Aedes larvae can develop very rapidly in the spring, even in ponds still partly covered by ice.

Only one ecologically fundamental process is clearly not covered by the above considerations-photosynthesis in green plants. Photosynthesis

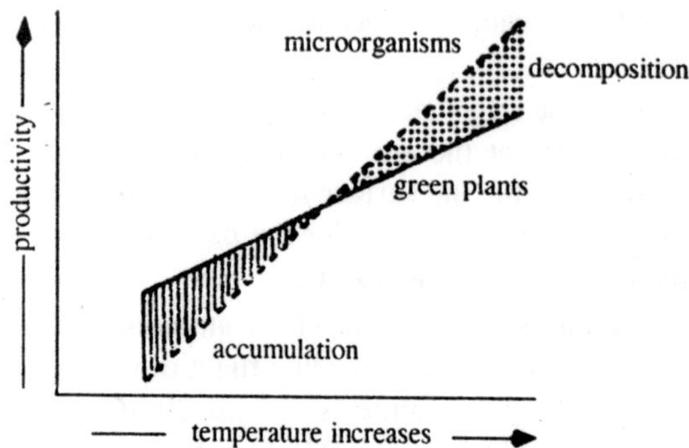

Figure 4.5: The influence of temperature on production by green plants and on the processes of decomposition by respiration in animals and microorganisms. In a tropical warm-moist climate plant matter is decomposed more rapidly than itis synthesized: the layer of humus on the ground is but a thin film covering the mineral soil, and in a few months it can be completely eroded. In cool regions the humus layer is. potentially much thicker.

is not a simple biochemical process; to a considerable extent it involves photochemical events and is thus not so dependent on temperature. The Q_{10} of photosynthesis is less than 2, distinctly lower than that of biochemical reactions in general (with a Q_{10} of 2-4).

Hence photosynthesis can operate at low temperatures, and at higher temperatures does not increase to the same degree as respiration or any. of the functions of animals and microorganisms. Figure elsewhere in this chapter illustrates a basic ecological phenomenon: in the moist, warm tropics dead organic matter is rapidly decomposed, whereas in cool regions decomposition occurs slowly.

However, the production of organic matter by the green plants is not very different in the two locations. This fact was remarked upon by Darwin in his book about the voyage of the Beagle. In comparing the jungles of thez,Amaion and of Tierra del Fuego, he writes that the tropical rainforests appeared to him as a symbol of life, full of power and growth; the forests at the southern tip of the continent seemed like a symbol of death, full of dead tree trunks, branches and twigs.

Forests with dead trees are characteristics of temperature and cool zones, because at low temperatures the dead wood remains intact for a long time. In a tropical rainforest fallen trees decay so rapidly that they are hardly noticeable.

From the different slopes of the two lines in Figure elsewhere in this chapter we would also predict that plant productivity at -consistently high temperatures cannot be much higher-and in certain circumstances may be even less-than at temperatures in the intermediate range. At high temperatures the steady losses due to respiration are so large that the balance between photosynthesis and respiration may show a deficit. Again, of course, the temperatures of interest are not those in the meteorological reports.

If the plants have access to enough water, massive transpiration can hold the leaf temperature well below that of the surrounding air. Warming by heat radiation, such as occurs in animals, plays no role in the leaves of plants; essentially all the infrared radiation passes through the leaf oris reflected by the chlorophyll.

So far we have been considering only the period ; in which :plants and animals are active. In climates with a cold winter the organisms face the problem of surviving freezing temperatures-and sometimes temperatures well below the freezing point.

Many animals can avoid exposure by moving to parts of the water or soil that do not freeze, but many others cannot do this; in the permafrost regions of the arctic such a strategy is entirely impossible. Very few orgaisms can tolerate freezing of their body fluid or of their cells.

At the lowest temperatures which they can survive, nearly all organisms manage to keep their internal Milieu in the liquid state. This fact, together with the photochemical nature of photosynthesis, explains the ability of green plants to assimilate carbon dioxide with a positive balance even in winter.

Cold-weather assimilation has been demonsstrated in the coniferous forests of the taiga and even more strikingly in antarctic lichens, but it also occurs elsewhere-for example, in the high-mountain plant Ranunculus glacialis. How is this prevention of freezing achieved? The organisms ptoduce substances that lower the freezing point, and accumulate them in their body fluids and cells.

A particularly well-known antifreeze agent in animals is glycerol, those of plants include the sugar hamamelose. There are a number of chemically similar substances that tend to produce the same effect. Because of these, some beetles can tolerate temperatures of -80°C or lower.

When an organism is so well adapted it would seem irrelevant whether the winter temperatures stay above zero or fall to-20° or-30°C. In fact there is an additional complication; at temperatures between the freezing point and about + 10°C ectothermic animals and plants lacking green parts use up a great deal of energy in respiration; in the temperature range 6°-10°C many animals can even more actively about.

But only predatory organisms can, under certain conditions, cover these losses, since the nutrients in animal tissue are readily utilizable. Herbivores and detritus feeders cannot eat enough to replace the lost energy at those temperatures.

It is considerablyy better for them if the winter temperatures remain well below the freezing point, so that none of their stored energy is used up. The paucity of species in maritime regions (for instance, Schleswig-Holstein or the British Isles) is in part explainable on this basis; the winter. is not warm enough for feeding, but not so cold that animals can retain all of their stored energy.

In this regard -continental climates are more favourable. The great variety of =insects in the northern United States and central Russia is partially due to this effect. On the other hand, the very warm summers of continental regions are naturally more favourable' to ectothermic animals than the rather cool summers of maritime regions with the same average annual temperature.

Bony fishes in the ocean face a special problem in surviving the winter. As mentioned previously, their osmotic pressure is lower than that of their surroundings. The water in, the open ocean freezes at a temperature of -17°C, whereas a fish would freeze at only-1°C.

Here we have yet another price paid for adaptation to a new

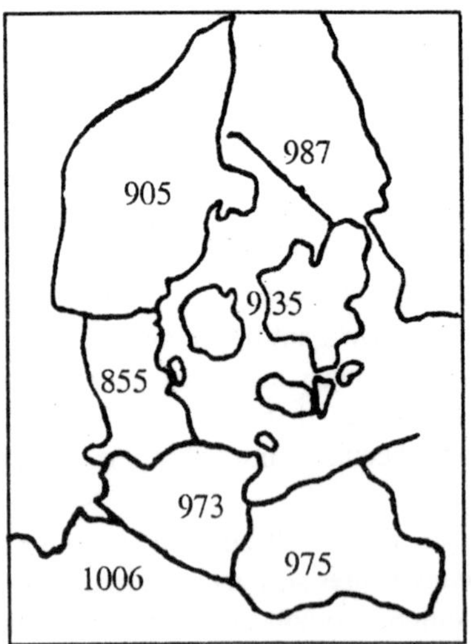

Figure 4.6: The number of species of wild flowering plants in northern Germany and Denmark; it is lowest in the region with the most pronounced maritime climate. The regions with many species have areas of continental climate, so that they also include continental species.

habitat. Arctic and antarctic fishes solve the problem by moving to deeper levels during the winter or by raising the osmotic pressure of the blood to approximately that of the medium. In so doing, however, the evidently enter a sort of dormant state in which they take hardly any food.

Species less well adapted in some situations-for example, when ice crystals are stirred into deep water by violent storms-die in massive numbers. Warm-blooded animals are in a quite different situation. These are organisms with a greatly elevated metabolic rate and concomitant high energy consumption and heat production.

The heat is a side product of metabolism which may be given off from the body or, with suitable insulating mechanisms, can be retained. By changing the insulation properties of the body surface as environmental conditions change, such an animal can achieve a constant body temperature between 35° and 42°C, depending on the species.

When the external temperature is very high cooling mechanisms involving the evaporation of water come into play. As a result the animals are largely independent of the surrounding temperature; they can remain fully active even at low temperatures and colonize regions from which most ectothermic animals are excluded.

Such regions include the antarctic continent and, to a considerable extent, the tundra of the far north (around latitude 80°N), where the temperature is so low and solar radiation so slight that ectothermic herbivores are practically negligible.

The price the warm-blooded animals have paid is that they require much more food than ectothermic animals of equal size. This requirement is in fact entirely a consequence of their temperature. Extrapolating the energy consumption per unit time of a crayfish at 20°-30°C, one obtains precisely the energy consumption of a warm-blooded organism that weighs the same.

But the advantages of warm-bloodedness are easy to see. Food that is hard to utilize fully (all plant matter!) is processed a good deal more successfully in the warm digestive tract of such animals (in some cases with the aid of specially adapted microorganisms) than by any , ectothermic animal.

A warmb ooded herbivore thus exploits its food more thoroughly than does an ectotherm. On the other hand, much of the energy obtained is lost in maintaining the necessary temperature. In effect, then, an ectothermic organism produces mere animal matter than a warm-blooded animal does, for a given amount of plant matter consumed.

It is not surprising that attempts have been made to reduce this high energy requirement. The technique of insulation has been brought to perfection by some organisms-arctic animals consume hardly any more energy when the environmental temperature is low than when it is high.

But warmblooded animals, like ectotherms, still face the problem of minimizing the loss of energy during the least favourable seasons. A warm-blooded animal that simply took shelter when the weather was bad would lose so much energy because of its ongoing high metabolism that it could survive only briefly.

The conspicuous phenomenon of bird migration, and the comparable migrations of bats, show one way out of this dilemma. Another solution is periodically to reduce body temperature, as hibernators do. In the dormant state these animals can last out the unfavourable season without much loss of energy-but they lose the advantage of warmbloodedness.

Such experiments play a central role in ecology, however, so that they deserve a brief discussion here, in the context of temperature preferences. The first question to consider is whether the preferred temperature corresponds to the optimum.

This is by no means necessarily the case. Behavioural research has shown that brooding geese presented with eggs of different sizes will choose one much larger than their own. Here the preferendum is far from the optimum. And we know that similar discrepancies can occur in the realm of ecology.

The Mediterranean cricket Gryllus bimaculatus has a tempera. ture preferendum in the region of 34°C. But the optimum for this species is much lower, between 25° and 31°C. This range is so wide because the measured optima differ, depending on the function being analyzed-egg production, the quantity of reserve substances in the eggs, the rate of development to the imago stage, the final size of the imago, or the level of mortality.

But in the life of the animal there are no distinct optima. The best indication one can give of the effective optimum temperature is a range of temperatures within which all the vital functions can operate more or less efficiently. An added complication is that in the field the temperature fluctuates. Such fluctuation has a positive effect on egg production.

However, the crickets do not (as tiger beetles do) seek out locations at different temperatures at different times of day. Finally, the food supply can modify the effect of temperature. We may well ask whether animals live within their optimum range at all. To what extent may other factors encountered under field conditions force them into a range of temperatures we would not consider optimal? We cannot answer this question here, but will return to it in the discussion of competition.

Range of Temperature Tolerance

The different species of plants and animals vary greatly irr the limits of temperature that they can tolerate. Plants and animals, which can tolerate very large fluctuations in temperature, are called as eurythermal, (e.g., cyclops, wall lizard, grass snake, toad, man, etc.) whereas others which can tolerate only a small variation in temperature are termed stenothermal (e.g., fishes, snails, coral reefs, etc.).

In organisms all metabolic processes necessary for life begin at a certain minimum tempe-e rature and increase with rise in temperature until they reach the maximum level at a temperature called optimum temperature. Further rise in temperature beyond optimum brings about decrease in metabolic rate, until it ceases at a temperature called maximum temperature. This is of great ecological significance and limits the distribution of plants and animals.

Minimum Temperature

The lowest temperature at which an organism can live indefinitely in an active state is termed minimum effective temperature. If an animal or. plant is subjected to a temperature below the minimum effective limit it enters into a condition of inactiveness called chill coma.

The activities of all animals and plants in chill coma can be restored by warming them to minimum effective temperature. The lowest temperature, at which the survival is possible, is called, as

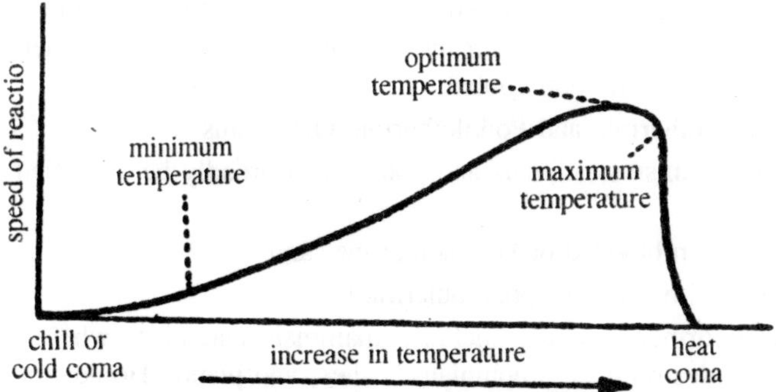

Figure 4.7: Graph showing effect of temperature on the physiological activity of animals.

Minimum survival temperature. The minimum survival 'temperature depends very much upon time.

For example, in an experiment the eggs and larvae of fruit fly Ceratitis capitata were killed after 7 weeks when kept at 7°C, after 3 weeks at 4°C, and after 2 weeks at 1°C. The minimum survival temperature is generally slightly above 0°C, because at 0°C the water freezes and this produces mechanical harm in the form of rapture of cell walls and in the stoppage of circulation.

But certain animals and plants have certain adaptations, where by they can tolerate temperatures even below 0°C. For example, a green alga Chlorella can withstand a temperature of-182°C for an hour without any harm. Similarly, Alaskan black fish can recover to normal activity after an exposure to -20°C for 40 minutes.

Optimum Temperature

When the temperature is increa·sed above the level of minimum temperature, there is also an increase in the physiological activities of animals and plants. The temperature at which the physiological activities of animals and plants are at the maximum is called as optimum tempera.ture. This optimum temperature also varies in different species at different times.

Maximum Temperature

The maximum temperature varies very much in different plants and animals. Generally the maximum temperature, which the animals can tolerate, is 48°C, but certain plants found in desert regions can tolerate a temperature of 70°C. The maximum temperature at which a species can live indefinitely in an active state is called as maximum effective temperature.

If the temperature is raised above maximum effective temperature the animals or the plants enter into the heat coma, a state of inactivity, but will recover if soon cooled.

Homoiothermic and Poikilothermic Organisms

All organisms (animals and plants) can broadly be classified into two groups:

(a) warm-blooded or homoiothermic, and

(b) cold-blooded or poikilothermic.

The former category includes mammals and birds whereas the later includes reptiles, amphibians, fishes, and plants. Homoiothermic animals are those animals which maintain the body temperature at a constant level irrespective of the environmental temperature. The body temperature of such animals can be higher or lower than that of the environment. In case of man we find the body temperature is normally maintained at a constant level at 37°C or 98.4°F. Poikilothermic animals are those in which the body temperature is same as that of environment and fluctuates with the temperature of the environment. For example, the body temperature of fish will be the same as that of water in which it is found.

EFFECTS OF TEMPERATURE ON PLANTS AND ANIMALS

Temperature plays a very significant role in shaping the structure, guiding physiological processes, behaviouristic patterns, and distribution of most of the species of plants and animals. The important effects of temperature 'on the plants and animals are as follows:

Effect on Metabolism

All chemical reactions going on inside the body of plants and animals are collectively called as metabolism. Most of these reactions are under the control of ,enzymes, which in turn are influenced by temperature.

Increase in temperature, upto a certain limit, brings about increased enzymatic activity, resulting in an increased rate of metapolism. For example, the activity of enzyme liver arginase which acts upon agrigine

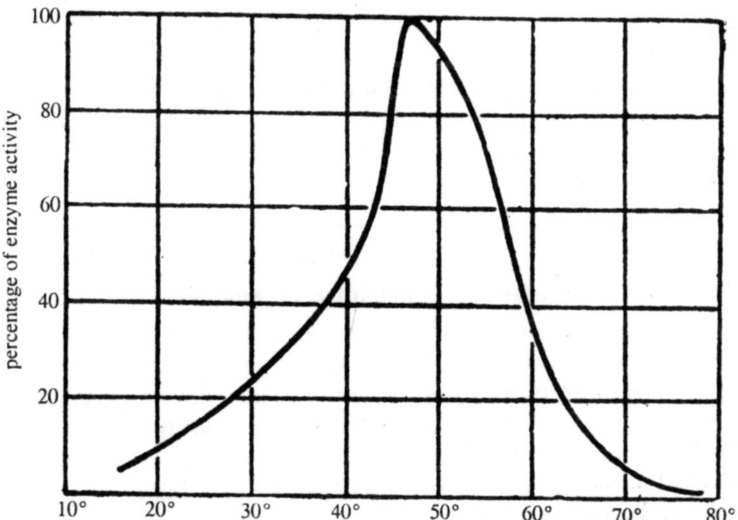

Figure 4.8: Graph showing effect of temperature in regulating the rate of transformation produced by enzyme liver arginase upon arginine amino acid.

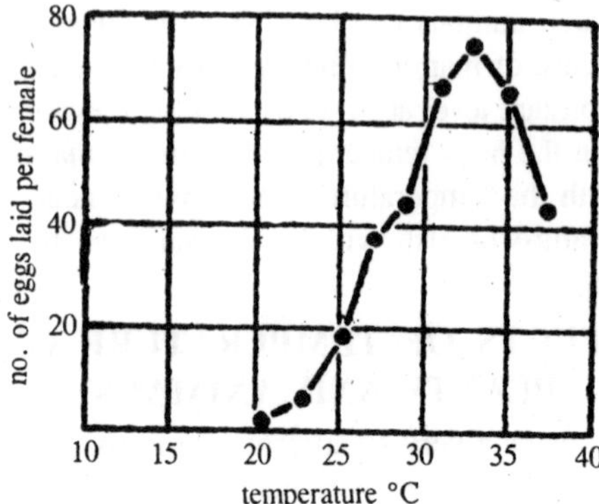

Figure 4.9: Graph showing effect of temperature on the number of eggs laid per female in blow-fly, Calliphora sericate.

(aminoacid), goes on increasing when the temperature is increased from 17°C to 48°C. But increase in temperature beyond this limit (48 °C) brings about retardation in the activity of the enzyme. Accordingly there is reduction in the rate of metabolism dependent upon this enzyme.

Effect on Sex-Ratio

In certain animals, such as rotifers and daphnids, the sex-ratio is also affected by temperature. Under normal temperature daphnids give parthogenetic eggs which develop into females. In increased temperature daphnids give sexual eggs which after fertilization develop either into males into females.

Effect of Temperature on Reproduction

In some animalsthe sex ratio is considerably affected by the temperature of the environment. Under normal conditions, daphnids produce parthenogenetic eggs which develop into females. But when the temperature of the environment is raised, they give rise to· sexual eggs which, after fertilization, may develop either into males or females.

Effect of Temperature on Distribntion of Animals

The importance of temperature as a limiting factor in the geographical distribution of animals has long been recognised.. Temperature affects the distribution of poikilotherms, or the so-called cold-blooded animals whose body temperature is mostly dependent 'on that of the environment temperature is not a limiting factor for most birds and mammals and this is, the reason why only birds and mammals occur in the coldest as well as in the warmest parts of the world.

Animals with a narrow range of temperature tolerance are restricted to specific parts. For example, coral reefs require a minimum temperature

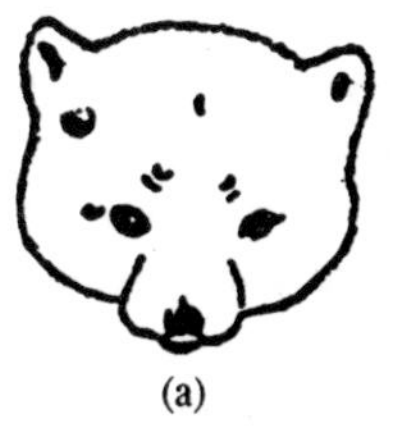
(a)

(b)

(c)

Figure 4.10: Heads of (a) arctic fox (Alopex lagopus, (b) red fox (Vulpes vulpes), and desert fox (Megalotis zerda) showing variation, in size of ears.

of 21°C for their existence, hence they are not found in the colder regions of the globe, Pecten groenlandicus is never found above 0°C., Generally aquatic animals have a narrow limit of temperature tolerance than land animals.

Temperature and Moisture

The interaction of temperature and, moisture depends on the relative as well as the absolute values of each factor. Thus, temperature exerts a more severe limiting effect on organisms when moisture is either very high or very low, than when it is moderate.

Similarly, moisture plays more critical role in the extremes of temperature. For example, the cotton boll weevil cannot develop if the relative humidity is less than 40 per cent or more than 88 per cent, no matter how favourable the temperature may be. Similarly, the animal remains dormant, regardless of humidity, if the temperature is lower than 10°C or higher than 39°C.

Within these ranges the speed of development depends upon the values of both factors. At a temperature of 28°C, for example, the boll weevil requires 21 days to develop under a relative humidity of 40 per cent,But it develops in only 11 days if the humidity is between 60 to 65 per cent.

The two factors acting together produce the limitation, and may be referred to as a "limiting combination." According to Shelford, limiting combinations probably operate under natural conditions more frequently than we realize.

Effect of Temperature on Animal Behaviour and Structure

The directive effect of temperature influences the animal behaviour to a considerable extent. Certain animals may be positive to one stimulus at one temperature and negative to the same stimulus at a different temperature. Temperature changes -are also known to affect structural changes.

Experiments show that Drosophila may undergo structural modifications at high temperatures. The vestigial wings of one of the mutants will develop into normal wings at high temperatures. Evolutionary changes in the same fly may be induced by temperature. Some of the changes induced by radiation in Drosophila can, to some extent be, duplicated by temperature effects.

Similarly, colour patterns in many insects can be induced or changed by regulating the temperature under which they develop. Many of the differences in the colour pattern of animals of the same species living in different environments may be thus explained.

Other Effects of Temperature

If extreme, the effect of temperature may be lethal. There may be many more results of the effect of temperature. It has been found in Drosophila that temperature may affect the mechanism of heredity by affecting the position of genes and the behaviour of chromosomes. Mutations also occur under certain temperature.

According to Jordan's rule fishes living in cold waters are said to have more vertebrae than those which occur in warm waters. Temperature also induces several other structural modifications in animals.

Effects of Cold, Heat and Lethal Temperatures

The thermal tolerance is not the same in all animals. They can tolerate extreme temperatures only to a limited extent. Even with a very slow increase in temperature, we reach an absolute upper lethal limit for the particular animal beyond which it cannot adjust to a father increase. Similarly, the absolute lower lethal limit is that point beyond which no further decrease in temperature is tolerated.

MORPHOLOGICAL AND PHYSIOLOGICAL ADAPTATIONS TO MEET TEMPERATURE EXTREMES

Animals and plants during the course of evolution have developed several ingenious methods to overcome the harmful effects of extremes of temperature. Some of the methods include:

Formation of Spores, Cysts, Seeds etc.

Some of the animals and plants produce cysts, eggs, pupae, spores, and seeds that can tolerate temperature extremes. Seeds of rye are active even at 0°C and can germinate at that tempera ture. Similarly, Amoeba, in encysted conditions, can tolerate even temperatures below 0°C. Encystment is very common in freshwater communities.

Removal of Water from Tissue

This is another method which enables the animals and plants to tolerate the extremes of temperature. Dried seeds, spores and cysts avoid freezing because there remains no liquid in them that can freeze. It has been observed that dry seeds can germinate even after exposure for 3 weeks to -190°C. Some of the bacterial cysts have high thermal resistance.

Dormancy

It is another special adaptation. The term dormancy includes two phenomena called hibernation and aestivation.

Hibernation

Over-wintering in a dormant state is known as hibernation. Animals which pass winter in a lethargic state are said to be hibernating. True hibernation consists of winter hypothermia accompanied by sleep. Hibernation occurs in poikilothermic animals as well as homoiothermic animals particularly micropterous bats (e.g., Myotis, Rhinolophus, Plectus, Macrotus, etc.), hedgehogs, ground-squirrels, and juming mice.

This is characterised by reduced metabolic rate, low body temperature and reduced heart beat rate. In pioikilothermal animals the body temperature is equal to that of environmental temperature, whereas in mammals it is 1°C above the environmental temperature. On the approach of favourable conditions the animals come out of sleep and their body temperature rises.

Aestivation

Dormancy in summer when high temperature excessive dryness and/or shortage of food may occur is called as aestivation. It is very common among insects, some invertebrates, plants, lung-fishes, amphibians and in certain mammals.

Lungfish Protopterus, during summer, burrows into the mud, secretes a cocoon of slime around itself and lies dormant in this condition in insects aestivation takes .place in the form of diapause, during which growth and development are suspended, or greatly retarded.

As we see dormancy is co-related with severe environmental conditions hence even insects belonging to same species undergo hibernation and aestivation during different periods of year in different parts of the world. This is beautifully illustrated by Coccinella septempunctata.

In London, it hibernates from January to May and from October to November, whereas, between the period ranging from June to September the normal development takes place. There is no aestivation period. In Moscow, it hibernates between January to April, normal development takes place in May, it aestivates in June, in July and August there is normal development, and from September to December it again hibernates.

In Formosa, the development takes place from January to May and from October to December whereas aestivation' period range-, from June to September. There is no hibernation.

Homoiothermy

It is a special device for dealing with temperature extremes while in active conditions. Birds and mammals are able to maintain a constant body temperature (within certain limits) despite variations in temperature of the environment. In summer evaporation of water from their bodies takes place, this brings about cooling effect, and hence brings the body temperature to normal values.

In cold weather the relative high temperature of their bodies is maintained due to insulating action of fur (mammals), feathers (birds) and fats (birds and mammals) and also with the help of certain physiological adjustments.

Thermal Migrations

This takes place in animals only. The journeys taken by animals that enable them to escape from extremely hot or cold situations are referred to as thermal migrations. The distance travelled by the animals during these journeys may vary from few centimeters to several hundred miles.

Thermal migration in fishes have been studied by tagging methods. Desert animals move to shaded places to avoid the scorching heat, whereas, some of desert animals become nocturnal and thus avoid the heat of the day (e.g. desert reptiles and snakes).

The frogs, turtles and other amphibious forms make short trips into or out of water and this provides cooling or warming as needed by the animal concerned. Burrowing animals, such as rodents, escape from ligh temperature by burrowing deep into the soil.

Light

Light is the factor that permits life to exist on earth at all. But it is difficult to distinguish among various habitats on this basis, for there is enough light to support photosynthesis over theearth's entire surface.

Very few habitats-the ocean depths, the caves-do not receive enough light for plants to be productive. Everywhere else in the biosphere there is light in adequate amounts and with the correct spectral composition.

It is only natural, then, that the quantitatively significant production of organic matter everywhere is in the final analysis based on the same mechanism-photosynthesis by means of. chlorophyll.

The different kinds of chlorophyll, as far as we know, hardly differ at all in productivity. We can consider them as a singleentity. The chief natural sources of light are the sun, the moon, the stares and the bioluminiscent organisms.

However, all the. energy of importance for organisms, under natural conditions, is derived directly or indirectly from the sun. Light is an environmental factor of great ecological and physiological significance. On light depends the synthesis of food by green plants, which inturn support all animal life on the earth.

Light is a highly directional factor, its intensity, quality and duration

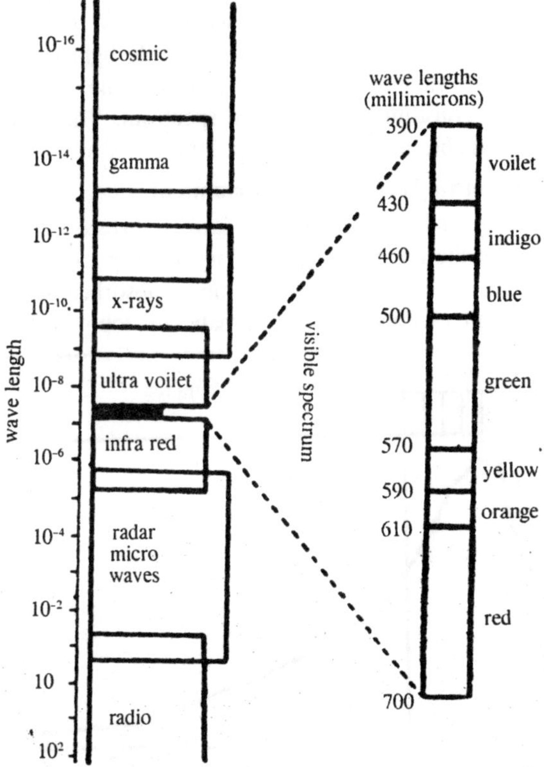

Figure 4.11: The spectrum of radiant energy and visible light (or visible spectrum).

all have influence on plants and animals. It is also responsible for directing and controlling various structural peculiarities and behaviour patterns in organisms and acts as a limiting factor in many activities of organisms.

Composition of Radiant Energy and Visible Spectrum

Solar energy consists of electromagnetic waves that extend from very short or high frequency wavelengths, to very long low frequency wavelengths. In solar energy high frequency short wave radiations, from 390 millimicrons (nm) downwards are ultravoilet rays, X-rays, gamma rays and cosmic rays.

Low frequency long wave radiations from 70G millimicrons upwards are infrared, radar micro-waves and radiowaves (with frequency more than 1000 microns).

A segment or part of solar energy, which can be perceived by the human eye, is called as visible light. This visible light is made up of a series of colours ranging from voilet through blue, green, yellow, orange and red, constituting the visible spectrum. The frequency of wavelengths in visible light ranges from 390 to 700 millimicrons.

Light in Relation to Terrestrial Environment

The intensity of light reaching the earth's surface varies greatly. The variations in the intensity, quantity and quality are caused by the angle of incidence, degree of latitude, amount absorbed and dispersed by atmosphere and a number of other climatic and topographical factors

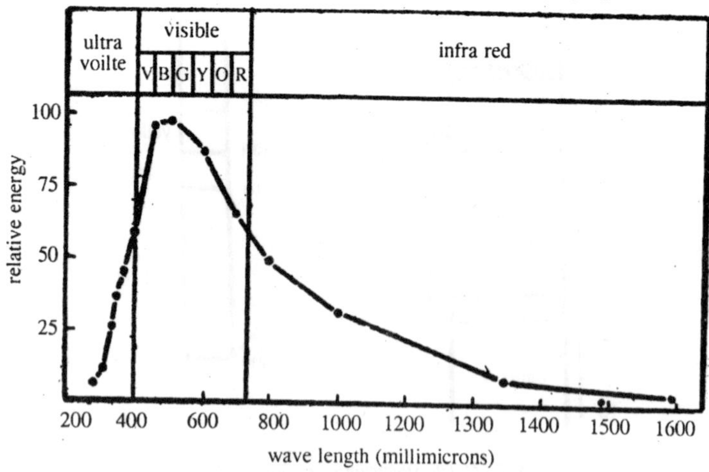

Figure 4.12: Spectral distribution of solar energy at the earth's surface, showing the ultravoilet, visible and infrared portions.

such as fog, clouds, suspended water drops and dust particles, etc. When the angle of incidence is smaller, light rays have to travel by a longer distance through the atmosphere which causes reduction in intensity. Light intensity also becomes smaller and smaller with the increase in degree of latitude.

Atmospheric gases, such as nitrogen and oxygen, also .absorb and disperse a small portion of light (mainly shorter wavelengths as ultravoilet) as it passes through the gaseous layer surrounding the earth.

Other factors such as atmospheric moisture, clouds and suspended dust particles in the atmosphere exert great influence on the intensity of light. Topography and layers of vegetations, such as forest connopy, also bring about some modifications in light intensity. For example, in a pine forest the amount of light reaching the earth's surface is maximum in summer and minimum in winter.

Light in Relation to Aquatic Environment

The light which enters the water, comes from the air, and hence has been subjected to all the changes imposed upon it by the conditions above the water surface. In addition, the light is further modified by water medium in respect to intensity, spectral composition, angular distribution and time distribution.

Nearly 10 per cent of the light falling on the water surface is reflected back. The phytoplankton, zooplankton, particles of organic and inorganic matter suspended in water and turbidity of water either reflect or absorb the light rays. For example, red and orange rays are completely absorbed upto the depth of 20 meters. Yellow rays may penetrate up to 50 meters where as green and blue rays penetrate 50 to 100 meters

As an initial consideration, we can take it that light energy is a factor in excess. Plants make use of but a small fraction of the incident radiation; the efficiency of light utilization is always less than 5 per cent and usually 1 per cent of the available energy.

It follows that productivity within a habitat is usually not dependent on the amount of light-there is always enough. The level of production is dictated by temperature and water supply, as well as by the presence of minerals.

Therefore it must be possible to calculate the level of production possible. Under the same conditions of soil, nutrient availability, and climate all plant communities must in theory exhibit roughly the same production, and observations have shown that in fact they do. Studies carried out in the Solling Project (supported by the German Research Foundation as part of the International Biological Programme) showed that the production of organic matter in a meadow, an area of coniferous forest, and an area of beech forest was quantitatively comparable.

CHART I: Production by a Field of Maize, as an Example of theCalculation of Primary Production

Total dry weight of the maize from 0.4 ha (=1 acre) (10,000 maize plants)		6,000 kg
Ash (inorganic components) subtracted		- 300 kg
Total weight of organic components		5,700 kg
Their equivalent in glucose		6,700 kg
Plus organic matter lost by transpiration appropriate to the season (expressed as the glucose equivalent)		2,000 kg
Total weight of the glucose formed by 0.4 ha maize		8,700 kg
Energy required for synthesis of 1 kg glucose		3,800 kcal
Energy required for synthesis of 8,700 kg glucose	ca.	33×10^6 kcal
Total solar energy available to 0.4 ha		$2{,}040 \times 10^6$ kcal
% utilization of the available energy		

$$= \frac{33,000,000 \times 100}{2,040,000,000} = 1.6\%$$

Theoretically possible annual maximum yield (kg dry matter/ha, from de Witt as cited by Baeumer, 1971)	Location	Number of sheep theoretically supportable by this amount of energy (per ha per year)
25,000	Stockholm	68
30,000	Berlin	80
51,000	Puerto Rico	140
57,000	Tropical Australia	156

This fact is hard to accept. We know, after all, that there .are shade plants and sun plants. We know of plants that carry on photosynthesis during only part of the year-spring flowers, for example, which later die back into the ground. How can we reconcile such things with the above claims regarding uniform productivity and a single basic biochemical process?

The only difference between shade leaves and sun leaves is that the former contain more chlorophyll; the same is true of shade plants as compared with sun plants. The greater amount of chlorophyll compensates for the lower relative light intensity.

Greater amounts of chlorophyll are obtained at a price; there is room for them in the leaf only if the thick epidermis and cuticle are eliminated. Therefore shade plants are very vulnerable to drought. In their normal habitat this is irrelevant, because shade is practically always associated with ample moisture.

The essential point here is that the mechanism of photosynthesis is identical to that of the sun plants. The assertion that productivity of different plant communities is similar under similar conditions does not refer to single species within the communities; no one could maintain that productivity is the same among different species.

Differences at this level are inevitable in view of the variations in length of growing season, which is controlled by other factors. The comparison here is between one plant community composed of many species and another of equally complex composition.

The overall production in such a community results from the activity of different plants occurring at different times; but because the underlying biochemical system is the same in all cases, the total production of the community per unit area and per unit time is the same.

To recapitulate: the uniformity in the productivity of different plant communities under the same conditions is ultimately based on the fact that the amount of chlorophyll exposed to the light is independent of the species composition of the community.

The modern high-yield varieties developed for agricultural purposes produce no more organic matter than the wild varieties, but what is produced is differently distributed. Instead of an extensive root system and strong stems more is produced of the part usable by humans—the kernels of grain. There is one exception in principle to the uniform—productivity rule one which leads to a slightly but distinctly increased productivity.

Whereas the first product of normal photosynthesis is a triose, a sugar with three carbon atoms (hence the term "C_3 plants" for those with this form), in a number of plants the CO_2 taken up is first coupled to phosphoenolpyruvate-a C_3 molecule-to form oxalacetate, a C_4 molecule. Since the first product of photosynthesis here is a C_4 molecule, these are called C_4 plants.

Later the oxalacetate is split up again; the carbon dioxide becomes available to the normal photosynthetic apparatus and is further processed in the normal pathway of photosynthesis, described previously.

This procedure uses up more energy than normal photosynthesis, and it is probably for this reason that C_4 plants are restricted to regions where solar radiation is very intense. But it conveys advantages. The limiting factor for the plants is carbon dioxide.

Phosphoenolpyruvate (PEP) carboxy se has a higher affinity for carbon dioxide than the ribulose-diphosphate (RuDP) carboxylase that acts as the acceptor for the CO_2 molecule in normal photosynthesis. As a result, more carbon dioxide can be fixed per unit time and productivity can he greater than that possible with normal photosynthesis.

Examples of plants with this kind of photosynthesis can be. found among the grasses, and dicotyledons (e.g., Atriplex) in very sunny regions which (usually) have an irregular water supply. The familiar crops maize and sugar cane are in this group, as well as aggressive, wide-spreading tropical weeds.

Because the difference between the two photosynthesis types is not clear-cut but gradual (all plants can bind slight amounts of carbon dioxide to PEP), a number of attempts are currently being made to find and cultivate varieties of other crop plants. with C_4 photosynthesis. The superiority of C_4 plants over C_3, plants is based on yet another principle: C_3 plants have so-called photorespiration.

That is, they lose considerable quantities oforganic matter by respiration even during the day-in fact, the daytime respiration level is about 5 times as high as that at night. The enzymes involved are not located in the mitochondria, but in the very small peroxysomers.

For a long time there has that RuDP carboxylase, which couples carbon dioxide to the RuDP molecule, often "confuses" oxygen with carbon dioxide, especially at high oxygen concentrations. When this happens the ribulose diphosphate is oxidized to form phosphoglycerate and phosphoglycolate.

The latter is oxidized to glyoxylic acid;, the hydrogen peroxide produced in this reaction is converted to water by peroxidase. During photorespiration-the oxidation of glycolate-the plant obtains no energy; the process represents a pure waste. The entire pathway is probably explicable only as a "historical relict."

It originated at a time when the oxygenconcentration was still significantly lower and that of carbon dioxide higher than today. The C_4 plants, with their higher specific affinity for carbon dioxide, have solved the problem of CO_2 deficiency, but the C_3 plants have not. On the other hand, the C_4 plants require greater amounts of energy for their actual photosynthesis-a higher level of solar radiation per unit time. For this reason they cannot spread into regions too far from the equator.

A very similar modification, but complicated by introduction of a timing factor, is found in many succulent desert plants. Their stomata are opened only at night at this time they bind. carbon dioxide to PEP as the C_4 plants do. Most of the oxal-acetate is converted to malate and stored in the vacuoles.

As it accumulates during the nignt, the pH of the vacuole contents falls dramatically with the increasing concentration of organicacids. In the morning the stomata close, and carbon dioxide is split off from the malate and enters the normal photosynthetic pathway. The pH of the cell sap again approaches the alkaline range (diurnal acid rhythm).

By keeping the stomata closed in the daytime the plant loses no water vapour during the period of greatest heat and low relative humidity-and for desert plants, water conservation is important.

It may be that the C_4 pathway of photosynthesis gives stilt another selective advantage. In the high-performance plants conversion of the C_4 acids to carbon dioxide and pyruvate occurs in specific bundle-sheath cells that are indigestible by ectothermic herbivores. Grasshoppers that eat such grasses excrete undigested bundle-sheath cells.

These plants are therefore a relatively unprofitable source of food for such animals (warmblooded herbivores have no difficulty in digesting the bundle-sheath cells). The pronounced daily rhythm of acidity in the succulents may also provide protection from plant-eating animals, but this possibility has not yet been documented.

As far as ecology is concerned, a crucial aspect of productivity is the site of incorporation of the organic matter produced by a vascular plant-does the new substance take the form of nectar, seeds, leaves, roots or wood?

Evidently the different plants vary in this regard; annuals differ from perennials. In addition, there are endogenous control mechanisms, most conspicuous and self-explanatory in biennial plants. And within a given species "resource allocation" depends very much on external factors.

A well-fertilized and well-watered plant develops only a small root systems, whereas under water stress or conditions of mineral scarcity a larger, and usually deeper, root system is elaborated. Flowers and seeds account for a smaller proportion of the total growth of a plant when water is abundant than when it is in short-supply.

This may be an absolute rule for some species; these form flowers and seeds only under conditions of water stress. Finally, the growth of a plant is critically affected by the amount of light received (photomorphogenesis, the regulatory hormone phytochrome).

These considerations lead us to the effects of light on animals. For animals, light is almost never a source of energy; it is most significant with respect to orientation of an animal -in space (via the eyes) and in time (the alternation between light and darkness acts as a timing signal for the daily and annual rhythms of animals).

Light thus appears not to be a factor necessary for animal metabolism, so that one would expect there to be no problem in raising animals in permanent darkness if other conditions were favourable. Such experiments have been done with only a few species, and most of them have failed.

Drosophila, terrestrial chironomids and cicadas, for example, have very high mortality rates in maintained darkness. No one knows why. As a model of the ecological effect of light in the context of the physiology of metabolism, consider Vitamin D. This is taken up as 7-D-hydrocholesterol; in the skin, by the action of short-wavelength sunlight, it is converted into cholecalciferol.

This corversion does not occur if insufficient light reaches the skin. When the supply of Vitamin D is inadequate the skeleton is incomsymptoms of rickets in children. Rickets is found predominantly at northern latitudes, where the winters are long and dark and UV radiation is weak even in summer.

In tropical regions with intense sunlight the illness is essentially unknown. Dark-skinned humans living in the north are particularly subject to rickets, because most of the limited radiation available is absorbed by their skin pigment and cannot be used for conversion of the precursors into the vitamin.

Conversely, people with light skins exposed to she strong tropical sunlight are in danger of excessive ossification. The problem of insufficient irradiation can be simply solved by taking vitamin pills, but so far no means have been found by which overproduction of Vitamin D can easily be prevented.

This example suggests that the distribution of animals may be closely related to light, but there is as yet practically no confirming evidence. It also appears plausible that animals of valleys and the high mountains might differ in their radiation requirements and tolerance. Such a possibility has often been proposed, but again evidence is almost entirely lacking. Gluck (1979), however, has shown that there is a clear correlation between the locations where birds breed successfully and the amount of light falling on their nests.

He found that the nests of chaffinches, goldfinches, and hawfinches were located where the total irradiation was relatively high, whereas greenfinches, serins, and linnets choose nest sites with a distinctly smaller amount of light.

Some animals-unlike plants-are active at night. The cause of noctural activity is frequently the higher relative humidity that prevails at night. In this case; then, light acts solely as a timing signal.

EFFECTS OF LIGHT ON THE PLANTS

Light plays a very important role in plant life. Nearly all the aspects of plant life, like structure, form, shape, physiology, growth, reproductions, development, local distribution, etc., are controlled by it. Based on light factor alone, plants can be divided into two groups: shade tolerant species called sciophytes and shade intolerant species i.e., heliophytes. Sciophytes have lower growth rate and lower respiration rate. The role of light on plant life may be summarized as follows:

Effect on Photosynthesis

The most important role of light is in photosynthesis. Photosynthesis is the only efficient means by which energy from abiotic world is trapped for utilization by the biotic world. The trapping of solar energy is mainly accomplished by means of chlorophyll.

Radiant energy, particularly the blue, voilet (wavelength 440 nm) and short red with wavelength 655 nm, is absorbed by chlorophyll a and b. Chlorophyll a is most directly concerned in photosynthesis, for only this form is capable of transforming energy to power carbohydrates building reactions.

$$6CO_2 + 12H_2O \xrightarrow{\text{Light Energy}} \underset{\text{Glucose}}{C_6H_{12}O_6} + 6H_2O$$

Light intensity effects the primary production in autotrophic layers. Thomas (1955) derivea the relationship of light intensity to photosynthesis in terrestrial and aquatic ecosystems and showed that there is linear increase upto a certain optimum level, called light saturation, followed by decrease at very high light intensities.

Effect on Vegetative Shape of the Plant

The intensity and direction of light have a great effect on the shape of the plant. Light inhibits the production of auxins or growth hormones as a result of which the shape and size of the plant are influenced.

Plants grown in insufficient light or in the total absence of light produce maximum amount of growth hormones, as a result of which they are elongated with weak pale yellow stem, and very few branches. The tissues are poorly developed and there are no supporting structures like xylem and phloem. The leaves ate represented by scales. Roots are also poorly developed.

Effect on Differentiation of Plant Tissue

Light affects the formation of certain specific chemical sub-stanc es, that effect the differentiation of specialized cells and organs. This can be illustrated by the development of palisade tissue in leaves and growth of storage organs and roots.

It has been seen that leaves of herbs and shrubs that grow regularly in deep shade consist entirely of spongy tissue. Cells that normally form palisade tissue in the sun develop into spongy parenchymatus cells in shade. Conversely, spongy cells under strong illumination develop into palisade.

The heliophytes grown under strong illumination have thick palisade tissue (length palisade tissue) or double layer or both. Intercellular spaces in heliophytes are smaller while in sciophytes they are larger. Leaves of the same plant also differ in the amount of palisade depending. upon the amount of light they receive.

Effect on the Production of Chlorophyll

Light is necessary for the formation of plant pigments. A primary response of the plant to light is the production of" chlorophyll. Plants with plastids produce chlorophyll only in light and the chlorophyll practically disappears in continued darkness.

However chlorophyll does not develop, in responseto light, in bacteria, fungi. Thalesia, Cuscuta and some otherparasites and saprophytes. In these the power to make chlorophyll has never been attained or has been lost in consequence of parasitic or saprophytic habits. Seedlings of most conifers, young fern fronds, some mosses and one-called algae are other exceptions as these become green (develop chlorophyll) in the absence of light.

Effect on Number and Position of Chloroplasts

Light has a very strong influence on the number and position of chloroplasts. The upper part of the leaf which receives full sunshine has larger number of chloroplasts which are arranged in line with the direction of light. These chloroplasts arrange themselves in a number of layers and screen each other from .the full effect of radiant energy. In leaves of plants which grow under shade, chloroplasts are very few in number and are „arranged at right angle to the light rays, thus increasing the -surface of absorption.

The leaf structure undergoes greatest modifications in response to light than any other organ of the plant. Differences in the thickness of leaves grown in the sun and the shade are usually very clearly marked. Thickness of the leaf increases with the .increasing light intensity.

The form of the leaf is largely determined by the action of the light upon the chloroplasts and consequent chages in the form of cells that contain them. Light also effects the differentiation of palisade tissue and spongy parenchymatus tissue in the leaves, (as discussed earlier in details).

Spongy cells tend to produce an extension of the leaf at right angle to the incident light, while palisade cells extend the leaf in the direction of the incident light. Hence leaves that contain excess of spongy tissue are relatively broader while those in which palisade is more are relatively thicker.

Effect on Stomatal Movement

Stomatal movement is greatly modified by light. In nearly all the plants stomata open in the presence of light, when other conditions are favourable. However, in unfavourable conditions, She influence of light is very different. For example, when water supply becomes low, stomata may close even of light.

Effect on Transpiration

When a plant is exposed to light its temperature rises. This rise in temperature increases the rate of transpiration. Martin (1935) derived a linear relationship between water loss (transpiration) and light intensity in a wide range of conditions for Helianthus (sun-flower) and showed, as the intensity of light increased there was increased water loss in transpiration.

Effect on Growth

Growth is the most common manifestation of life. In strict sense, growth implies the permanent accumulation of materials. utilized by the plant for the building up of new tissues. Light s necessary for growth, yet stems show greater elongation in the darkness than in the light. More rapid growth takes place at night.

In dicot plants grown in continued darkness, the s ms elongate rapidly but remain delicate and weak with long internodes. Plants grown in strong light remain short and stocky and present a healthy look.

Growth it also affected by the quality of light. Different parts of radiant spectrum affect growth differently. Plants grown under red light attain maximum height and appear to be etiolated, whereas plants grown under blue light are small and compact but otherwise show normal growth.

Effect on Development of Flowers, Fruits and Seeds

Intensity of light has very pronounced effect on the development of flowers, fruits and seeds. Diffused light or reduced light promotes the development of vegetative structures and causes delicacy. Vegetative crops like potato, carrots, turnips and beets give highest yield in regions with high percentage of cloudy days.

Tobaco plants are grown under artificial shading to get larger leaves needed for making cigars. Intense light favours the development of flowers, fruits and seeds. The great profusion of flowers in grass-lands throughout the growing seasons in largely due to strong light.

Similarly larger number of bright coloured red flowers is found in apline meadows where the light is very intense. The countries which produce highest yield of grains and fruits, in the world, are only with high percentage of sunny days.

Effect on the Distribution of Plants

According to Krebs (1972), light does not acts as a limiting factor in geographical distribution of plants. Light does, however, play an important role in determining local distribution of plants. Plant species become adapted to live in a certain kind of habitat and in this process evolve a series of characteristics (e.g., shade tolerant and shade intolerant spp.) which prevent them from occupying other habitats.

Grime (1966) suggested that light may be one of the major components -directing these adaptations. However, the local distribution of plants is affected by the duration and intensity of light. In sea, for example, the vegetation differs at different depths as light intensity goes on decreasing. Similarly, on land, the vegetation in polar regions is different from other regions.

EFFECTS OF LIGHT ON ANIMALS

The visible light represents a small fraction of the whole radiant spectrum. The shares many of the properties of other wavelengths specially of those just longer or just shorter than it. Light is one of the

-complex environmental factors that has far reaching effects on the animals. The visible light acts as an important limiting factor for many multisided activities of the animals.

It effects a number of biological processes like pigmentation, reproduction, development, growth, locomotion, migration, etc. and some other structural and behavioural characteristics of animals. The important effects of light on the animals may be discussed as follows.

Effects of Light on Metabolism

Visible light is indispensable for photosynthesis. The chlorophyll of Euglena like organism furnishes the mechanism by which CO_2 is combined with H_2O to form carbohydrates and to store the energy obtained from the sunlight:

$$6CO_2 + 6H_2O + \text{sunlight} \rightarrow C_6H_{12}O_6 + 6O_2$$

However, the above formula generally used to explain the formation of a carbohydrate does not give an idea of the intermediate steps and is only a sum of many reactions, but it is certain that light plays an essential role in the process even though some steps may be completed in the dark.

The rate of photosynthesis varies somewhat with different wave lengths of light. In terrestrial ecosystems the quality of light does not vary enough to have an important differential effect on the rate of photosynthesis.

But as light penetrates water, the reds and blues are filtered out and the resultant greenish light is poorly absorbed by chlorophyll. However, phycoerythrings (supplementary pigments) of the red algae enable them to utilize this energy and to live at greater depths.

The relationship of light intensity to photosynthesis in both aquatic and terrestrial plants and Euglena like organism follows the same general pattern of a linear increase upto an optimum or light saturation level, followed in many instances by a decrease at very high intensities.

Effects of Light on Colour and Structure

Light induces chemical changes resulting in the formation of pigments. The absence of light results in the loss of colour among the cave animals. The role of pigmentation and protective colouration are well known in terrestrial animals.

Many inhabitants of caves, where light of course has no ecological significance, generally have vestigial eyes, or they may be absent. Numerous animals of the deep sea are blind or have reduced eyes and -some have telescopic eyes.

Thus, it becomes clear with these examples, that light affects certain structures, especially the eyes.

Among green plants light is required for the production of chlorophyll in the chloroplasts. Plants grown under insufficient light do not develop their normal green colour. On the other hand, excessive light causes destruction of chlorophyll.

Effects of Light on Development

Salmon larvae undergo normal development only when they get sufficient light. In the absence of light their development is not normal and mortality is the result.

Effects of Light on Locomotion and Orientation

In certain lower animals the speed of locomotion is considerably influenced by light. This phenomenon is known as photokinesis. For example, according to Welsh (1932), the larvae of pinnotheres move fast in the increased light intensity. When the intensity of light is decreased, they move slowly.

Locusts immediately stop their flight if the sun is hidden by the clouds. Light also plays a significant role in orienting the growth or locomotion of animals and plants. Orientation is brought about either by the differential growth or movement of parts of the organism or by a change in the direction of locomotion of the whole organism.

If the orientation of plants is toward gravity, it is called geotropism. On the other hand, the orientation of locomotion of motile organisms is explained by the terms geotaxis, phototaxis etc. In the aquatic environment the buoyant action of water often reduces the effect of gravity so that primary orientation is toward light or current.

Other Effects of Light

The response of organism to daylength is known as photoperiodism. The latter plays an important role in the life cycle of several animals and plants. In these organisms the reproductive phase of the life cycle is initiated by days that are shorter or longer than certain critical lengths.

Plant species that flower only when the days are longer than a certain number of hours and the nights are correspondingly short are known as long-day plants. On the other hand, short-day plants flower only under conditions of short days and long nights. However, the reproductive cycle, of some plants is not affected by day length. These are referred to as intermediate or indifferent or day-neutral plants.

The ecological understanding on responses of plants to different conditions of light is of great practical significance. For example, the crop of betel leaves (paan) in our country is grown in artificial shading. This results in greater expansion of leaf with less of hard tissue and chlorophyll.

The betel leaves that are soft, palatable and yellowish white fetch more price. The knowledge of photoperiodism is of great practical utility in selection of species and season of its cultivation depending upon the plant parts which are economically important.

Photoperiodism similarly plays an important role in the life cycles of many animals. For example, wing production in aphids, metamorphosis in mosquitoes, etc. are influenced by day-length. Trout that ordinarily spawn in December can be induced to lay their eggs in August by artificially changing the day-length.

According to Farner (1950), the light also affects the migration of birds. The length of the day has been shown to influence breeding, migration, and colour change in many birds and mammals.

Effects of Light on Terrestrial Organisms

Light affects the distribution, colour, and some structures, etc. in terrestrial animals. It influences their pigmentation in several ways. Skin colour may be indirectly affected by light through themediation of eyes or other receptors Vertebrates sess an adaptation to ultraviolet light in which the outer la of the skin are thickened and develop keratin, pigments, and corns,. etc., all of which help to absorb the sunshine and reduce the penetration of light of all wavelengths.

Lizards of the genus Ctotapbytus expand the dark pigment of their skin to absorb sunlight until they reach an optimum temperature, after which they contract the dark pigment and expand the: light-coloured pigments for light reflection. The absence of light results in the less of colour in cave animals.

According to Rasquin, blind cave amphibians and fishes develop pigments in-the, skin after exposure to normal daylight. The role of protective colouration and mimicry is well known in terrestrial animals, including insects. In birds the light affects reproductive activities through colouration, protective, resemblance, and migration.

The latter in birds is evidently a secondary effect of the influence of light. The light factor also affects the orientation behaviour and the normal day-to-day activities of many terrestrial animals. The bee does not fly directly toward or away from the sun but orients at an angle to the changing azimuth of the sun.

The bee's compound eye has been shown to be sensitive to the angle of polarization of sky light and the bee apparently uses this information in combination with other orienting forces to determine the proper line of flight when the sun is obscured. Locuts also stop their flight when the sun is hidden by the clouds.

The attraction to light is so strong in insects such as moths that they fly into the source of light that may prove lethal to them. According to Kramer (1952) certain species of birds may use the direction of sun light as a means of orientation and are able to follow the change in the sun's position .during the day.

However, the positive and negative orientations are not the only forms of behaviour influenced by light. But the level and type of activity may also be affected. Decreasing light intensity draws nocturnal moths, owls, bats, and many small mammals out of their,hinding places, and the twilight before sunrise drives them back, again.

The fact that numerous species of insects interrupt the . development of the young stages in summer, despite the apparently favourable high temperatures and abundance of food, and enter a resting phase (diapause) can definitely be attributed to the influence of light.

The latter sets in motion certain hormonal regulatory mechanisms evolved in association. with the climatic or other peculiarities of the animal's environment and thus during the resulting diapause .the seasons unfavourable to development and reproduction ate passed over.

Though diapause may be elicited directly by light, but in some cases it is "preprogrammed", in the sense that light conditions to which early developmental stages (such as larvae still within the egg) are exposed include diapause indirectly later on in the pupal stage.

For example, if caterpillars of Apatele rumicis are exposed to short periods of day light, less than 15 hours, all the pupae that develop enter diapause. But if the light period is increased to more than 16 hrs, the pupae omit the resting stage.

Among other structures the light affects eyes or vision most. There is a correlation between the types of eyes and the nature of light that they perceive. Among terrestrial animals with well developed eyes, some of the eyes are so located on opposite sides of the head as to view the entire surroundings of the animal, whereas other animals have their eyes facing in one direction so that both eyes may focus upon one object.

Nocturnal animals usually have large eyes for gathering faint light, or small eyes where other means of guidance are available. The burrowing habit and the deficiency of light in the environment similarly leads to the reduction of eyes in many burrowing animals.

Effects of Light on Aquatic Organisms

Light is certainly one of the major factors controlling the distribution, movement (speed and direction of swimming), colouration, and the development of certain structures in aquatic organisms.

Primary food production in the marine environment is virtually confined to the illuminated surface layers of the sea where there is sufficient light to support plant life. The depth of this photosynthetic or euphotic zone varies from about 40 to 100 metres.

Plants are restricted to the euphotic zone due to their dependence upon light for energy. As animals drive their food directly or indirectly from plants, they are also-most numerous in or near the surface layers.

Below the euphotic zone, there is little or no light in dysphotic (100200 m) and aphotic -zones (below 200 m). Hence plants are aknost absent and animals are almost entirely dependent upon food Sinking to them from above.

However, many organisms do not remain consistently at one level but perform vertical movements which are related to changes of light. Another effect of light on animals and plants is exhibited by a 24 hour cycle in their activities or diurnal periodicity.

Themost fundamental diurnal rhythm is that of photosynthesis itself which fluctuates due to daily change of light. Many plant& exhibit other more specialized reactions because of change of light, such as the opening and closing of flowers and folding of leaves.

Diurnal changes of distribution are shown by a great variety, organisms of both plankton and nekton, including medusae, siphonophores, ctenophores, chaetognaths, pteropods, copepods, cladocerans anphipods, mysids, pelagic decapods, and some cephalopoda and fish.

The moon light and the lunar cycle also control many animals activities. For example, marine alga, Dictyota produces. its gametes at the time of full-moon spring tide. Similarly, in some marine polychaete worms spawning takes place at a particular period of the moon.

The colouration of marine organisms is also related to the illumination of their surroundings. The fish of shallow water are usually protectively coloured, being dark on the upper surface and whitish underneath. Deep water creatures which, often come to the surface may have a reflecting surface or be almost transparent.

In the total darkness of the sea there are numerous nonpigmented forms. The common occurrence ofbioluminescence in the sea is probably the result of much lower intensities of light in the sea. According to Harvey (1952), bioluminescence may be used for one or more of the following functions: recognition, illumination, lure warning,, prey-catebing, etc.

In marine environment there may be a correlation between the-type of.colouration, bioluminescence and the occurrence of eyes. The latter are well developed among animals of the surface layers of the ocean. At deeper levels the eyes of the fish become enlarged or 'telescopic' and at greater deepths they are often degenerate of absent.

However, some deep sea fish possess both well developed eyes and luminescent organs. But bioluminescence is definitely an adaptation to the absence of light in the sea.

Oxygen Supply

Organisms need oxygen to break down organic matter and thus obtain energy. When no oxygen is available other temporarily when there is a sudden marked increase in energy consumption (this probably happens only in animals), or it can be a maintained condition; there are organisms capable of living in a milieu extremely low in oxygen or permanently lacking it. Such a situation arises only underwater or in the coil; actual terrestrial organisms never encounter it.

On the land—that is, in the air—there is always .an adequate supply of oxygen. It is limkted to a certain extent in the high mountains. Here birds and mammals find it very difficult to achieve peak performance. Land animals seem to have had hardly any success in evolving hemoglobin with greater oxygen affinity.

This fact is remarkable, in that aquatic animals have been able to take this evolutionary route; modifications utilizing the Bohr effect and the- Root effect have made it possible for the oxygen to be released to their organs as required despite the high oxygen affinity of their hemoglobin.

Adaptation to the high mountains mainly involves an increase in the amount of hemoglobin in the blood, so that more oxygen is transported. To some extent this increase in blood hemoglobin content is a .simple acclimatization acquired after a prolonged stay at altitude, but in some cases genetic factors play a role.

At the moment it is impossible to decide whether these measures-a slightly increased oxygen affinity of the hemoglobin and a greatly increased hemoglobin concentration-really represent the only response of animals to the low oxygen supply at great-heights. Relevant findings are few, although an intensive programme of physiological research is currently underway. Data are particularly scarce for all ectothermic animals and for plants.

To permit brief bursts of high-performance activity, with short-term high oxygen consumption, many animals store oxygen in their musculature. Oxygen is transferred from the hemoglobin in the blood to the muscle tissue of these animals a red colour, and enabling the animals to run rapidly or fly over long distances.

The breast musculature of pigeons, falcons, curlews and gulls is, because of its myoglobin, as red as the muscles of hares, deer and antilopes. By contrast, animals that move at top speed only briefly, and then hide, do not store oxygen in their musculature; such muscles (those of rabits, for example, and the pectoral muscles of most fowl) are white.

They consist entirely of contractile fibres, and are capable of maximal activity only for a short time. Oxygen is also stored in the myoglobin of whale muscles, which are a deep red; whales dive without first filling their lungs with air and so must rely on the oxygen in the myoglobin while they are under water.

There are additional ways of supplying energy where it is needed during such "active oxygen deficiency," via metabolic pathways other than the normal glycolysis followed by citricacid cycle and respiratory chain. These alternative pathways are present in bacteria and thus do not represent recent evolutionary acquisitions.

We must assume that they have been carried along during evolution as a "genetic load," until it suddenly again became selectively advantageous to use them. Chief among them in warm-blooded animals is lactate fermentation; here glycolysis does not feed into the citric-acid cycle but branches off with the conversion of pyruvate to lactate and ends there.

The yield of energy is only 2ATP per mole of glucose, as compared with 38 ATP for the classical pathway. This alternative may be more widespread than was previously thought. It has been demonstrated, for example, in marine worms.

During the escape movements of cephalopods and molluscs octopine fermentation occurs, another strictly temporary, lowyield alternative. Octopine, like lactate, is subsequently reconverted under normal conditions and returned to the metabolic pool.

If an oxygen deficiency should arise in the surrounding medium many organisms can switch, for prolonged periods or even permanently, to other means of obtaining energy. Familiar examples are the fermentation of acetic acid or alcohol in microorganisms and that of succinate by worms parasitic in the intestinal canal.

These forms appear to have discarded the "normal" (and phylogenetically younger) pathway by which energy is derived. But recently it has become increasingly evident that many aquatic animals are very flexible; whereas they ordinarily operate with the citric-acid cycle and the respiratory chain, they can use fermentation pathways under shortor long-term environmental oxygen deficiency.

This is true of Arenicola, many marine and fresh-water clams, Tubificidae and earthworms-and no doubt of many other organisms. The alternative pathway as a rule involves conversion of succinate to propionate; a small fraction of the malate is converted via pyruvate to lactate or to acetate.

The energy yield of succinate fermentation is probably 8 ATP, higher than that of lactate fermentation though not as high as is obtainable with the citric-acid cycle and respiratory chain. It suffices to guarantee the existence of many aquatic animals for relatively long periods in a medium lacking oxygen.

One must bear in mind, however, that in all these cases there is not only a reduced energy yield but a very high food requirement. The increased food supply cannot be actively provided, for any extra activity would use up more energy.

The amount of food immediately available must therefore be extraordinarily high if the alternative pathways described are to mean more to the animals than just survival with loss of energy.

In the ocean, oxygen deficiency occurs primarily in the tidal zone during ebb tide; clams and mussels close their shells, thus shutting off the flow of fresh oxygenated water past their 'gills as effectively as it is shut off from the tubes occupied by -crustaceans and polychaetes.

In fresh water and in enclosed bodies of sea water (the Baltic and Black Seas) the conditions bringing about oxygen deficiency are of particular current importance of humanity. The oxygen in the water is derived from two sources. First, it can diffuse into the water from the air.

This is a slow process, and it supplies oxygen to underlying layers only if the surface water moves into the depths. In lakes such circulation is brought about only by high winds; because such strong wind is rare during the warm summer months, there is hardly any stirring of the water at the time when the temperature is high just when the metabolic rates of all the organisms, and thus their oxygen consumption, are especially high.

The second supply of oxygen comes from aquatic plants, especially algae floating in open water, in the plankton. These are of course restricted to the upper, illuminated water levels. If the body of water contains abundant nutrients for the plants, a particularly large mass of planktonic algae develops.

The consequence is increased turbidity of the water, so that light penetrates less deeply and photosynthesis is concentrated in the uppermost layers. When the water is heavily fertilized, then, it is precisely the most endangered levels that are deprived of oxygen.

The danger is increased in that during such a "bloom" dying planktonic algae sink to the depths in vast numbers. There they are decomposed by bacteria-a process that naturally requires oxygen.

The oxygen at the bottom of the river or lake can be used up completely, so that all the animals living there die. This is the reason why eutrophication of inland waters is such a severe threat; fertilization here has effects quite different from those on land.

In a lake poor in nutrients light penetrates deeply planktonic algae can carry on photosynthesis an d produce oxygen at depths of more than 50 m. The end result is that fish production in a nutrient-poor lake is higher than in a lake rich in nutrients.

Of course, there are lakes that have a high nutrient concentration even without human intervention. Reichholf (1975) showed that flocks of ducks overwintering on nutrient-rich reservoirs along the Inn River graze off all the water plants, removing from the water organic material which otherwise would sink to the bottom and rot there-a process that would use up oxygen.

The ducks themselves, being air breathers, withdraw no oxygen from the lake. The important point is that the ducks must not be disturbed, so that they will remain in large numbers. They will then prevent loss of oxygen from the water and thus postpone the reversion of the lake to land.

Fire

Fire is a regularly recurring factor in many natural ecosystems. Spontaneous combustion and lightning are its most common causes. Fires at regular intervals are a feature of the, dryer parts of the tundra, throughout the taiga, in all savanna and steppe regions, and in all Mediterranean plant communities in the broadest sense-including the chapparal of California and the pine forests of Florida as well as the sclerophyll woodland .around the Mediterranean Sea.

Some eucalyptus forests in Australia are also exposed routinely to fires of natural origin. The detailed investigation Zaekrisson (1977) made of the burn scars on very old trees showed that in the northern European taiga, before humans intervened to protect it, the forests were swept by about two fires per century. Similar figures have been obtained for the Canadian tundra and the tundra of Alaska.

Fires are still more frequent in savannas, steppes, and the Mediterranean regions. To simplify matters, one can say that in :general pines (the genus Pinus), oaks (Quercus) and all the Ericaceae are typical "fire plants". Because fire in a regular event in their natural habitats, they have become highly :modified in adaptation to such conditions.

Their thick bark gives excellent protection. against fire, allowing them to survive without difficulty. If large regions of bark should be destroyed by the fire, regeneration hardly ever presents a problem. The seeds of pines and of the heather Calluna agerminate particularlyy well after being subjected to heat stress.

Indeed, the cones of many pine species release theseeds only after they have been warmed to 70°-80°C. Germination thus occurs after competitors have been eliminated; the, seedlings of pines and of Calluna are very sensitive to competition.

The lichens Lecidea anthracophila and Lecidea friesii. grow only on charcoal and are therefore strictly dependent on forest fires for their existence. Similar adaptations to fire are exhibited by the animals inhabiting these regions. Beetles of a; number of species seek out very warm wood in which to lay their eggs.

One metallic wood borer has actually been found to have infrared sensors that enable it to find freshly burned over areas. The health that germinates and grows rapidly after a fire. provides very many birds and mammals (hares, especially) with far better food than old or cut heath.

For centuries the heath in Scotland has been burned regularly to keep the population of willow grouse and alpine hare large; the effect'on black, grouse populations is similar. The new growth of heath after a fire contains more nutrients and appears to be more palatable to animals than either old heath or the new growth following mowing.

In the pine savannas of the southeastern United States the parts of the plants that grew out after either fire or cutting were found to contain distinctly more N, P, K, Ca, and Mg, and the amounts of N, Ca, and Mg were greater after fire than after cutting. Not until 4-6 months had elapsed did the mineral content of these plant parts return to normal.

Other species are extraordinarily sensitive to fire-spruce;, for example, and most deciduous trees such as beech and linden. Pure spruce forests or beech forests catch fire only after strong winds have blown sufficient combustible material to the ground. It is generally valid to say that fire is not a. natural event in most deciduous forests (apart from oak woods. and Mediterranean sclerophyll regions).

Fire plays a leading role in determining the composition of plant communities. The northern European-Siberian taiga belt, in which spruce and pine predominate in different proportions, is a product of fire. Without repeated burning the forests here, where it is not too dry, would consist exclusively of spruce.

The recurrent fires do severe damage to the spruce trees, and it is only for this reason that the pines can maintain themselves. Fire resistance could be regarded as a direct mechanism for competition; pines shed a great deal of burnable material onto the ground, where it accumulates in loose piles.

The firesweeps, rapidly through this fuel, injuring the spruce as it goes. By contrast, a dense stand of spruce is practically invulnerable to fire. The short needles become tightly packed in the ground and so are almost impossible to set alight.

Once it covers a certain minimal area, then, a spruce forest is to a great extent protected from burning. The situation is similar in the oak savanna of North America, where the oaks (like the cork oaks in the Mediterranean region) develop specific kinds of bark that enable them to survive even intense fire. When the acorns germinate, they are free of competition.

The wellknown oscillation of hare (and thus of lynx) populations may perhaps be associated with fire cycles. Man has fought fire wherever he could. As a result, the frequency of fires in all regions inhabited by humans soon declined sharply. The result was a drastic change in the composition of the local plant communities.

In northern Europe the range of spruce distribution expanded, and in the North, American oak savanna brush displaced the original oaks. Bushes also invaded the savannas of Africa. Specifically fire adapted animals became rare. To offset such changes, a system of controlled burning wass introduced some time ago in North and South America, Africa, and recently in Europe.

Because of this conservation measure the oak savannas of North America have regenerated in many places. Fire has also been used to keep the spruce population down in parts of northern Europe and in the national parks of North America, where the growing spruce were slowly inhibiting germination and growth of the giant sequoias the parks were established to protect.

In the Florida Everglades, too, fire has been and is being widely employed to maintain the natural vegetation. Today we know how to light very cool fires, with an effect like that of mowing, under certain moisture conditions; we can also laay very hot fires that burn off part of the raw-humus layer and speed up the breakdown to real humus.

We know the difference between hot fires that go with the wind and the relatively cool fires against the wind. The insect world suffers to varying degrees from the different kinds of fire, but in general the effects are less severe than was expected.

Nutrition

Unfortunately, it is practically impossible to give a description of plant nutrition that will satisfy the physiologist. Only minute quantities of the essential nutrients are freely available in the soil and water. Even fertilization causes little change in this situation, for the added nutrients are immediately adsorbed on soil particles or react with other components of the soil and water.

It requires activity of the plant (through the roots of which hydrogen ions and organic acids can be excreted) to make these nutrients accessible. Other nutrient ions are immediately incorporated by microorganisms and are thus out of reach of the plants, but when a microorganism dies—if it does so in close proximity to a root—the ions liberated become temporarily available.

The advantage of this situation to the plant is that although the supply of nutrients is small at any moment it is quite uniform in the long term. The best example is given by the primeval forests of the Amazon basin, which thrive on soil that is practically free of nutrients, with ground water containing no nutrients at all. These forests have been compared with a firm that holds no funds in reserve, but keeps its entire capital in the business.

The same can be said of aqatic environments. When a body of water is fertilized to increase the yield of fish, what happens to the fertilizer? It rapidly disappears from the water, sometimes in less than a week. In part this is due to the plants, which utilize it immediately, and in part to mud particles, to which the fertilizing substances adhere and from which releaseis slow.

The latter fraction must be regarted as temporarily lost. This withdrawal of substances makes it impossible even in water to find the true relationship between the amount of minerals supplied and the resultant plant growth. Such experiments are feasible only in hydroculture, but then the results cannot readily be applied to the field situation.

Only a rough idea can be obtained—for example, that diatoms thrive at mineral concentrations lower than those necessary for dino flagellates, so that there is a strong tendency for them to take the plate of dinoflagellates in nutrient-poor waters.

The physiologist himself, on the other hand, cannot establish precisely the minimal or maximal concentrations for plant growth, to say nothing of the optima. In practice thelimiting concentrations vary greatly, depending on the nature of the sail and its water supply. Furthermore, plants respond differently to variations in nutrient availability.

Under nitrogen deficiency the roots of the plants are elongated and driven deeper into the soil. When nitrogen is abundant root penetration it· limited to the top soil stratum, but there it is much, more extttisive. (As a result, fields under intensive cultivation which art heavily fertilized are extremely vulnerable to brief periods, of' drought. Shallow rooting is also the cause of the greaterdslnger of 'erosion in intensively cultivated regions such as Icelandic pastures.

In an ecological context, the uptake of nutrients involves, micro-organisms to a· large extent. This involvement is especiallyAar in the case of the many land plants associated with symbiotic microorganisms or fungi that live in or near their roots. Here hardly anything can be said about the requirements of the individual species; the system fundamentally comprises- two species.

In considering the nutrition of animals, we must distinguish between the qualitative and the quantitative aspects. Let us -first turn to the qualitative nutrient requirements of animals.

Usually food specialization is evident in the, structure of an animal. Carnivores all have shorter digestive tracts than herbivores, even when they are members of the same species. The intestine of a plant-eating tadpole is very long, whereas that of the adult, carnivorous frog is very short.

The modification of the forelimbs of arthropods to form a great variety of mouthparts-biting, licking, piercing-sucking-is a well-known phenomenon. Specialization can lead to extreme selectivity; the snake Dasypeltis scaber subsists entirely on the eggs of birds, and some nematodes eat only diatoms.

There are a particularly large number of specialists among the insects, some of which are restricted to one or a few species of plant. Such obligate feeding is based predominantly on secondary substances in the plants. But it has been established that only a few animals really require these secondary plant substances. In actuality the alkaloids, terpenes, and phenols were developed in evolution as defense mechanisms against grazing.

Through coevolution specific animals developed resistance to these defense substances, and at the same time they came to use the substances as a means of recognizing their specific plant. If the sense organs on the mouthparts of the tobacco-moth caterpillar are destroyed it no longer feeds exclusively on tobacco, as before, but will eat and thrive on a great variety of other plants.

These specialists have "made a virtue of necessity". Not only do they tolerate the poisonous secondary plant substances; most can store them in their bodies and as a result become unpalatable, inedible or even toxic to predators. In fact, not only herbivores protect themselves in this way.

Marine slugs that feed on coelenterates with nematocysts not only are unharmed by these' stinging organs but carry them in their own body walls, in' firing condition; these "kleptocnids"'make life difficult for the slugs' predators. The animals that have coevolved to tolerate the defense substances of plants are not physiologically dependent on them, although they benefit from a food supply in accessible to other herbivores under the competitive conditions in the field.

But not all secondary plant substances are dispensable. It is a familiar fact that animals have lost the ability to synthesize a great many biologically important materials, which they must then obtain in their food. A few remarkable cases, of interest in the ecological context, deserve mention. Brancles (Balanus balanoides) can use a great variety of living or dead foods, which they filter out of the water, for growth.

But to reach sexual maturity they need the planktonic diatom Sceletonema costatum. Without this food they can attain a normal size but cannot reproduce. Similarly, the marine isopod Idotea requires green algae plus the attached diatoms to get through the first stages of growth, whereas later the green algae alone suffice.

The butterfly Iphiclides podalirius enters diapause in the fall, when the days become shorter. The mechanism that elicits diapause functions better when decreasing day length is accompanied by the availability of autumn leaves as foodwhich ordinarily occurs in nature.

But autumn leaves can also have a diapause-triggering effect if provided when the days are growing longer. The males of many danaid species were found to be utterly unattractive to the females under laboratory conditions. It turned out that the male imagines are incapable of synthesizing the pheromones that stimulate the. females unless given the opportunity to suck on dried Boraginaceae (Heliotropium), from which they obtain the precursors of the pheromones.

Normally the food consumed by an adult butterfly or moth is considered, a negligible element among the insect's ecological requirements. But it is quite significant apart from its, energy contribution. This example demonstrates that a plant that is not food for the larvae and is not, alive during the flight phase of the imagines (the males suck on the dried stems) can be crucial to the existence of the species.

The subtle requirements of animals for particular, food constituents imply, adaptations of sense organs and nervous system that are now receiving greater attention from neurobiologists. Toads, for instance, when presented with a horizontal stripe moving along its long axis (a sight resembling an earthworm), respond with prey-capture behaviour; they exhibit no interest when the stripe is moving in the perpendicular direction.

Grasshoppers have a specific grass receptor. Even with respect to the basic nutrients-carbohydrate, fat and protein animals make qualitative demands on their food. These substances must be available in a form the animal can utilize and in the right proportions, and they must contain the right amounts of the essential amino acids and fatty acids.

Roe deer fed with the highest quality meadow hay, on which red deer and cows thrive, lose weight and eventually die. The roe-deer rumen is very small, and cannot break up the cellulose of the cell walls fast enough. Roe deer need food that is much more easily digestible, containing little cellulose or lignin.

In the field, therefore, they subsist almost entirely on the buds of leaves and flowers. It is because of this diet that they have such an impact on the ecosystem—an effect far greater than would be expected from the number of animals and the amount of energy each requires.

Other animal species have been less thoroughly studied. But we can take it as established that the specialization of the different angulates on the African steppe to different plants or plant parts has similar causes, at least to some extent.

And the situation is no doubt similar with nonmatltmalian animals birds and ectotherms. In the case of ectotherms, the degree to which plant food can be utilized is also strongly temperaturedependent. The lignin and cellulose that make old leaves harder to digest than fresh buds (which' contain very little) cause great difficulty to the ruminant digestive system. It is not a matter of breaking the substances dt wrt, but of doing so as rapidly as possible; otherwise tnore energy is used up than is gained.

When an organism selects its food on the basis of digestibility it uses much energy in looking for the food but does not need any to digest it, and'very little ballast material is consumed. The alga-eating chironomids are less sbibetive, and consume farther than they utilize; many algal cells leave the gut of such an insect undamaged and fully capable of further growth.

Special significance attaches to the composition of food. If this is not appropriate, animals (e.g., some that suck plant juices) may be assisted by symbionts; in other cases, considerably more food is eaten than the energy requirements of the organism demand.

The surplus components in the food are· absorbed in the intestine but then eliminated. This phenomenon: has become famous in the case of the aphids, which excrete "feces" in which sugar is highly concentrated and can be used by other animals such as bees.

Aphids are forced to excreteso much sugar because their food contains such great amounts in comparison with the low content of protein or amino acids. Similar relationships can be found with regard to many nutrients. Herbivorous mammals living in regions with a long winter or a long dry season must make do for extensive periods with food of very low quality consisting almost entirely of lignin and cellulose.

In the animals' very warm intestinal canals this food is broken down with the help of symbionts, so that it provides sufficient energy but not enough protein or amino acids. When mammals with several-chambered stomachs (kangaroos, camels and llamas, ruminants) are restricted to· such a diet, can recycle nitrogen.

The urea formed in the liver is transported to the stomach, taken into the rumen, and there converted by microorganisms to amino acids and protein that can be used by the animal. As a result,. the urine contains hardly any nitrogen.

This sort of nitrogen, processing has been shown to occur in kangaroos, camels, and most ruminant groups. The animals also conserve water in this. way; it is not necessary to produce urine in order to get rid of* nitrogenous products of metabolism.

Naturally this procedure is not used on a permanent basis, for it does not permit growth. But it does permit an animal to maintain the status quo for fairly long periods of time.

Nagy and Milton (1979b) showed that the howler monkey (Alouatta palliata) is adequately supplied with minerals only if its food is very diverse. The figs and young leaves of Ficus insipida that constitute the most important food of these animals during the dry season do not contain enough copper, sodium, or phosphorus; these minerals must be obtained from other food.

Many tropical animals leave the crowns of the trees to supplement their diet with minerals from the soil. Howler monkeys do not descend to the ground evidently they can find the appropriate nutrients in the treetops.

The alternative approach to specific nutrient scarcity-eating enough to supply the scarcest substance and eliminating the excess of the' others, as the aphids do-does not seem to be realized in other animals.

The regulation of amount eaten appears to be based entirely on .energy requirement. Naturally animals choose the qualita tively best food available; but if this contains too little protein either recycling occurs or the animals show deficiency symptoms.

Hyperphagy in, insects, has not yet been completely explained. When given food deficient in protein crickets eat distinctly more than they do of better balanced food. But this hyperphagy cannot compensate for the protein deficiency, because it begins only when the protein content of the food is extremely low.

However, some.leaf beetles are said to be able to compensate !for the low nitrogen content of leaves by hyperphagy. This complex of questions deserves considerably more attention in the future, because of the abundance of trace elements present in widely, varying amounts in potential food sources.

The ecological effect of animals in a system could, under certain circumstances, be increased many times by hyperphagy—but no more than this can be said with the limited data now available.

Experiments along these lines can be laborious and frustating. Hahn and Aehnelt (1972) were able to demonstrate that the fertility of male domestic rabbits and cattle was greatly reduced when the animals were fed on hay from a heavily fertilized meadow in which only one grass species was growing.

Animals fed on varied sorts of hay from unfertilized meadows .bad considerably more reproductive success. The search for ions responsible for this difference in the various foods gave consistently negative results. This is the problem that confronts us everywhere: minute differences can have marked effects.

One can speculate further, that a massive increase in the size of the herbivore population leads to increasing unformity of the plant community. Is this uniformity in food one of the factors responsible for the collapse of a herbivore population.

Recently we have begun to appreciate the significance of the discovery that many marine animals can nourish themselves directly on dissolved substances (amino acids, carbohydrates). Such a capacity seems obvious in the relatively large pogonophorans, which lack a gut, but it also plays a considerable (though not decisive) role in many other animals.

Sea anemones (Actiniaria, Cnidaria), for example, bear on the body surface an absorbing epithelium with microvilli, and molluscs and polychaetes take up dissolved substances from their surroundings. Calculations by Schlichter (1975) have shown that the quantity of such dissolved substances is quite sufficient to supply the -entire nutrient requirement of these animals.

In fresh water -and on land, this principle is probably of no importance. One reason is that such direct absorption is more difficult in view of the osmotic gradients involved; furthermore, the numerous bacteria in fresh water remove from it essentially all of the free -.amino acids and carbohydrates (most of which are derived from the metabolism of planktonic algae and lower animals).

The fresh-water clam Pisidium does take up glucose even when it is present only at the concentrations found in the natural environment. But the amounts so accumulated meet less than 0.05 per -cent of the animal's energy requirement-in marked contrast to the marine situation, in which 100 per cent of the required energy can be obtained from dissolved substances.

Nor can the fresh-water sponge Ephydatia meet its requirements; it takes up dissolved proteins by micropinocytosis, a method quite different from the enzymatic uptake by marine animals. Statements about the biomass of animals in a habitat, then, are not in themselves informative.

At least the mean body size of the species must be given. The relatively higher food consumption and the relatively higher metabolic rate of small organisms naturally finds expression in other fundamental' ecological parameters. Small organisms, for example, grow more rapidly than larger animals (this is also indicated in Kleiber's table); the productivity per unit time is greater and the rate of reproduction is higher.

The consequence of all this is that small organisms are more likely to starve, and do so more quickly, than large ones. Shrews must eat at intervals of at most two or three hours; they cannot follow a light/dark cycle of rest and activity. Field mice, too, must leave their burrows at least once every 2-3 h, although their chief activity period is at night.

An ecological consequence of this distributed activity is that both nocturnal predators (owls) and those that hunt by day (buzzards) can feed on the same prey. Small animals are also better suited than large animals to take advan-. tage of the sudden occurrence of favourable conditions by reproducing very rapidly.

Large animals are not so flexible, but they are better able to survive unfavourable periods without serious losses. We shall return to these questions in considering predator-prey relationships.

Animals	1 cow	300 rabbits
Total body weight	600 kg	600 kg
Daily food consumption	*7,5 kg* hay	30 kg hay
Daily heat loss	20000 kcal	80000 kcal
Daily weight increase	0,9 kg	3,6 kg
Weight increase pert hay	108 kg	108 kg
Meadow with 3 t hay suffices in theory for	1 year	90 days

Figure 4.13: A cow weighs as much as 300 rabbits. The ecological effects of the two, however, are quite different.

The next step is a detailed analysis of the food requirements of an animal in the laboratory or in captivity. First, the validity of the general formula can be tested; it can be expanded by determination of the additional food required when the animal is regularly in motion.

With small animals (for example, insects or clams), the quantitative food requirement estimated in the field can be made relatively precise. But correction factors must be introduced to allow for the complicated effects of temperature; at higher temperatures food is more readily utilized, metabolic rate rises, and the amount of food necessary increases (development is more rapid).

Such effects present no problem in the case of warm-blooded animals; on the other hand, with warm-blooded animals it is more difficult than with most zectotherms to transfer the data obtained in captivity to field -conditions. For many animals-from filter-feeding clams to fish, frogs, birds, and mammals—there is great uncertainty as ·to how the two situations compare.

Some plant-eating insects have been usefully studied in the field, with analysis of both the plant substance utilized and the excreta produced. Under favourable circumstances feces production by mammals and birds can be determined in the field, and such data can be used to infer consumption if the digestibility of the food is known.

This approach has been moderately successful with wild geese in Iceland and reindeer on Spitsbergen. A promising new method of estimating energy requirement in the field has been developed by Nagy and Milton. They captured howler monkeys (*Alouatta palliata*) and injected them with weakly radioactive (*tritium-labelled*) water.

The blood thus acquired a certain initial level of radioactivity. Because water is continually produced by *metabolism* and then eliminated, the radioactivity in the blood steadily declines, providing a measure of metabolic rate.

The results implied that the active howler monkey under field conditions uses up about twice as much energy as when at rest. But there are still many gaps in our knowledge. Consider, for example, the uncertainty that prevails in the current estimates of consumption by mammals.

A widely used procedureis simply to multiply the basal metabolism by 3 and take that as the food consumption of herbivorous mammals. Recently, with no particular justification, people have begun to regard a factor of 1.5 as sufficient. In the case of roe deer there areindications that a factor of 4 is more realistic.

But probably there is no generally applicable factor. Rate of locomotion. need by no means be linearly related to energy consumption, Birds have an optimal flight speed well above the minimum; slower flight costs more energy. The relatively quick "fivelegged" shuffle of a kangaroo looking for food on the ground costs considerably more energy than the smooth forward leaps it uses for long-distance travel.

It will probably be impossible to find any general solution to these problems. The particular feeding strategy of a species has a marked effect on its energy consumption in its habitat. A "sit-and-wait" animal needs little more than its basal turnover, as experiments of wolf spiders have indicated.

And the extra energy required by a web-building spider is only that needed for the construction of the web. Studying a pair of snowy owls with young in a zoo. Ceska (1974) found the same food requirement as measured for snowy owls with an equal number of young in Alaska When the lemming population is in the exploding phase, at least, the owls do hardly any physical work when hunting.

Things are quite different for the roe deer, which accepts only the most fresh and delicate buds and must therefore hunt for each separate bite. An animal feeding by this method is in constant motion. The fact that metabolism is regulated by size: also implies that no simple factor is applicable.

Movement increases the metabolic rate of a small animal much more than. that of a large animal. Finally, short-term analyses of an animal's food requirements. are extremely uninformative. Even adult animals undergo great. changes in food requirements during the year, although the supply may be constant.

This is true of both birds and mammals. The situation is doubly complicated in that the quality of the food in the natural habitat changes during the year. And the feeding strategy and energy consumption of a given' species is not always the same; in a dry summer the grasshopper studied by von Gyllenberg (Chorthippus parallelus) had to travel further than before to find favourable food, so that Gyllenberg: (1969) had to expand his population model by adding an "activity block."

The activity of roe bucks and does during the mating season expends considerable effort and they lose weight correspondingly; later this loss is made up by increased food. consumption. Of course, the nutrient content of food-whether itschemical composition or its caloric value-is also subject to,change.

When a wild mouse is caught and fed in.the laboratory,, the energy content of its body rises distinctly after only a few days because of the accumulation of fat; laboratory mice have - a higher caloric value (per unit weight) than wild mice. The composition and caloric value of plant parts change in thecourse of a year and even during a day.

As important as the problem of quantitative animal nutrition is to ecology, then, it is still far from a solution. Very rough estimates can be made on the basis of approximate calculations of basal metabolism, if the feeding strategy of the animal is known so that the required locomotor activity can be taken into account.

But for any more precise estimate one would have to know the energy budget of each individual from birth to death, and this information is available only for certain plant-eating insects. In the International Biological Programme studies of this sort have been done and a number of appropriate formulas and units established; on this basis, an ecosystem analysis can be undertaken.

There are hardly any detailed analyses of the degree to which animals satisfy their needs. The few studies of wild mammals, birds, springtails and crickets, though, indicate that "the normal animal is a hungry animal." Times of abundance probably occur everywhere, but only rarely. The normal freeliving wolf is undernourished, just like the normal springtail.

The choice of suitable food for larvae is determined not only by quality, but by quantity as well. Parasitic wasps are famous in this regard, for in general they check very closely whether their victim has already been invaded by parasities or not.

When Trichogramma finds a host egg already parasitized, it adds no eggs of its own. Most other insects behave in the .same way. The number of eggs laid by the beetle Oryzaephilus depends on the mass of food on which they are deposited and which the larvae will eat; only about as many eggs are laid as the mass could feed.

Flies and gnats with larvae that live in a rotting substrate (Drosophila, Limosina, Pseudosmittia) also measure out their eggs with relative precision. If there are already very many eggs in the substrate, no more are laid.

The eventual disposition of the energy acquired by feeding is of fundamental ecological interest. Some of the food is digested and incorporated into the body, some is used up in respiration, and some is excreted as feces. In simplified terms, one can define assimilation as production plus respiration: $A=P+R$.

In times of a world nutritional crisis it is of course not a matter of indifference what capacities animals have for assimilation. Simplifying the situation greatly, we can say that warm-blooded animals assimilate 80 per cent to 90 per cent of the energy in the food they eat.

Similar values are reached by ectothemic predators, which feed on easily digestible, high-protein flesh. Ectothermic herbivores, by contrast, in general can assimilate only 20 per cent to 40 per cent of the energy they take in. Departures from this rules occur, for example, when warmblooded herbivores receive food extremely hard to utilize; then their assimilation efficiency can fall as low as 30 per cent.

Of the assimilated energy, some must be used to maintain the normal vital processes, and some of the remainder goes into production of new matter (growth and reproduction). It costs a great deal of energy to maintain a high body temperature, so that the ratio of consumption to production in warmblooded animals is incomparably worse than that in ectotherms.

For this reason it has occasionally been suggested that instead of raising warm-blooded domestic animals for meat, ectothermic herbivores should be provided with favourable food and used as a source of protein. But this suggestion is not realistic. The composition of the protein in ectothermic animals is not as suitable for our needs as that of warm-blooded animals.

If we relied on ectothermic an mals for protein we would need more than we would if the protein came from a warm-blooded animal. Instead of the effect we were hoping for, we would achieve the reverse.

Data on ecological efficiencies should never be taken too literally. When food is abundant, owls dissect their prey and eat only certain parts; the American badger (Taxidea taxus) has a digestion efficiency of 85.6 per cent when food is scarce and only 72.2 per cent in times of plenty.

A general rule of thumb is that an animal uses 1-10 per cent of the food eaten to synthesize new matter for its own body. Up to 90 per cent to 99 per cent of the food assimilated is burned in metabolism. The end products water and carbon dioxide are eliminated.

Other components of the food (protein contains nitrogen) are given off as excreta. It is on the picture of energy flow through an organism so obtained that subsequent calculations and discussions in the realm of ecosystem research are based.

Materials that can neither be burned nor be eliminated accumulate in the body. Examples of such substances are DDT. PCBs, lead, and mercury. When one animal is eaten by another and that by a third, there is a progressive accumulation of these substances in the food chain. This is the physiological basis of the danger inherent in modern environmental poisons.

There is an additional consideration. Because predators are always fewer in number than their prey, the predator population is more likely to be affected by any biocide application than the prey it controls. The consequence of any generalized poisoning will thus, from the outset, probably be a mass multiplication of the pest, for the predators that had previously kept its numbers down will have been destroyed.

Finally, the much higher number of prey individuals has yet another effect. The probability that offshoots resistant to our poison will appear rises, the greater the number of individuals. Such poisoning, then, brings the danger of eradicating the predator and making the prey immune.

The spatial distribution of food is highly significant. A densemono-culture—whether animal or plant—is easter for a predator or grazer to exploit than a very irregular distribution, which requires an animal to spend considerable time and energy in finding a suitable food source. There is a certain minimum food density below which the effort per unit time to obtain enough to eat is prohibitive.

Here, again, we have the problem of cost vs benefit. If the water flea Daphnia pulex is offered the diatom Scenedesmus acutus as food, it filters the diatom from the water and eats it.

A 1-mm-long water flea in water at 10°C can survive if 0.04 mg carbon is available per liter of water (1 mg carbon corresponds to about 20 mg animal matter). Water fleas 3 mm long at 25°C need much more to maintain themselves-1.9 mg carbon per liter.

Copepods filter-feed more effectively and can live even in nutrient-poor lakes, in the winter and at depth; in this regard they are superior to water fleas. Quantitative data of this kind are scarce; there are only a few other examples.

In some places redshanks feed primarily on the crab Corophium, which is found in enormous numbers in mud flats. If the density of the crabs is about 200 animals/m2 or less,. the redshank switches to polychaete worms which provide more food for a given amount of time spent searching. The sanddwelling shrimp Crangon feeds chiefly on polychaetes (Nereis, Nephthys). But experiments by Gerlach (1969) showed that this laborious, bunting strategy costs more energy than it brings in, so that the weight of the shrimp slowly declines.

Badgers (Meles) in southern England feed almost exclusively on earthworms (Lumbricus), catching them on the surface of the ground by night. There are vast numbers of these worms everywhere in the soil, but they do not come to the surface everywhere, and not enough are available to the badgers to satisfy their needs.

Therefore no relationship can be established between the density, of the earthworm population and that of the badgers. The sole decisive factor is the availability of the food, which depends on specific geomorphological features.

In the case of colony-breeding sea birds, a relationship has been found between reproductive biology and the distance that normally must be travelled to find food. Terns usually lay three eggs and feed the young until they can fly. They can manage this only if there is a good feeding site without 5 km of the nest, where they can fish without losing time. Among the auk species one can find a progressive series of brood-feeding behaviour.

The black guillemot is the only bird in this family to lay two eggs; it breeds individually near the coast and usually finds its food by diving in the water just off the coast. The fish it catches are brought directly to the young, which very soon leave the nest and go along on the fishing expeditions.

The other species breed in very large colonies and each bird lays only one egg. The parents usually fish relatively far from the coast; they feed their young until they have grown to about one-quarter of the adult size. Then the young leave the nest and follow their parents out to sea. The puffin flies out to the high seas in its search for food. Its young live in holes in the ground and are thus particularly well protected; they are fed for a very long time.

This sort of behaviour is taken to the extreme by the tube-nosed albatrosses and their relatives. These birds also lay only one eggs; they hunt for food on the high seas, out of sight of the coast. Therefore the young can be fed at most once a day, and those of many species are fed only every second day.

The adult birds fly at great speed; their feeding grounds in general lie between 30 and 200 km from the nest, and it is quite possible for them to extend to even greater distances. Among the larger forms, then, the period during which the young are fed lasts more than three months. By that time the young bird has grown to a weight greater than that of the adult.

The young of most species at this stage leave the brood-hole at night and wander independently out to sea, where they develop their flying skills. Some other species (for example, the arctic fulmar. Fulmaris glacialis) are fledged while still in the nest, with marked loss of weight, for the adults have already stopped coming to the nest rocks and feeding them.

The young bird is fully fledged when it leaves the nesting site. The large procellariids and albatrosses can breed only every second year; the breeding ground is occupied each year, however, by different pairs of birds in alternation. The price these birds pay for the opportunity to exploit' the food offered by the high seas is a reduction in rate of reproduction (only one offspring per reproductive season) and an' extremely long breeding period. They can afford this cost because their life span is so long.

5

LIGHT AFFECTING PLANT LIFE

Various kinds of plant germinate, grow, flower and fruit at different times in the year, each in its own season. Thus some plants flower in the spring, others in the summer and still others in the autumn. And in the autumn, trees and shrubs stop growing in apparent anticipation of winter, usually well before the weather turns cold.

What is the nature of the clock or calendar that regulates these cycles in the diverse life histories of plants? Some 40 years ago it was discovered that the regulator is the seasonal variation in the length of the day and night. Since this is the one factor in the environment that changes at a constant rate with the change of the seasons, in retrospect the discovery does not seem so surprising.

But how do plants detect the change in the ratio of daylight to darkness? The answer to this question is just now becoming clear. It appears that a single light-sensitive pigment, common to all plants, triggers one or another of the crises in plant growth, from the sprouting of the seed to the onset of dormancy, depending upon the plant species.

This discovery is a major break-through toward a more complete understanding of the life processes of plants, and it places within reach a means for the artificial regulation of these processes. The pigment has been called phytochrome by the investigators who discovered it at the Plant Industry Station of the U.S. Department of Agriculture in Beltsville, Md. It has been partially isolated, and it has been made to perform in the test tube what seems to be its critical photosensitive reaction:

changing back and forth from one of its two forms to the other upon exposure to one or the other of two wavelengths of light that differ by 75 millimicrons.

A millimicron is a ten thousandth of a centimeter). Phytochrome appears to be chemically active in one of its forms and inactive in the other. In the tissues of the plant it functions as an enzyme and probably catalyzes a biochemical, reaction that is crucial to many metabolic processes. The first step toward the discovery of phytochrome was taken in the 1920's, when W.W. Garner and H.A. Allard of the Department of Agriculture recognized "photoperiodism".

They showed many -plants will not flower unless the days are of the right length' some species fowering when the days are short, some when the days are long. Indeed, some plants seem to react not simply to seasonal changes but to changes in the length of the day from one week to the next.

Photoperiodism explained why plants of one type, even though planted at different times, always flower together, and why some plants do not fruit or flower in certain latitudes. Other investigators soon reasoned that if a plant needs a certain length of day to flower; then keeping it in the dark for ,part of the day would inhibit its flowering.

They tried to demonstrate such an effect in the laboratory. Nothing happened: the plants always bloomed in the proper season. The riddle was solved when the reverse experiment was tried, that is when the night was interrupted with a brief interval of light.

Chrysanthemums, poinsettias, soybeans, cocklebums and other plants that flower during the short days and long nights of autumn and early winter remained vegetative (i.e., nonfloweiing). Moreover, they could be made to bloom out of season, when the night was lengthened by keeping them it the dark at the beginning or the end of a long.summer day.

Conversely, a brief-interval of light interrupting the Gong winter night induced flowering in petunias, barley, spinach and other plants that normally bloom in the short-night summer season. Artificial lengthening of the short summer night kept these plants vegetative. Interrupting or prolonging the night time darkness correspondingly affected stem growth and other processes as well as flowering in many plants.

It was evident that light must act upon a photoreceptive compound, or compounds, to set some mechanism that runs to completion in darkness. As a first step toward elucidating the chemistry of the process H.A. Borthwick, Marion W. Parker and Sterling B. Hendricks of the Department of Agriculture in 1944 set out to determine the wavelength or colour of light that is most effective in inhibiting flowering in long-night plants.

They exposed each of a series of Biloxisoybean plants from which they had stripped all but one leaf, to different wavelengths of light from a large spectrograph. Several days after the treatment the plants were examined for the effect of this exposure upon the formation of buds. Red light with a wavelength of 660 millimicrons proved to be by far the most effective inhibitor of flowering.

The cocklebur and other long-night plants gave the same response. By plotting on a graph the energy of light required to inhibit flowering at various wavelengths, the investigators obtainthe "action spectrum" of the mechanism that inhibits flowering. This showed that to interfere with flowering, much more light energy is required at, for example, 520 or 700 millimicrons than at (or very near) 660 millimicrons.

The wavelength at which the unknown substance absorbs light most efficiently was thus shown to be 660 millimicrons. Borthwick and his associates then turned to short-night plants. The same spectrographic experiments yielded exactly ,the same action spectrum. But in this case the effect of the exposure was to promote—not inhibit—flowering!

Since the same wavelength of light caused the greatest response in both cases, the investigators could only conclude that a single photoreceptive substance was involved in these two diametrically opposed responses. Subsequent experiments implicated the same compound in the control of stem elongation and leaf growth.

Recent work has shown that light at 660 millimicrons also acts upon mature apples to turn them red by enabling them to make the pigment anthodyanin. The same red light controls the production of anthocyanin in a number of seedlig plants. With the collaboration of a research group headed by Eben H. Toole, Borthwick and his associates next set out to determine which wavelengths of light trigger germination in those seeds that must be exposed to light in order to grow.

Many weed and crop seeds are of this type. The action spectrum for the promotion of seed germination turned out to be essentially the same as that established for other plant responses. Whereas. about 20 per cent of the seeds germinated in the dark or when they were exposed to green, blue and other shorter-wavelength colours, more than 90 per cent sprouted after irradiation by red light at 660 millimicrons.

This finding led the two groups of investigators to the study of an entirely different effect of light upon germination. It had been observed in the late 1930's that germination was inhibited when seeds were exposed to the longer wavelengths of far-red light which are invisible to the human eye. That observation was speedily confirmed, In fact, seeds that had been pushed to maximum germinative capacity by exposure to red light failed to germinate when they were subsequently irradiated with farred light.

The plotting of the action spectrum for this effect showed that far-red light at 735 millimicrons wavelength is the most potent in inhibiting the germination of seeds. Still more interesting was the discovery that the diametrically opposed effects of red and far-red light upon germination are fully reversible.

After a series of alternate exposures to light of 660 and 735 millimicrons, the seeds responded to the light by which they were last irradiated. If it was red, they germinated; if far-red, they remained dormant. Now all phenomena of growth and flowering had to be re-examined for the effect of far-red as well as of red light.

In each case the experiments demonstrated that irradiation by far-red light reversed the effects obtained by irradiation with red light. The reversibility of these reactions and the clear definition of their action spectra strongly suggested that a single ligntsensitive substance is at work in every case and that this substance exists in two forms.

One form, which was designated .phytochrome 660, or P_{660} absorbs red light in the region of 660 millimicrons. When P_{660} is irradiated at this wavelength, it is transformed into phytochrome 735 (P_{735}) which absorbs farred light at 735 millimicrons. When P_{735} is irradiated with light at 735 millimicrons, it reverts in turn to the P_{660} form.

In order to substantiate these deductions phytochrome had to be extracted from the plant. This required a method for detecting the presence of the compound other than the responses occur at sharply defined wavelengths, there was reason to expect that phytochrome itself would prove to be more opaque,.or "dense," to light at the wavelengths of 660 and 735 millimicrons when examined in a spectrophotometer—an instrument that measures the intensity of transmitted light at discrete wavelengths.

The transformation of phytochrome from one form to the other would also show up well. Measuring the very small amounts of phytochrome present in plants was not a simple task. K.H. Norris and one of the authors (Butler), respectively an engineer and a biophysicist in the Department of Agriculture, had been studying the pigment composition of intact plant-tissue, and had developed some sensitive spectrophotometers that measured the absorption of light by leaves and other plant parts. With Hendricks, a chemist and H.W. Siegelman, a plant physiologist who had been investigating the chemistry of phytochrome, they formed a research group' to look for the reversible pigment. Initially the absorption of light by plant parts failed to reveal the presence of phytochrome.

The plant tissue, however, contained large amounts of chlorophyll, which absorbs strongly at 675 millimicrons. Apparently the absorption of light by chlorophyll—at a wavelength so near the phytochrome absorption peak of 660 millimicrons—was masking the absorption by phytochrome.

It was no great problem, however, to get around this obstacle. Seedlings can be sprouted in the dark and can grow for a while on the food energy stored in the seed, they do not begin to synthesize chlorophyll until they are exposed to the light. Corn seedlings were accordingly grown for several days in complete darkness.

They were then chopped up and exposed to red light to put the phytochrome, into the P_{735} form in which it absorbs far-red light. In the spectrophotometer a weak beam of light at 735 millimicrons was projected through the sample, weak light being used so that the phytochrome would not change form.

The absorption spectrum showed that the phytochrome was indeed absorbing light at 735 millimicrons; the same sample passed light at 660 millimicrons. On the other hand, after exposure to relatively bright far-red light the chopped seedlings were found to absorb more light at 660 millimi Irons and less light at 735 millimicrons. Repeated demonstration of this reversibility fully confirmed all that had been predicted from the responses of whole, growing plants.

No doubt remained that a single compound was resposible for the reversible changes in growing, plants. The spectrophotometer measures the changes in "optical density" with such high sensitivity that it can be used to assay the amountt of phytochrome in plant tissue.

Thus with the help of this instrument a search was instituted for a plant that would supply phytochrome in sufficient abundance for' chemical separation. Certain plant tissues, such as the flesh and 'seed of the avocado and the head of the cauliflower, showed a relatively., high concentration off phytochrome.

The cotyledons' (the first leaves, which feed the seedling) of most legumes synthesize phytochrome, and the concentration reaches its maximum about five days after the seeds start soaking up, water. The growing shoot, or hypocotyl, as well as the first leaves of the legumes, contain less phytochrome than the cotyledons. In cabbage and turnip seedlings that have been sprouted in the dark the cotyledons are also a good source of phytochrome.

However, fiveday-old, dark-grown corn seedlings proved to be the best source because they develop a high phytochrome. content, have large stems and are easy to grow and harvest. The preliminary 'and partial chemical isolation of phytochrome was easily accomplished. Corn shoots were ground up in a blender along with water and a mild alkaline buffer, and a clear solution was separated from the solid material by filtration.

This extract exhibits exactly the same reversible optical-density changes at 660 and 735 millimicrons as the chopped seedlings. themselves. Thorough study of the partially purified material has developed no evidence that any compound other than phytochrome participate in the photoreaction.

Though phytochrome has not yet been isolated in pure form, the outlook is favourable. The compound shows all the properties of a relatively stable soluble protein, and Hendricks and Siegelman are now using the techniques of protein chemistry to purify it. They have subjected it to dialysis (diffusion through a porous membrane), and it has retained its photochemical activity. Oxidizing and reducing agents do not affect it.

Moreover, the photoconversion occurs at zero degrees centigrade as readily as at 35 degrees, as would be expected of a strictly photochemical reaction. Higher temperatures denature the protein and destroy its photochemical activity. Measurements of the amount of red' and far-red light necessary to bring about the conversion show that P_{660} consumes only one third as much energy in being transformed to P_{735} as $P_{i;3b}$ consumes in being changed into P_{660}.

In both cases, however, the energy consumption is relatively small, indicating that the phytochrome absorbs light efficiently. The pigment should turn out to be a blue or blue-green, the colors complementary to red, but the concentration achieved so far has been too low to make the colour visible.

Experiments with growing plants had indicated that P_{735} slowly changes back into P_{660} in darkness, whereas red-absorbing P_{660} is stable. Direct measurement of the changes in the form of phytochrome in intact corn seedlings have confirmed these indications. In seedings that have never been exposed to light, phytochrome occurs entirely in the red-absorbing, or Peso, form. These seedlings are exposed briefly to red light to convert the P_{660} to P_{735}. They are then returned to the darkroom and -are examined with the spectrophotometer at intervals thereafter. Such measurements show that it takes about four hours at room temperature for the P_{735} to change back into P_{660}.

This conversion in the absence of light is apparently mediated by enzymes. It is markedly retarded by lowering the temperature, and it does not occur at all in the absence of oxygen. In the partially purified clear liquid extracts of seedlings, however, P_{735} is stable in the dark, indicating that the darkconversion enzyme system has been removed.

Half the phytochrome activity is lost in intact seedings during the dark conversion of P_{735} to P_{660}. After a second illumination with red light, total phytochrome activity declines still more. In continuous light, phytochrome activity is quite low, but is still detectable. It was fortunate that the presence of chlorophyll made it necessary to grow seedlings in darkness for the early experiments.

If the seedlings had received even small amounts of light, the unstable P_{735} would have formed and would have soon lost its activity to such an extent that phytochrome might never have been detected. How phytochrome exerts its manifold influences on plant growth is still unknown.

P_{735} seems to be the active form, while P660 appears to be a quiescent form in which the plant can store the potentially active compound. At the close of any period of exposure to light, phytochrome is predominantly in the far-red.absorbing form. The rate at which P_{660} is then carried through the dark conversion back to P_{735}, provides the plant with a "clock" for measuring the duration of the dark period.

The rate of conversion probably varies from one plant to another, and must depend in part upon such factors as temperature. The effective dark period might be the time required for the complete conversion, or it might be the time in darkness after the conversion is finished. In either case a brief interval of light in the middle of the dark period would cause a plant to respond as though the dark period were short.

Phytochrome is undoubtedly an enzyme—a biological catalyst. Its ability to control so many kinds of plant response in so many different tissues suggests that it catalyzes a critical reaction that is common to many metabolic path-ways. Several reactions of this kind are known. One is the reaction that forms the so-called acetyl coenzyme-A compounds.

These compounds are essential intermediates in fat utilization and fat synthesis, in cellular respiration and in the synthesis of anthocyanin and sterol compounds. The regulation to the supply of acetyl coenzyme-A compounds would provide an ideal control for growth processes. More than three fourths of all the carbon in a plant is incorporated in this coenzyme at some stage or other.

The extraction and partial purification of phytochrome is the starting point of a major forward movement in the under-standing of plant physiology. Further research on this remarkable protein, ubiquitous in the plant world, should answer many questions concerning germination, growth, flowering, dormancy and colouring. It should also provide a means to control all of these plant processes to the great benefit of agriculture.

The progress of each group's flower-bud development was directly proportional to the excess of its dark period over eight .and a half hours, up to a certain limit. What does this mean? The simplest and most plausible explanation is that the plant synthesizes the flowering hormone in the late stages of the dark period, and the more time it has for synthesizing the hormone, the faster the flower bud will develop.

However, diminishing returns set in after about 12 hours of darkness; in fact, it appears that when the dark period is prolonged to 20 hours or so, the hormone begins to be destroyed. This brings us to the somewhat controversial next step. The cocklebur will often flower even if it is left in the dark for nine days. But James Lockhart and Hamner, working at the University of California at Los Angeles, have found that for full flowering development the plant seems to need a re-exposure to high-intensity light, e.g., sunlight, after the dark period.

Consequently it may be that this exposure represents an other chemical step in the normal flowering process: the light may be needed to "stabilize" the flowering hormone or to stop some process in the leaves that destroys the hormone. A very simple experiment has disclosed another distinct stage in the requirements for flowering: namely, transport of the flowering hormone from the leaves to the growing stem tips where the flowers form.

If a cocklebur's leaves are removed at the end of the critical dark period, the plant will not flower. This must mean that the flowering hormone is still in the leaves and none has yet reached the stem tips. Finally, there are obviously two more steps in the flowering process; the flowering hormone acts upon the cells in the rowing tips in some way to transform, or differentiate, them from the vegetative to the flowering form of growth, and the bud then develops into the specific structures that make up a flower.

To sum up, the flowering of a plant has been resolved so far into about eight steps:

1. the build-up of needed substances in the plant by photosynthesis,
2. conversion of a pigment in the leaves to the noninhibitory form in darkness,
3. another preparatory reaction in the darkness,
4. synthesis of the flowering hormone, also in darkness,
5. a possible further chemical reaction requiring exposure to intense light,
6. transportation of the flowering hormone from the leaves to the growing stem tips,
7. alteration of the vegetative cells there to the flowering mode of growth,
8. development of the flower bud.

All this gives us only a tantalizing general view of the process, as if we were watching the building of a house and could see the foundation, floors, walls and roof go up but were too far away to see any of the details (wiring, plumbing, etc.) that make it a living home. We long for a more intimate view, which means a closer and more direct look at the chemical reactions involved in generating a flower.

At Colorado State University we have recently been doing some experiments which are opening some enticing new avenues of approach. Mainly these experiments take the form of testing the effects of various chemicals applied to the plant before, during or after the dark period.

Some chemicals, known to be general inhibitors of plant growth (e.g., maleic hydrazide), have proved to inhibit flowering in our cockleburs regardless,of when: they were applied. Others seem to exert a more specific action. For example, the growth, hormones (auxins) interfere with flowering only if they are applied before the flowering hormone has traveled from the leaves to the growing tips.

Our experiments suggest that they may play some part in destruction of the hormone in the leaves. Another chemical, the growth inhibitor dinitrophenol, prevents flowering only if it is applied to the cocklebur during the dark period. We think that it probably blocks synthesis of the flowering hormone. Dinitrophenol is known to interfere with the production of energy-rich phosphate bonds.

If such bonds are the source of energy for the synthesis of the flowering hormone, dinitrophenol may exert its inhibiting effect by cutting off the power supply, so to speak. One of our most useful tools for dissecting the flowering process has been the ion of cobalt.

This chemical inhibits flowering only if applied during the early hours of the dark period. Thus we can narrow down its action to interference with one of two processes: the conversion of the pigment involved in flowering or the "preparatory reaction." Furthermore, among all the chemicals tested so far the cobalt ion is the only one that affects the length of the dark period needed for flowering.

In some experiments plants treated with cobaltous chloride did not flower unless their dark period was at least 11 hours long. In other words, cobalt slows down the clock that ticks off the critical night for the cocklebur.

With refined probing tools such as cobalt and other specific growth regulators we have hopes of eventually being able to pinpoint the substances and reactions that bring the cocklebur to flower. But already the experiments have opeded wider horizons.

The specific wavelengths of orange-red and far-red light that so powerfully influence the flowering of cockleburs seem to control many other plant processes—not only the flowering of many plants but also the colouring of tomato skins, the germination of lettuce seeds, the growth of seedlings in the dark, the winter dormancy of tree buds, and so on.

Perhaps we are on the track of a key pigment which plays a large role in the plant kingdom, and possibly even among some species of the animal kingdom.

THE PATH OF CARBON IN PHOTOSYNTHESIS

The processes of life consist ultimately of the synthesis and breakdown of carbon compounds. Because a carbon atom can bind four other atoms to itself at a time and is thereby able to link up with other atoms-especially other carbon atoms—in chains and rings, carbon lends itself to the construction of a virtually endless variety of molecules.

These molecules derive their physical characteristics and chemical activity not only from their composition but also from their size and intricacy of structure. The rich variety of life suggests in turn that living cells have gone far in the elaboration of such compounds and the processes that make and unmake them. All these processes depend in the end on a first one.

This is the process of photosynthesis, which takes carbon and several other common elements from the environment and builds them into the substances of life.

The plant finds most of these elements already bonded to oxygen in oxides such as carbon dioxide (CO_2), water (H_2O), nitrate (H_2O) and sulphate (SO_2^-). Before the plant can bind the elements other than oxygen together as organic compounds, it must remove some of the excesss oxygen as oxygen gas (O_2), and this accomplishment takes a large amount of energy.

In the simplest terms photosynthesis is the process by which green plants trap the energy of sunlight by using that energy to break strong bonds between oxygen and other elements, while forming weaker bonds between the other elements and forcing oxygen atoms to pair as oxygen gas.

For example, to make the sugar glucose ($C_6H_{12}G_6$) the plant must split out six molecules of oxygen in order to combine tit, carbon and half the oxygen of six carbon dioxide molecules with the hydrogen of six water molecules.

The glucose and other 6rganic-compounds taken up in the chemical machinery of the.plants and the, animals that on plants serve both as fuel and as the raw materials for the synthesis of higher organic compounds. That considerable solar energy is bound by photosynthesis becomes apparent when wood or coal is burned.

In living cells the controlled combustion of respiration extracts this energy to power the other processes of life. Both kinds of combustion take oxygen from the air and break down organic compounds to carbon dioxide and water again. In its end result photosynthesis can be defined as the opposite of respiration.

Together these complementary processes drive the cyclic flow of matter and the noncyclic flow, of energy through the living world. From such generalizations about the effect and function of photosynthesis in nature it is a long step to the, explanation of how photosynthesis works. Yet much of the explanation is now complete.

The work has been greatly facilitated by the earlier and more nearly complete resolution of the chemistry of respiration. The two processes, it turns out, are in some ways complementary on the molecular scale, just as they, are on the grand scale in the biosphere.

Each involves some 20 to 30 discrete reactions and as many intermediate cmpounds; half a dozen of these reactions and their intermediates are: common to both photosynthesis and respiration. Only the first few steps in photosynthesis are driven directly by light.

The energy of light is trapped in the bonds of a few specific compounds. These energy carries deliver the energy in discrete units to the steps of synthesis that follow. The same or closely similar carriers perform corresponding operations in respiration, picking up energy from the stepwise dismemberment of the fuel molecule and delivering it to the energy-consuming processes of the cell.

Although the first, energy-trapping stage in photosynthesis remains to be clarified, it is now possible to trace the path of carbon from, the very first step in which a single atom of carbon is captured in the bonds of an evanescent intermediate compound.

The term "carbohydrate" recalls the deduction of early 19th-century investigators that photosynthesis made glucose directly by combining atoms of carbon with moiecules of water, as the formula for glucose suggests. In line with this idea it was thought that the oxygen transpired by green leaves came from the splitting of carbrn dioxide.

The progress of chemistry, however, failed to disclose any processes that would aecomplish these results so simply. Accumulating evidance to the contrary became convincing some 30 years ago, when C.B. van Niel of Stanford University discovered that certain bacteria produce organic compounds by a process of photosynthesis similar to that in plants but with one important difference.

These bacteria use hydrogen sulphide (H:S) instead of water and liberate elemental sulphur instead of gaseous oxygen. The otherwise complete similarity of the two processes strongly suggested that the oxygen evolved by green plants must come from the splitting of water.

The Capture of Light

Photosynthesis' could now be described in terms of familar chemistry. The splitting of water would be accomplished by the process of oxidatian (which means the removal of hydrogen atoms from a molecule), with oxygen gas as the product of the reaction.

The free hydrogen atoms would then be available to carry through the equally familar and opposite process of reduction (which means the addition of hydrogen atoms to a molecule). By the addition of hydrogen atoms (or electrons plus hydrogen ions) the carbon dioxide would be reduced to an organic compound.

It is during the first, energy-converting stage of photosynthesis that the water molecule is split. Initially the energy of light impinging on the plant cell is transformed into the ; chemical potential energy of electrons excited from their normal orbits in molecules of the green pigment chlorophyll and other plant pigments.

A large part of this energy eventually goes into the splitting of water as electrons and hydrogen ions are transferred from water to the substance triphosphopyridine nucleotide (TPN+), which is thereupon reduced to the form designated TPNH. The TPNH thus becomes not only a carrier of energy but also the bearer of electrons for the subsequent reduction of carbon dioxide.

Along with the movement of electrons from water to TPNH, some energy goes to charging the energy-carrying molecule adenosine triphosphate (ATP), specifically by promoting the attachment of a third phosphate -group ($-OP0_3$) to adenosine diphosphate (ADP), the discharged form of the carrier. Both ATP and TPNH belong to the family of compounds known as cofactors or coenzymes, which work with enzymes in the catalysis of chemical reactions.

ATP, the universal currency of energy transactions in the cell, plays a significant role in respiration as well as in photosynthesis. Needless to say, the manufacture of each of these cofactors involves an intricate cycle of reactions. Although the cycles are not yet fully understood, it is enough for the purpose of the present discussion to know that ATP and TPNH, or closely similar compounds, furnish the energy for the second stage of photosynthesis, during which the carbon atom of carbon dioxide is reduced and joined to a hydrogen atom and a carbon atom in place of an oxygen.

The process of reduction goes forward in small steps. Each reaction brings about some change in a carbon compound until the starting material is at last transformed to the final product. For each reaction there is therefore an intermediate compound. Since every life process involves a more or less extended series of intermediates, cells typically contain a large number of intermediates.

Many of them turn up in two or more pathways leading to different end products. The tracing of the path of carbon in photosynthesis required first of all a technique for identifying the intermediates proper to it and for establishing their sequence along the path.

Samuel Ruben and Martin D. Kamen, then at the University of California, met this need some 20 years ago by their discovery of the radioactive isotope of carbon with a mass number of 14. This tisotope has a conveniently long half life of more than 5,000 years; over the time period of an experiment, therefore, carbon 14 has an effectively constant radioactivity.

Ruben and his colleagues recognized at once the potential usefulness of this isotope as a label for the identification of compounds in biological processes. They prepared carbon dioxide in which the carbon atoms were carbon 14. When they exposed green plants to an atmosphere containing this gas instead or normal carbon dioxide ($C^{12}O_2$), the plants took up the ($C^{14}O_2$), and made compounds from it.

The presence of the carbon 14 in these compounds could be detected by various divices, such as the Geiger-Muller counter, and by radio-autography on X-ray film. Unfortunately this work was cut short by the war and by Ruben's death in a laboratory accident.

In 1946 Melvin Calvin organized a new group at the Lawrence Radiation Laboratory of the University of California with the primary objective of tracing the path of carbon in photosynthesis with $C^{14}0_2$ as one of its principal tools.

Starting as a graduate student in 1947, I had the good fortune to participate in this work with. Calvin, Andrew A. Benson and". others The early experiments were quite simply contrived. We used leafy plants and often just the leaves of plants. After allowing a leaf to photosynthesize for a given length of time in an atmosphere of $C^{14}O_2$ in a closed chamber, we would bring biochemical activity to a halt by immersing the leaf in alcohol.

With the enzymes inactivared, the reactions converting one intermediate compound into another would story, and the pattern of labeling would be "frozen" at the point. We soon discovered, however, that photosynthesis proceeds too rapidly for completely reliable observation by such a procedure.

With few seconds delay in the penetration of alcohol into the cell, for example, the labeling pattern would be disarrayed and no longer representative of the stage at which we tried to halt the photosynthesis. Since rapid and precisely timed killing of the plant is important, we adopted single-celled algae-Chlorella pyrenoidosa and Scenedesmus obliquus-as the subject for many of our experiments.

In both species the plant consists of a single cell so small that it can be seen only with a microscope. Alcohol can quickly penetrate the cell wall and deactivate the enzymes. The algae offer another advantage: they can be grown in continuous cultures, asssuring us a supply of material with, highly constant properties.

An experimental sample is taken from the culture in a thin walled, transparent closed vessel. Illuminated through the walls. of the vessel and supplied with a stream of ordinary carbon dioxide, which is bubbled through the suspension, the algae photosynthesize at the normal rate. We shut off the supply of carbon dioxide and inject a solution of radioactive bicarbonate ion (carbon dioxide dissolved in our algae culture medium is mostly converted into bicarbonate ion). After a few seconds or minutes the cells are. killed. We then extract the soluble ,radioactive compounds from the plant material and analyze them.

The Reduction of CO_2

Calvin and his colleagues soon found that the carbon 14 label was distributed among several classes of biochemical compounds, including not only sugars but also amino acids; the subunits of proteins. As the exposure time was reduced to a few seconds, the first stable intermediate product of photosynthesis was found to be the three-carbon compound 3phosphoglyceric acid (PGA).

The next step was to determine which of the three carbon atoms in the first generation of PGA molecules synthesized in the presence of radioactive carbon dioxide bears the carbon 14 label. We first removed from PGA' the phosphate group and then diluted the free glyceric acid with glyceric acid containing the stable carbon 12 isotope in order to have enough material for analysis by ordinary chemical methods.

Treatment with reagents that severed the bonds between the carbons produced there different products, one from each carbon atom. By measuring the radioactivity of each of the products we were able to identify the labeled carbon.

In PGA from plants that had been exposed to labeled carbon dioxide for only five seconds we found that virtually all the carbon 14 was located in the carboxyl atom, the carbon at one end of the chain that is bound to two oxygens. This was not surprising because the carboxyl group most nearly resembles carbon dioxide.

The carbon is bound to the oxygens by three bonds, however, instead of four; the fourth bond now ties it to the middle carbon in the PGA chain. The transfer of this bond from one of the oxygens to a carbon constitutes the first step in the reduction of the carbon dioxide. This was evidence also that the reduction is accomplished by some sort of carboxylation reaction, a reaction in which carbon dioxide is added to some organic compound.

Ultimately, of course, the two other carbons of PGA must come from carbon dioxide. But it was some time before investigation disclosed the specific compound that picks up the carbon dioxide and the cyclic pathway that makes this carbon dioxide acceptor from PGA.

The discovery of the pathway intermediates was made much easier by a then comparatively new technique; two-dimensional paper chromatography, developed by the British chemists A.J. P. Martin and

R.L.M. Synge. Closely similar compounds can be distiuguished in this procedure by slight differences in their relative solubility in an organic solvent and in water.

The extract from the plant is dropped on a sheet of filler paper near one-cornor. An edge of the paper adjacent to the corner is immersed in a trough containing an organic solvent; the paper is held taut by a weight and the whole assembly is placed in a water-saturated atmosphere in a vapour-tight box.

The solvent travelling through the paper by capillarity dissolves the compounds and carries them along with it. As they move along in the solvent, however, the compounds tend to distribute themselves between the solvent and the water absorbed by the fibers of the paper.

In general the more soluble the compared with the organic solvent, the slower it travels. If the compound is also absorbed to some extent by the cellulose fibers, its movement will be even slower. As a result the compounds are distributed in a row in one dimension.

Depending on the solubility of the compounds and the nature of the solvent used, somecompounds may still overlap one another. Repetition of the procedure, with a different solvent travelling at right angles to the direction of the first run, will usually separate these compounds in a second dimension.

Since most of the compounds are colourless, special techniques are needed to locate them on the paper. Those that are radioactive will locate themselves, however, if the chromatographic paper is placed in contact with a sheet of X-ray film for a few days. The resulting radio-autograph will show as. many as 20 or 30 radioactive compounds in the substances, extracted from algae exposed to carbon 14 for only 30 seconds. Clearly the synthetic apparatus of the plant works rapidly.

CHROMATOGRAPHS AND RADIOAUTOGRAPHS

In order to identify these compounds we prepared a chromatographic map by running samples of many known compounds through the same chromatographic system and recording the locations at which we found them on the paper. The locations can be made visible in these cases by spraying the paper with a mist of some chemical that is known to react with the compound to produce a coloured spot.

Comparison of the radioautograph of an unknwon compound with the map yields a first clue to its identity. This can be corroborated by washing the radioactive compound out of the paper with water and mixing it with a larger sample of the suspected authentic substance. The mixture is applied to a new piece of filter paper and chromatographed. With enough of the authentic material to yield a coloured spot, comparison with a radioautograph of the same paper now shows whether or not the radioactive and the authentic material really coincide.

The possibility that the authentic material and the radioactive material are still not the same can be tested by using different solvent systems in the preparation of the chromatograph and by other means.

Over the years these procedures have established the identity of a great many of the intermediate and end products of photosynthesis. Some of the sugar phosphates labeled by carbon 14 proved to be well-known derivatives of triose (three-carbon) and hexose (six-carbon) sugars.

Other were discovered for the first time among the intermediates produced by our algae. Benson showed that among these are a seven-carbon sugar phosphate and also five-carbon phosphates, including in particular rihulose-1, 5-diphosphate.

The rapid building of carbon 14 into the more familiar triose and hexose phosphates suggested certain biochemical pathways already established in- studies of respiration. It seemed likely that PGA might be linked to these phosphates by the reverse of a sequence of respiratory reactions first mapped many years ago by the German chemists Otto Meyerhof, Gustav Embden and Jakob Parnas.

In the respiratory pathway hexose phosphate is split into two molecules of triose phosphate, with the split occurring between the two carbon atoms in the middle of the chain. The triose phosphate is then oxidized to give PGA.

The electrons from this energy-yielding operation are picked up by diphosphopyridine nucleotide (DPN+), which is thereupon reduced to DPNH. The DPN+ is a close relative of the TPN+ that turns up in photosynthesis. In addition this oxidation yields enough energy to make a molecule of ATP from ADP and phosphate ion.

In the reverse pathway of these reactions in photosynthesis Calvin concluded, the plant uses the cofactors ATP and TPNH, made earlier by the transformation of the energy of light, to bring about the Teduction of PGA to triose phosphate. In the first step the terminal phosphate group of ATP is transferred to the carboxyl group of PGA to form a "carboxyl phosphate" (really an acyl phosphate).

Some of the chemical potential energy that was stored in ATP is now stored in the acyl phosphate, making the new intermediate compound highly, reactive. It is now ready for reduction by TPNH. This reducing agent donates two electrons to the reactive intermediate. One carbonoxygen bond is thereby severed and the oxygen atom, carried off with the phosphate group, is replaced by a hydrogen atom.

In this way the carboxyl carbon atom is reduced to an aldehyde carbon atom; that is, it now has two bonds to oxygen instead of three and one bond each to carbon and hydrogen. This is the point in the cycle at which most of the solar energy captured in the first stage of photosynthesis is applied to the reduction of carbon.

The Unstable Intermediate

The next development in the plotting of the carbon pathway came from a series of experiments first performed in our laboratory by Peter Massini. He hoped to see which intermediates would be most trongly increased or decreased in concentration by turning off the light and allowing the synthetic process to go on for a while in the dark.

In order to establish the concentration of the various intermediates when the reaction proceeds in the light, he bubbled radioactive carbon dioxide through the culture for more than half an hour. At the end of this period every intermediate was as highly radioactive as the incoming carbon dioxide. The radioactivity from each compound therefore gave a measure of the concentration of the compound.

He then turned off the light and after a few seconds took another sample of algae in which he measured the relative concentration of compounds by the same technique. zComparison with the compounds sampled in the light showed that the concentration of PGA was greatly increased.

This finding could be readily explained turning off the light stopped the production of the ATP and TPNH required to reduce PGA to triose phosphate. Of the sugar phosphates present, only one, the five-carbon ribulose diphosphate, was found to have changed significantly; its concentration dropped to zero. Because the PGA had simultaneously increased in concentration, it was apparent that ribulose diphosphate was consumed in the production of PGA.

This finding was of great significance because it indicated for the first time that ribulose diphosphate is the intermediate to which carbon dioxide is attached by the carboxylation reaction. For this reaction ribulose diphosphate is prepared by an earlier reaction that goes on in the light and in which ATP donates its terminal phosphate group to ribulose monophosphate.

The more reactive diphosphate molecule now adds one molecule of carbon dioxide by carboxylation. The details of this reaction remain

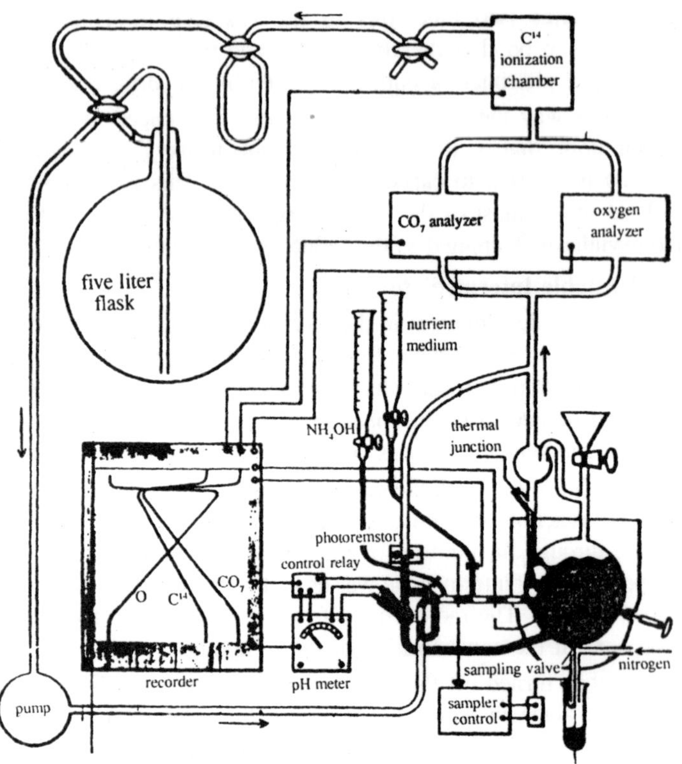

Figure 5.1: Steady-State Apparatus permits experimental control and study of photosynthesis. The algae are suspended in nutrient in a transparent vessel (lower right). A gas pump circulates a mixture of air, ordinary carbon dioxide and labeled carbon dioxide (when needed) to the vessel, where it bubbles through the suspensions. Labeled carbon can also be added in theform of bicarbohate (HC"Os). Measurements of the oxygen, carbon dioxide and labeled carbon levels in the gas are recorded continuously. The pH is maintained at a constant value by means of the pH meter. The sampler control allows removal of samples into the test tube.

obscure because the resulting six-carbon intermediate is so unstable that we have not been able to detect it by our methods of analysis. As its first stable product this sequence of events yields two three-carbon PGA molecules.

Massini's experimental results were confirmed by a parallel experiment devised by Alex Wilson, then a graduate student in our laboratory. Instead of turning out the light Wilson shut off the supply of carbon dioxide. In this situation one might expect to find an increase in the concentration of the compound that is consumed in the carboxylation reaction; ribulose diphosphate showed such an increase.

Corrrespondingly, one would look for a decrease in the concentration of the product of this reaction; PGA did in fact decrease in concentration. The first steps along the path were thus established. The photosynthesizing plant starts with ribulsose monophosphate and converts it to ribulose diphosphate, using chemical potential energy trapped from the light in the terminal phosphosphate bond of ATP.

Carbon dioxide is joined to this compound, and the resulting six-carbon intermediate splits to two molecules of PGA. With energy and electrons supplied by ATP and TPNH, PGA is reduced to triose phosphate. In the next step, it was apparent, two triose phosphates must be joined end to end in the reverse of a familiar respiratory pathway to form a hexose phosphate.

The pathway from hexoseto pentose phosphate remained to be uncovered. We continued the carbon-by-corbon dissection and analysis. of these chains by the methods that had earlier shown the carbon 14 in PGA to be located first in the carboxyl carbon.

In the hexose molecules we had found the labeled carbon concentrated in the two middle carbons, just where it should be if two triose molecules mode from PGA were linked together by their labeled ends. We also took apart the seven carbon and five-carbon sugar phosphates to establish the position of the carbon 14 atoms in their chains.

As the result of these degradations we were able to show that the over-all economy of the photosynthetic process starts with five threecarbon PGA's, variously transforms them through three-, sixfour-and seven-carbon phosphates intermediates and returns three five-carbon ribulose diphosphates to the starting point [see illustrations on pages 192 and 1931.

From carboxylation of these three chains and their immediate bisection, the cycle at last yields six PGA molecules. The net result, therefore, is th: conversion of three carbon dioxide molecules to one PGA molecule.

The Calvin Cycle

With these steps filled in, the carbon reduction cycle in photosynthesis, called the Calvin cycle, was complete. The intermediates formed in the cycle depart from it on various pathways to be converted to the end products of photosynthesis.

From triose phosphate, for example, one sequence of reactions leads to the six-caabon sugar glucose and the large family of carbohydrates. Because the cycle had been established primarily by experiments with algae and the leaves of a few higher plants, it was important to see whether or not the cyele prevailed throughout the plant kingdom. Calvin and Louisa and Richard Norris carried out experiments with a wide variety of photosynthetic organisms. In every case, although they found variation in the amounts of particular intermediates formed, the pattern was qualitatively the same.

It also had to be shown that the path-way we had traced out is quantitatively the most important route of carbon reduction in photosynthesis. To this end Martha Kirk and I undertook an intensive study of the kinetics of the flow of carbon in photosynthesis. Our study has helped to solve other general problems, particularly the question of how carbon enters into the pathways leading to the synthesis of proteins and fats.

The biological materials for this work are supplied by an algae culture system under automatic feedback control. In this apparatus we are able to maintain the photosynthetic process in a steady state, with nutrients supplied at a constant rate and with temperature, density, salinity and acidity held within narrow limits.

At the start of a run we inject radio-active bicarbonate ion .into the culture medium along with radioactive carbon dioxide gas and so bring the ratio of carbon 14 to carbon 12 immeditely to its final level in both the gas and the liquid phase. An .automatic recorder measures the rate at which carbon is .absorbed by the photosynthesizing cells.

We take samples every few seconds and kill the cells immediately by immersing them in alcohol. After we have chromatographed the photosynthetic intermediates and measured their radioactivity we then plot the appearance of labeled carbon in each of these compounds as a function of time.

By the end of three to five minutes, our records show, all the stable inter-mediates of the cycles are saturated with carbon 14. Taking the total amount of carbon thus fixed in compounds and comparing it with the rate of uptake of carbon in the culture, we found that the cycle accounts for more than 70 per cent of the total carbon fixed by the algae.

A small but significant amount is also taken up by the addition of carbon dioxide to a three-carbon compound, phosphoenolpyruvic acid, to give four-carbon compounds From the earliest work with carbon 14 in our laboratory, it had been apparent that carbon dioxide finds its way rather quickly into products other than carbohydrates in the photosynthesizing plant.

This was at variance with traditional ideas about photosoynthesis that regarded carbohydrates as the sole organic products of the process. It was important to ask, therefore, whether fats and amino acids could be formed directly from the cycle as products of its intermediates or whether these noncarbohydrates were synthesized only from the carbohydrate end products of photosyntesis.

Our kinetic studies show that certain amino acids must indeed be formed from the intermediates and must therefore be regarded as true products of photosynthesis. The amino acid alanine, for example, shows up labeled by carbon 14 at least as rapidly as any carbohydrate; it would be labeled with carbon 14 much more slowly if it were made from carbohydrate, since the carbohydrate would have to be labeled first.

We have been able to show that more than 30 per cent of the carbon taken up by the algae in our steady-state system is incorporated directly into amino acids. There is some evidence that fats may also be formed as products of the cycle. The discovery that plants make these other compounds as direct products of photosynthesis lends new interest and importance to the chloroplast, the subcellular compartment of green cell that contains pigments and the rest of the photosynthetic apparatus.

It has been known for some time that this highly structured organelle is responsible for the absorption of light, the splitting of water and the formation of the cofactors for carbon reduction. More recent studies have shown that it is the site of the entire carbon-reduction cycle. Now the chloroplast emerges—as a complete photosynthetic factory for the production of just about everything necessary to plant's ,growth and function.

6

Aquatic Ecosystems

About three quarters of the earth is covered by oceans, lakes, ponds, rivers, or streams. Not only is water all around us, but it is underground, too. When it rains, part of the water runs off into streams, but much of it seeps into the soil. As it does, particles absorb and hold some water near the surface.

Usually it is this soil water that plants use. Some of the water trickles down through subsoil until it is eventually stopped by an *impenetrable* barrier of rocks. Unable to drain further, *groundwater* accumulates on top of the *impervious rock*.

The upper surface of groundwater is the water table, which; more or less parallels the surface of the land. *Water fills* every pore and crevice between the water table and the underlying rock. *Swamps*, springs, and other bodies of water develop wherever the water table is high enough to *intersect* the *surface*.

Groundwater, rainwater and runoff water all participate in the water cycle driven by the sun. Solar energy evaporates tremendous amounts of water every day. This evaporation draws water from the soil, from plant leaves through *transpiration*, ande from each body of water, large or small.

Once in the atmosphere the water falls again to earth as rain or snow. Thus there is *continuous recycling* of *moisture* between earth and atmosphere and back again. *Falling* rain and snow are *powerful* erosive forces. Most landscapes, even those of arid *countries*, are carved by water action. Water freezing in tiny crevices splits mighly boulders, and glaciers grind wide, smooth valleys between knife-sharp ridges, violent steams dig *narrow canyons* that in time become *flat plains* through which a much-tamed waterway bmeanders to the sea.

Without doubt the sun that powers the water cycle and the precipitation that condenses from water *vapour* are amont the mighties forces on earth. *Oceans*, *lakes* and *rivers* are only a *part* of this great system.

THE OCEANS: THE BIGGEST PART OF THE WORLD

Water returning to the oceans from the land carries huge amounts of sediment. The buildup of these sediments, together with erosion of shores by pounding waves, has created the conainental shelves that border the coasts. In general, a *sharp drop*, the *continental slope*, marks the edge of the continental shelf and the *boundary* of the deep *oceanic basins*.

The shelf, slope,and in many places the ocean bottom are covered with a fine mud or ooze consisting of silt, minerals precipitated from sea water, and the *microscopic shells* of dead *marine animals*. Much of the ocean;floor is a broad abyssal plain.

Here and there the floor is studded with underwater mountains, often of volcanic origin. Where these seamounts just above, the water they form-small, isolated islands, such as those of Hawaii. Also interrupting the flatness of the abyssal plain are deep trenches and mountainous submarine ridges. The Japanese islands are the exposed. tops of gone such ridge.

Drifting Continents and Changing Oceans

Recently it has been widely agreed that the continents were puce jointed, together, and that the present oceans were formed after the continents drifted apart. This is the theory of plate tectonics, or as it is more popularly known, continental drift. There is a significant body of evidence in support of this theory. Equally important, it explains many previously puzzling features of the earth's surface.

Close inspection of a world map reveals that some continental coastlines have *complementary shapes*." Like pieces of a *jigsaw puzzle*, they seem to fit together. Furthermore, the present occean floors appear to be relatively young. *Examination* of cores *drilled* from bottom sediments suggests that the *Atlantic Ocean* formed only about 200 million years ago.

Figure 6.1: Continental Fit. Although the physical fit of South. America and Africa is quite remarkable if one considers only the surface features as shown, the result is even more striking if the undersea continental margins at the edge' of the continental slopes are taken into consideration. Using this same technique, one finds that the eastern coast. of the United States fits very nicely along the western shore of Africa.

That was probably when the Americas began to separate from africa and Europe. The separation was a slow process, which still continues.

Drifting of continents from one climatic zone to another may be part of the explanation for why dinosaurs and lush tropical vegetation once existed in what are now temperate areas of the United States and Europe. It certainly explains distribution of closely related species on distant continents-for example, thesouthern *beeches* found only in Chile, *New Zealand*, *Tasmania*, and *Australia*.

Are you asking yourself how *continents* move?

Crustal Plates

It is clear that the earth has an unstable crust. Catastrophic earthquakes and volcanic eruptions all too often reveal the tremendous forces at work inside the earth.. Luckily for us, most internal stresses, such as those that fold' the earth's crust into mountain ranges, act so slowly that they do not affect us during our lifetime. Yet these forces move: continents.

Present information indicates that the earth's crust is not air unbroken skin. Instead it consists of at least six-and probably more-fairly rigid blocks or plates. These plates do not correspond exactly to any of our customary geographic boundaries but often include both continental masses and ocean bottom.

Being composed of rather light rock, these crustal plates float on top of the heavier, more plastic material beneath. And like ice cubes floating in water, adjacent plates rub together and slide past or over each other as they are pushed apart by upheavals of molten rock from below.

Tectonics Means Building

The Atlantic Ocean floor is spreading as the result of activity at mid-oceanic ridges. Here new crustal material seems to be seeping out from fissures and forming additional sea floor. This, in turn, pushes the continents, apart. In other oceans similar crustal plates are also growing. But since the earth is not expanding in circumference, old parts of the crust must be undergoing destruction.

This seems to be happening at Pacific Ocean trenches. among other places. Such oceanic trenches, some more than six miles deep, develop when one plate is focused under another. In places, molten crust comes to the surface, forming volcanoes. *Volcanoes* are particularly common along ocean ridges at places where the plates are growing.

Volcanoes also appear near trenches where one crustal plate is slipping over another. In such locations, strings of volcanoes create island arcs. Not surprisingly, earthquake zones are associated with these island arcs as well as being common along other plate margins. Collisions between plates are also responsible for folded mountains.

The union of India (which once was an island) with Asia is believed responsible for the crumpled crust we know as the Himalayas. Crustal movements are an ongoing characteristic of the earth, extending far back in time. Before the Old and New Worlds were united in one supercontinent, there was a time when they were separated by a body of water called the Protoatlantic Ocean.

Considering the behaviour of the *crustal plates*, no marine environment is changeless, although some are exceptionally -stable compared with most habitats.

Ocean Habitats

Salts are constantly added to the ocean in river water and rainwater runoff. Depending on drainage, currents, and temperature, the saltiness of the oceans varies at different locations. The *average salinity* is about 3.5 per cent, or about 35 parts by *weight* of salt to each 1000 parts of water. Most of the salt in seawater is *ordinary* table salt (sodium chloride), but sulphate, magnesium, calcium, and potassium salts are also abundant. In .fact, seawater contains traces of just about every element.

These accumulated salts make seawater much denser than fresh water. This is the reason it is easier to swim or float in the ocean than in a river or a lake. It also means that salt water has a much lower freezing point than fresh water.

In addition to salt, seawater also contains dissolved atmospheric gases. But seawater has less oxygen than fresh water, since salt decreases the solubility of oxygen in water.

Ocean Layers and Life

The sun heats and illuminates the ocean, although few of the sun's rays penetrate very deep into the water. As a result, water temperature, illumination, and salinity (which is temperature dependent) are related to depth. Of course, all these characteristics influence the kind of organisms to be found at a given location, but light is of special importance.

Because photosynthetic plants need light in order to live, they are found only in shallow water and in the surface layer of the open ocean. Almost all photosynthesis occurs in the upper 80 meters (260 feet) designated as the euphotic (good light) zone. Underneath the euphotic zone is a region of ever-deepening twilight.

No sunlight penetrates below. 600 meters (1967 feet). As a result, most of the ocean is in perpetual darkness and can be inhabited only by animals and decomposer bacteria and fungi.

Life at the Top

Microscopic floating algae, known collectively as phytoplankton, are the main producers in the oceans. Diatoms and dinoflagellates are the most prominent phytoplankton.

Their collective biomass far outweighs that of the more obvious algae known as "seaweeds." Most seaweeds are attached to rocks near the coast.

Phytoplankton are never evenly distributed. Not only are they limited to the top layers where there is light, but within that layer their density follows distribution of minerals. Organisms that die in deep water usually drift to the bottom.

Similarly, faces settle out, and the valuable nutrients they contain are lost from surface waters. Currents and diffusion only slowly return precious nitrogen and phosphorus from the bottom to the euphotic zone.

Shallow water over the continental shelves is usually fairly well mixed and contains more nutrients than surface water over the open ocean. Here the deep water is quite undisturbed, and minerals are concentrated far below the euphotic zone.

During the winter, because sunlight striking temperate waters is less intense than at other seasons, photosynthesis is limited to the top few meters of water. With the coming of spring the phytoplankton multiply rapidly in response to increasing illumination.

Exploding plankton populations are termed plankton blooms, because the masses of algae often colour the water bright red, brown, or green. Although clearly visible, marine plankton blooms are never as dramatic as .those of freshwater lakes. This difference in productivity may result from mineral. deficiencies in illuminated marine waters.

'Microscopic animals, often referred to as zooplankton, feed on phytoplankton. Copepods and krill, tiny relatives of crabs and shrimp, are among the most abundant zooplankton. Others are numbered among the unicellular protozoa and include foraminifera and radiolarians. Typically, zooplankton bear numerous projections that increase their surface area and help suspend them in the water, Most zooplankton both swim and float.

For the most part, relatively small fish, such as anchovies, herrings, and sardines, prey on zooplankton. There are exceptions, however. In the cold but fertile water around Antarctica the penguins, fish, squid, and even baleen whales feed directly on krill.

The amount of zooplankton consumed by a large animal can be astounding. A single blue whale can eat three tons, of krill' a day.

The Briny Deep

Beneath the productive upper layer of the ocean lies as much as six miles of water. Throughout most of this space, life is sparse. Food from the top decomposes quite slowly. Fish in deep, dark waters are mostly mouth. Good meals are rare here and few items are rejected as being too big.

This is the province of the famous angler fish, which is equipped with luminescent lures that attract prey into its gaping mouth. The low population levels in deep water makes finding a mate at the right time a chancy proposition.

In some species the males attach to the females during adolescence and maintain this parasitic relationship throughout life. As you might expect, the males of such species are tiny compared with their mates.

Rocks and Sand: Marsh and Muck

In contrast to the relatively uniform conditions of the open sea, a variety of habitats occur where water meets land. Each of these environments is unique; each is intriguing in its own way. Perhaps rocky shores are the most interesting. Here we find a diverse community attuned to the rhythmically changing environment.

Living between the Tides.

In the band that spans high and low tide, the first priorities are to stay put, to keep wet, and to avoid being crushed. Waves pound the shores so vigorously that delicate organisms can be destroyed or carried away. Alternately submerged and exposed, intertidal species (those that live between lowest low tide and highest high tide) must also withstand cold, heat, and a wide range of salinity.

Summer sun can cook tissues, and evaporation of seawater deposits a crust of salt on every surface. Only a few months later, winter tides pull the protective layer of water away and leave organisms exposed to freezing cold or to torrents of fresh water.

As adaptations to this extreme environment, intertidal organisms either cling tenaciously or dart about to find shelter. Their bodies are protected by shells, tough body walls, leathery surfaces; or muscus.

Since tidal exposure varies every day, there are distinct life zones along the shore. The following applies to the central California coast, but similar areas occur on rocky shores from Mexico to Alaska and along the coast of Maine and the Maritime Provinces, as well as on other continents.

A dark band of cyanobacteria (blue-green algae) marks the highest zone where there is much marine life. Here numerous periwinkles scavenge. A distinict band of white barnacles grows below the black zone. Barnacles lie on their backs, stuck to the rocks.

When the tide goes out, barnacles close their limy shells to conserve water. When they are submerged, they open their shell plates and feed, using delicate, jointed appendages to kick food into their mouths.

Limpets are abundantly distributed among the barnacles. These marine snails use a tremendous suction foot to pull their shells tightly against the rock. This traps water under the shells and prevents dehydration during low tide.

A crowded strip of 'mussels stands just below the mean-sealevel mark that coincides with the bottom of the barnacle region. The clamlike mussels spin proteinaceous fibers that attach their blue-black shells to the rocks. Tidal pools harbour rock crabs, hermit crabs, and large green sea anemones. Farther out, on the underside of large rocks and steep ledges hide sponges, sea cucumbers, sea squirts, chitons. and abalone. Shrimp and spiny lobsters lurk in the lowest tide pools.

No one has made a complete census of animals in the intertidal zone, but bioiogists familiar with the California coast estimate that there may be 3000 species there. The showy life of rocky shores appears missing from sandy beaches, but even though beaches appear barren, animals are present. It's just that most of them are hidden from view.

Burrowing, digging, and tunnelling creatures, among them clams, mole crabs, tube worms, and olive shells, bury themselves in the sand. Low tides expose some species periodically; others are permanently protected within their burrows. Typical residents below the low-tide line include whelks, swimming crabs, sand dollars, and hermit crabs.

Wetlands and Estuaries

Bays and river mouths, where fresh and salt water meet, are unusually fertile environments. The most valuable of such estuaries are broad, shallow basins created by silt deposits. Here mud flats and tidal marshes line channels of open water.

Most of the silt and organic matter dumped from the river becomes trapped in its estuary. Slow currents, a large surface for evaporation, and presence of rooted vegetation all help make estuaries places where nutrients tarry.

Salt marsh grasses, eel grasses, and other rooted pl ints take advantage of rich water and soft bottoms. Algal scums cover mud flats, larger plants, and every solid surface, and dense phytoplankton blooms colour the water.

There is so much food that only a tiny part of the photosynthetic product finds its way directly into the mouths of herbivoures. Instead, most plants die and, in the absence of swift currents, simply sink to the bottom and rot.

The abundant organic matter supports a teaming broth of bacteria and fungi that use all available oxygen from the muddy bottom. As a result, other anaerobic microorganisms thrive there and release hydrogen sulphide. This noxious gas blackens marshland mucks and imparts a characteristic stench.

Their tremendous photosynthetic productivity and extensive decomposer food chain permit estuaries to literally teem with life. Microscopic decomposers are eaten by filter-feeding zooplankton, as well as by larger filter feeders, such as worms, clams, and oysters. Estuaries serve as nurseries for numerous coastal fish. Menhaden, striped mullet, summer flounder, king whiting, croakers, striped, bass, smelt, and sturgeon are all commercially important species that rely on estuaries sometime during their lives.

The shrimp fisheries also depend on this resource, because young shrimp require the estuary habitat. Oysters, blue crabs, and several commercially valucable elam species are permanent estuarian residents. Furthermore, saltwater marshes are the natural home of most waterfowl.

As valuable as they are in their native state, estuaries are often prized more for their land. To take advantage of a protected harbor, most seaports are built on estuaries.

As early ports grew, the surrounding marshes and mud flats were usually drained, and regions of shallow water were dredged or filled to provide areas for docks, industries, airports, and even residences.

In Washington, D.C., only the Tidal Basin remains to remind us that the Jefferson Memorial, Lincoln Memorial, and Washington Monument were built on land "reclaimed" from a marsh.

Once leached free of their load of salt, drained tidal marshes become fertile farmland. Over the centuries, carefully engineered diking and pumping schemes created much of the Netherlands.

But present generations seem little aware of how much humans are responsible for familiar shorelines and of how important estuaries are in the schemes of aquatic life. Even now, many of our least-modified estuaries are threatened with "development" into resorts.

LAKES: QUIET CHANGES

In many ways lakes resemble oceans. Of course, lakes are much smaller, and they usually contain fresh water. Diatoms and desmids are the most abundant phytoplankton of lakes.

And though the shoreline and broad-leaved floating plants contribute much more to the productivity of fresh waters than marine seaweeds do to the oceans, zooplankton and fish are abundant in both habitats.

Probably the most distinctive animal components of the freshwater food chain are the many insects, especially in their juvenile stages. Variations in climate, fertility, shape, and bottom characteristics cause lakes to be quite different from one another. But ultimately all these factors translate into nutrient availability.

Unlike the oceans, temperature zone lakes are stirred regularly. As a result. there is efficient nutrient cycling. This is what accounts for the much greater productivity of many lakess compared with any ocean.

Seasonal Turnover

Swimmers know that lake water is warmer at the surface and colder at depths. Thus in the summer, lakes are stratified with lighter, warmer water at the top and colder, denser water toward the bottom.

As winter approaches, falling air temperatures and brisk winds slowly cool temperature zone lakes. The fact that fresh water is most dense at 4°C (39°F) permits cooling lakes to be thoroughly stirred. When surface waters cool to 4°C, they sink to the bottom and displace the warmer, less dense water there.

This turnover brings nutrients from the bottom and spreads ahem throughout the lake. At some point the entire lake is at 4°C and lacks any density stratification. Absence of stratification .allows the lake to be further stirred by the wind.

Only after the whole lake reaches 4°C may the temperature of the surface dip lower. When this occurs, the colder, less dense water floats and a layer of ice may eventually form. In the spring, the surface water gradually warms to 4°C.

Then, as during the fall-cooling, there is a period when all the water is 4°C and all of the same density. At this time winds 'blowing across the surface may set up currents that travel toward the shore and turn downward and move across the bottom.

As you can see, there are two turnovers a year, one in the spring and the other in the fall. Both stir bottom sediments, and both also replenish the oxygen supply at the bottom. With available nutrients and increasing sunlight and warmth, plankton blooms colour lake water beginning in the spring.

Changes in temperature and nutrient levels cause one phytoplankton species to bloom and die, only to be followed by a population burst of another. The exact succession of blooms is determined by the requirements of the various species.

Nutrients, Pollution, and Aging

Lakes have a relatively short life span. It may take thousands or millions of years, but most lakes that we know are in the process of disappearing. At the time of formation, a young lake is usually low in nutrients and sparsely inhabited.

As time goes by the lake is enriched by accumulation of river sediments and nutrients leached by rainwater from the surrounding land.

Further fertilization occurs as dead plants fall into the water and decay. This normal enrichment of a lake is known as eutrophication (addition of good food).

Eutrophication permits more and more organisms of increasingly different kinds to livein the lake. Clearly, the biological nature of a lake gradually changes as the lake ages. With time, lakes undergo a process analogous to succession on land. Eventually eutrophication may end with disappearance of the lake altogether.

The Fate of Lakes

As sediments build up, lakes become more shallow and vegetation encroaches. Filled-in lake margins develop into marshes or swamps. By definition a marsh is a wet grassland and swamps are wet forests.

Like their saltwater counterparts, freshwater marshes support diverse communities adapted to slight variations in water levels. So do swamps. And like marine wetlands, those of fresh water are gradually disappearing. Conversion of the rich muck into farmland is the goal of many government-funded drainage and stream channelization projects.

In cold climates lakes may eventually turn into spongy, wet bogs. Because of the cold, accumulated plant material decomposes poorly, and it is gradually transformed into peat. Humic acids derived from the peat further inhibit decomposition and' give the water a characteristic brown tinge. Peat is often dug up, dried, and burned as fuel.

Excess Eutrophication.

Although natural eutrophication is part of the aging process of every lake and tends to favour mineral accumulation, human. activities that accelerate the process can lead to early death of a lake. Fertilizer washed' into lakes from nearby farms and the addition of minerals in household or industrial sewage can create an overabundance of' nutrients in the water.

Under these conditions algal blooms deplete oxygen in the water. Fish and other animals may simply choke to death. Studies of the Great Lakes trace their "*cutrophication*" toexcess phosphorus. Experimental addition of phosphate to small lakes in the same region has produced responses similar to pollution in the Great Lakes.

Neither nitrogen nor carbon alone has a similar effect. Apparently simply removing phosphate from waste water, principally by banning phosphates in house hold detergents: would markedly improve conditions in many bodies of water.

RIVERS AND STREAMS: RUNNING WATERS

The continuous one-way flow of running waters distinguishes them from lakes. Indeed, many of the special characteristics of these waters are related to their turbulence. Because currents constantly bring new water into contact with a given organism, running water is effectively richer than still water in which a static, "*tired*" layer surrounds each individual. And to be sure, turbulence mixes air into running water and thus usually ensures a plentiful supply of oxygen.

The Food Web of an Open System

Rivers and streams inevitably reflect the land they drain. Stream water arises mainly from groundwater, and surface runoff provides most of the remainder. Water from both sources carries mineral nutrients and human additives, such as pesticides. But most of the organic matter that supports the food chains of running waters also washes in from the surrounding land. Or simply falls in.

Probably tree leaves supply more energy and more. carbon than any other single source. Additional sources -of carbon and energy ase adult insects that flounder into the water, earthworms, and other small soil animals. Except in quiet streams that closely resemble lakes or ponds, there are few phytoplankton in rivers.

Thus running waters are unusual ecosystems in that primary production accounts for but a small portion . of the energy needed. Most nutrients enter rivers and streams from the outside.

Adaptations of Currents: Dont's Get'Carried Away!

Only careful strategies prevent the current from carrying stream organisms to different and less suitable habitats. For example, diatoms of such habitats have stalks. Larvae of Blackflies and many other insects anchor themselves with holdfasts.

Yet other every insects spin sticky threads about themselves or burrow into the mud. Many stream animals are streamlined. They have compact and flattened bodies and usually live under stones, where the current is reduced and where they are less visible to predators.

Fish can expend a great deal of energy swimming against the current-so they don't. Fish survive by finding shelter. As anyone who fishes knows, the best place to catch trout is in a deep bottom hole or along the downstream side of large rocks or other obstacles. Generally, the larger the shelter, the larger the fish.

The adaptations of stream organisms truly illustrate the selective forces of this environment. But of course, environment is selective.

A SPECIAL WAY OF LIFE IN WATER

To an animal, the most fundamental difference between living on land and living in water is the scarcity of oxygen. Oxygen is so poorly soluble in water that it is hardly surprising that no warm-blooded animals can live submerged for more than short periods.

Aquatic mammals, such as whales, and aquatic birds, such as penguins, all breathe air and thus obtain enough oxygen to sustain the high metabolic rate associated with a constantly warm body. And surely the complexity of gills is related to the need for extensive surfaces for gas exchange with water.

Most often gills are located where water can be readily pumped past them to maintain a constant supply of oxygen. As we will see in the next chapter, the deadly effects of aquatic pollution can be traced to exhaustion of the oxygen supply.

Aquatic ecosystems are also unusual in that most producers are microscopic. Since so many people disregard anything they can't see, this may be why the structure of underwater communities escapes the understanding of many citizens.

Microscopic producers dominate in water, because they have a large surface area compared with their volume. This ensures efficient absorption of nutrients. Furthermore, vascular tissue is unnecessary in this habitat, and large plants are subject to damage by waves or current.

Finally, the high specific heat of water gives aquatic environments a temperature stability unknown on land. Water is slow to warm and slow to cool. Large bodies of water, especially, fluctuate little in temperature.

Not only are aquatic organisms freed from the usual problems of temperature regulation, but density changes associated with minor temperature shift account for lake turnover and also affect ocean currents. Remembering these facts can help us maintain the integrity of aquatic ecosystems. This is an important step toward ensuring stability of the biosphere.

7

THE ECOSPHERE

The great 19th-century French naturalist Jean Lamarck first conceived the idea of the biosphere as the collective totality of living creatures on the earth, and the concept has been taken up and developed in recent years by the Russian geochemist V.I. Vernadsky.

The word "ecosystem means a self-sustaining community of organisms—plants as well as animals—taken together with its inorganic environment. Now all these are interdependent. Animal life could not exist without plants nor plants without animals, which supply them with carbon dioxide.

Even the composition of the inorganic environment depends upon the cyclic activity of life. Photo synthesis by the earth's plants would remove all of the carbon dioxide from the atmosphere within a year or so if it were not. returned by fires and by the respiration of animals and other consumers of plants.

Similarly nitrogen-fixing organisms would exhaust all of the nitrogen in the air in less than a million years. And so on. The conclusion is that a self-sustaining community must contain not just plants, animals and nitrogen-fixers but also decomposers which can free the chemicals bound in protoplasm.

It is very fortunate from our standpoint that some microorganisms have solved the biochemical trick of decomposing chitin, lignins and other inert organic compounds that tie up carbon.

A community must consist of producers or accumulators of energy (green plants), primary consumers (fungi 'microorganisms, and herbivores), higher-order consumers (carnivorous predators, parasites and scavengers), and decomposers that regenerate the raw materials.

Organisms living on the face of the earth as it floats around in space can receive energy from several sources. Energy from outside comes to us as sunlight and starlight, is reflected to us as moonlight, and is brought to earth by cosmic radiation and meteors.

Internally the earth is heated by radioactivity and it is also gaining heat energy from the tidal friction that is gradually slowing our rotation. On top of this man is tapping enormous amounts of stored energy by burning fossil fuels.

But all these secondary sources of energy are infinitesimal compared to our daily sunshine, which accounts for 99.9998 per cent of our total energy income. This supply of solar energy amounts to 13×10^{23} gramcalories per year, or, if you prefer, it represents a continuous power supply at the rate of 2.5 billion billiom horsepower.

About onethird of the incoming energy is lost at once by being reflected' back to space, chiefly by clouds. The rest is absorbed by the atmosphere and the earth itself to remain here temporarily until it is re-radiated to snace as heat. During its residence on earth this energy serves to melt lice, to warm the land and oceans to evaporate water, to generate winds and waves and currents.

In addition to these activities. a ridiculously small proportion-about four hundredths of 1 per cent of the solar energy goes to feed the metabolism of the biosphere. Practically all of this energy enters the biosphere by means of photosynthesis.

The plants use one-sixth of the energy they take up from sunlight for their own metabolism, making the other five-sixths available for animals and other consumers. About 5 per cent of this net energy is dissipated by forest and grass fires and by man's burning of plant products as fuel.

When an animal or other consumer eats plant protoplasm, it uses some of the substance for energy to fuel its metabolism and some as raw materials for growth. Some it discharges in brokendown form as metabolic waste products for example, animals excrete urea, and yeast releases ethyl alcohol.

And a large part of the plant material it ingests is simply indigestible and passes through the body unused. Herbivores, whether they are insects, rabbits, geese or cattle, succeed in extracting only about 50 per cent of the calories stored in the plant protoplasm. (The lost calories are, however, extractable by other consumers flies may feed on the excretions or man himself may burn cattle dung for fuel.)

Of the plant calories consumed by an animal that eats the plant, only 20. to 30 per cent is actually built into protoplasm. Thus, since half of its consumption is lost as waste, the net efficiency of a herbivore in converting plant protoplasm into meat is about 10 to 15 per cent.

The secondary consumers–i.e., meat-eaters feeding on the herbivores-do a little better. Because animal, protoplasm has a smaller proportion of indi,gestible matter than plants have, a carnivore can use 70 per cent of the; meat for its internal chemistry. But again only 30 per cent at most goes into building tissue.

So the maximum efficiency of carnivores in converting one kind of meat into another is 20 per cent. Some of the consequences of these relationships are of general interest and are fairly well known. For example, 1,000 calories stored up by the algae in Cayuga Lake can be converted into protoplasm amounting to 150 calories by small aquatic animals.

In turn, smelt eating these animals produce 30 calories of protoplasm from the 150. If a man then eats the smelt he -can synthesize six calories worth of fat or muscle from the 30 if he waits for the smelt to be eaten by a trout and then eats the trout, the yield shrinks to 1.2 calories.

If we were really dependent on the lake for food, we would do well to exterminate the trout and eat the smelt ourselves, or, better yet to exterminate the smelt and live on planktonburgers. The same principles, of course, apply on land. If man is really determined to support the largest possible populations of his kind, he will have to shorten the food chains leading to himself and, so far, as practicable, turn to a vegetarian diet.

The rapid shrinkage of stored energy as it passes from one organism to another serves to make the study of natural' communities a trifle more simple for the ecologist than it would otherwise be. It explains why food chains in nature rarely contain more than four or five links. Thus in our Cayuga Lake chain the trout was the third animal link and man the fourth.

Chains of the same sort occur in the ocean, with, for example, a tuna or cod as the third link and perhaps a shark or a seal replacing man as the fourth link. Now if we look for the fifth link in the chain we find that it takes something like a killer whale or a polar bear to be able to subsist on seals.

As to a, sixth link-it would take quite a predator to make its living by, devouring killer whales or polar bears. We could, of course, trace food chains in other directions. Each species has its. parasites that extort their cut of the stored. energy, and these in turn support other parasites down to the point where there is not enough energy available to support, another organism.

Also, we should not forget the unused energy, contained in the feces and urine of each animal. The organic matter in feces is often the basic resource of a food chain in which the next link may be a dung beetle or the larva of a fly.

It is estimated that the maximum amount of protoplasm' of all types that can be produced on earth each year amounts to 410 billion tons, of which 290 billion represent plant growth and the other 120 billion all of the consumer organisms.

We see, then, that the availability of energy sets a limit to the amount of life on earth-that is, to the size of the biosphere. This energy also keeps the nonliving part of the ecosphere animated, largely through the agency of moving water, which is the single most important chemical substance in the physiology, of the ecosphere.

Each year the oceans evaporate a quantity of water equivalent to an average depth of one meter. The total evaporatian from land and bodies of fresh water is one sixth of the evaporation from the sea, and at least one fifth of this evaporation isfrom the transpiration of plants growing on land.

The grand total of water evaporated annually is roughly 100,000 cubic miles, and this must be roughly the annual precipitation. The precipitation on land exceeds the evaporation by slightly over 9,000 cubic rules, which therefore represents the annual runoff of water from land to sea.

It is astonishing to me to note that more than one tenth of this total runoff is carried to the sea by just two rivers-the Amazon and the Congo. Precipitation supplies'nonmárine organisms with the water which they require in large quantities. Protoplasm averages at least 75 per cent water, and plants require something like 450 grams of water to produce one gram of dry organic matter.

The water moving from land to sea also erodes the land surface and dissolves soluble mineral matter. It brings to the plants the chemical nutrients that they require and it tends to level the land surface and deposit the minerals in the sea.

At present the continents are being worm down at an average world-wide rate of one centimeter per century. The levelling process, however, apparently has never gone on to completion on the earth. Geological uplift of the land always intervenes and brings marine sediments above sea level, where the cycle can begin again. The rivers of the world are now washing into the seas some four billion tons of dissolved inorganic matter a year, about 400 million tons of dissolved organic matter and about five times as much undissolved matter.

The undissolved matter represents destruction of the land where organisms live, but thedissolved materials is of greater interest, because it includes such important chemicals as 3.5 million tons of phosphorus, 100 million tons of potassium and 10 million tons of fixed nitrogen.

Zn order to say what these losses may mean to the biosphere we must review a few facts about the chemical composition of the earth and of organisms. Every organism seem to require at least 20 chemical elements and probably several others in trace amounts.

Some of the organisms requirements are rather surprising. Penicillium is said to need traces of tungsten, and the common duckweed demands manganese and the rare earth gallium. There is a European pansy which needs high concentrations of zinc in the soil, and several plants in different parts of the world are so hungry for copper that they help prospectors to find the mineral.

Many organisms have fantastic abilities to concentrate the necessary elements from dilute media. The sea-squirts have vanadium in their blood, and the liver of the edible scallop contains on a dry-weight basis one tenth of 1 per cent of cadmium, although the amount of this element in sea water is so small that it cannot be detected by chemical tests.

But the exotic chemical tastes of organisms are compratively unimportant. Their main needs can be summed up in just five words-oxygen, carbon, hydrogen, nitrogen and phosphorus, which account for more than 95 per cent of the mass of all protoplasm.

Oxygen is the most abundant chemical element on earth, so we probably do not need to be concerned about any absolute deficiency of oxygen. But nitrogen is a different matter. Whereas protein, the main stuff of life, is 18 per cent nitrogen, the relative abundance of this element on the earth is only one 10,000th of the earth's mass.

It is apparent that our land forms of life could not long tolerate a net annual loss of 10 million tons of fixed nitrogen to the sea. Fortunately this nitrogen loss from land is reversible, so that we can speak of a "nitrogen cycle." Organisms in the sea convert the fixed nitrogen into ammonia, a gas which can return to land via the atmosphere.

Carbon also is not in too abundant supply, for it amounts to less than three parts in 10,000 of the total mass of the earth's matter. But once again the biosphere profits from the fact that carbon can escape

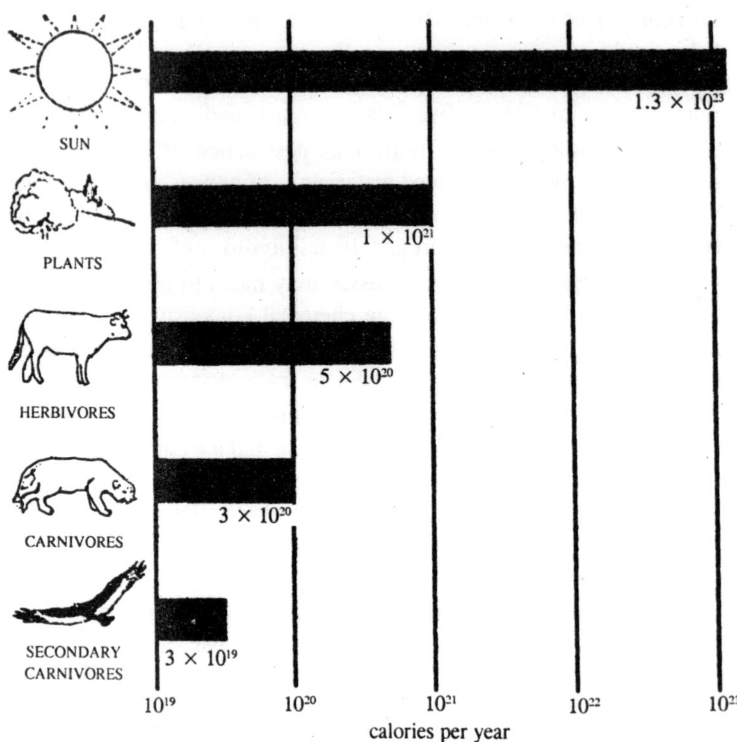

Figure 7.1: Utilization of Solar Energy decreases with each step along the food chain. These bars (on a logarithmic scale) show that plants use only .08 per cent of energy reaching the atmosphere; plant-eaters use only part of this fraction and flesheaters even less.

from the oceans as a carbon dioxide. This gas goes through a complex circulation in the atmosphere, being released from the oceans in tropical regions and absorbed by the ocean waters in polar regions.

Because some carbon is deposited in ocean sediments as carbonates, there is a net loss of carbon from the ecosphere. But there seems to be no danger that a shortage of this element will restrict life. The atmosphere contains 2,400 billion tons of carbon dioxide, and at least 30 times that much is dissolved in the oceans, waiting to be released if the atmosphere should become depleted.

Volcanoes discharge carbon dioxide, and man is burning fossil fuels at such a rate that he has been accused of increasing the average carbon dioxide content of the atmosphere by some 10 per cent in the last 50 years.

In addition, lots of limestone, which is more than 4 per cent carbon

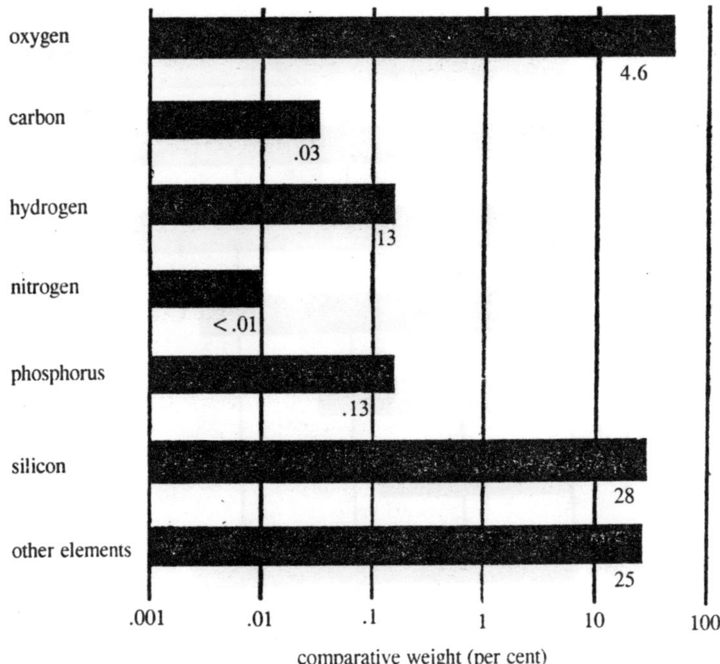

Figure 7.2: Estimated Relative Abundance of elements in the earth and its atmosphere (above) and in living matter (below) is compared in these charts; the scale is logarithmic. Silicon, with many stable compounds, is abundant on earth but rare in living organisms. Nitrogen, rare, on earth is important to life, making up as much as 18 per cent of proteins.

dioxide, has been pushed up from ancient seas by uplifts of the earth. The story of phosphorus appears somewhat more alarming. This element accounts for a bit more than one tenth of 1 per cent of the mass of terrestrial matter, is enriched to about twice this level in plant protoplasm and is greatly enriched in animals, accounting for more than 1 per cent of the weight of the human body.

As a constituent of nucleic acids it is indispensable for all types of life known to us. But many agricultural lands already suffer a deficiency of phosphorus, and a corn crop of 60 bushels per acre removes 10 per cent of the phosphorus in the upper six inches of fertile soil. Each year 3.5 million tons of phosphorus are washed from the land and precipitated in the seas.

And unfortunately phosphorus does not escape from the sea as a gas. Its only important recovery from the sea is in the guano produced by sea birds, but less than 3 per cent of the phosphorus annually lost from the land is returned in this way.

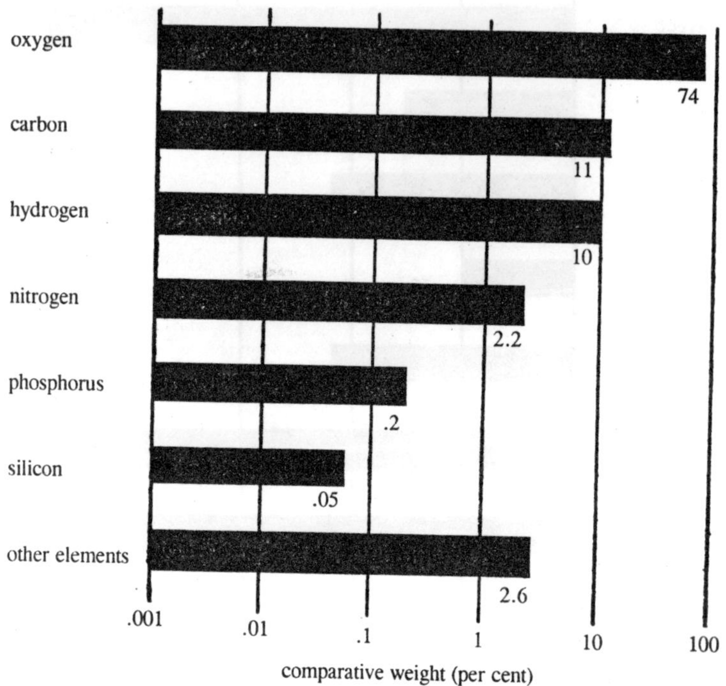

It must agree with agriculturalists who say that phosphorus is the critical limiting resource for the functioning of the ecosphere. The supply is at least shrinking (if dwindling is too strong a word) end there seems to be no practical way of improving the situation short of waiting for the next geological cycle of uplift to bring phosphate rock above sea level.

Perhaps we should also worry about other essential elements, such as calcium, potassium, magnesium and iron, which behave much like phosphorus in the metabolism of the ecosphere, but the evidence clearly indicates that if present trends continue phosphorus will be the first to run out.

This brings me to the close of a very superficial summary of dome of the physiological processes of the ecosphere. There are srastic oversimplifications in this treatment; the importance of

some processes may be overestimated and others (e.g., dumping. sewage in rivers and oceans) may not have received enough attention. The figures for the total quantity of energy received by the earth, for total annual precipitation and for the total supply of some chemical elements may overlook the very irregular distribution of these resources

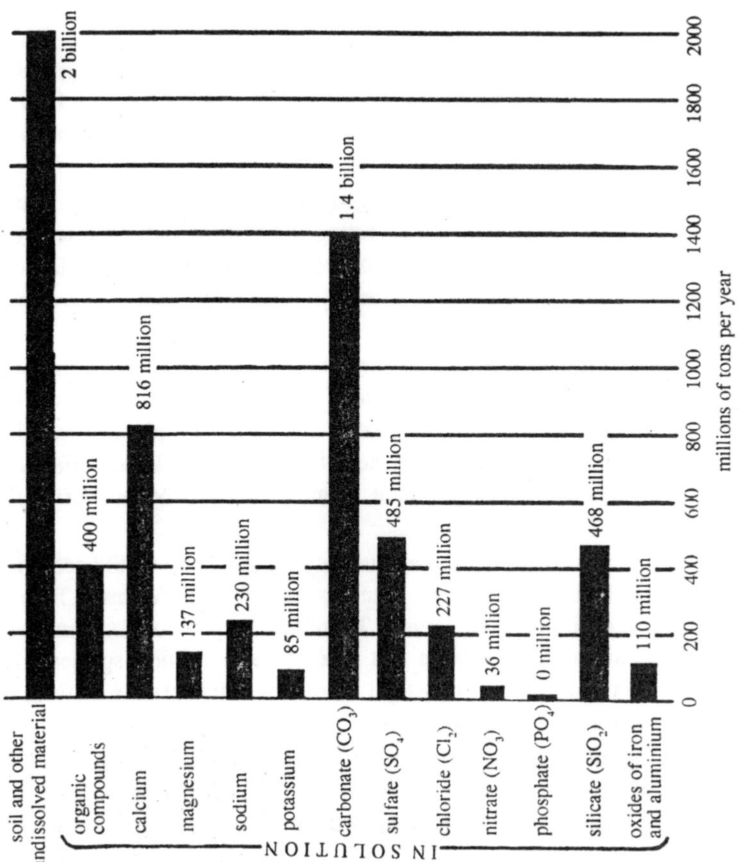

Figure 7.3. Annual Loss of minerals and organic matter washed into the sea amounts to billions of ions. Much nitrogen and carbon eventually return to the land via the atmosphere; the loss of phosphate is more serious since almost all of it remains in the oceans.

in time and space. Much solar energy falls on deserts and fields of snow and ice where it cannot be used by plants, and much precipitation arrives at unfavourable seasons or in such torrents that it does more harm than good to organisms.

Our survey suggests that man may be justified in feeling some real concern about the problem of erosion. It should also make us aware of the important role played by organisms that we might otherwise ignore or even regard as pests.

The dung beetles, the various scavengers and the termites and other decomposers all play important bit parts in this great production. At least six diverse groups of bacteria are absolutely essential for the proper physiological functioning of the nitrogen cycle alone. Man in his carelessness would probably neither notice nor care if by some unlikely chance his radioactive fallout or one of his chemical sprays or fumes should exterminate all of the microorganisms that are capable of decomposing chitin.

Yet, as we have seen, such a tragedy would eventually mean an end to life on earth. Finally, it is interesting to ask how large a role man plays in the physiology of the ecosphere. The Statistical Office of theUnited Nations estimates the present human population of the earth at 2.7 billion persons.

Each of these is supposed to consume at least 2,200 metabolizable kilocalories per day. This, makes a total food requirement of 22×10^{14} kilocalories per year. I have estimated that all of the plant growth in the world. amounts to an annual net of all 5×10^{17} kilocalories, of which not more than 50 per cent is metabolizable by any primary consumer.

Thus if man were to feed exclusively on plants he would require: almost exactly 1 per cent of the total productivity of the earth. To me this is a very impressive figure. There are more than one million species of animals, and when just one of these million species can corner 1 per cent of the total food resources, this form is truly in a position of overwhelming dominance.

The figure becomes even more impressive when we reflect that 70 per cent of the total plant production takes place in the oceans, and that our figure for productivity includes inedible materials such as straw and lumber.

8

Ecological Succession

If left alone, the fresh scar of bare earth left by a landslide will gather a mantle of green as grasses and herbs sprout. As the years pass, a procession of plants will file through the space, until after a few decades, only a practiced eye could discern that the vegetation had been disturbed. After a few centuries, all trace of the disturbance will have disappeared.

This recovery process that leads to the revegetation of an area is an example of ecological succession, but it is much more than the re-establishment of herbs and trees. When an ecosystem is disturbed, whether by fire, wind, oil spill, or chainsaw, the balance between the biotic and abiotic processes is changed.

The visible effect of disturbance may be dead trees, bare soil, or oiled birds, so it is natural to think first of the recovery of living things. However, the healing process has to include the restoration of the abiotic processes.

The re-establishment of ecosystem functions, such as nutrient cycles, carbon storage, microclimate, and the hydrological cycle, may be essential precursors to the reinvasion of the flora and fauna.

CLEMENTS AND THE SUPERORGANISM

In 1916, Frederick Clements proposed the concept of succession leading to a climax vegetation, and proposed that the successional stages and the eventual climax were a superorganism capable of shaping its surroundings. We now know this view to be mistaken, but his ideas have played such an important role in ecology and environmentalism that they are worth investigating.

After more than two decades of researching the regrowth of vegetation following disturbance, Clements proposed that each climate type would have a single *climax community*; an end point to the successional process.

Because the climate determined the climax community, all successions within that climate zone would produce the same climax community. In other words, microclimate, soils, depth of water table, and other habitat variables would, in the end, be shaped by the vegetation to produce the climax system.

For example, on the sand dunes around Lake Michigan, Clements believed (mistakenly) that successional sequences starting from a lake, or a sand dune, or an abandoned field would all lead *inexorably* to a beechmaple climax forest. *Clements* went a step further to liken the various stages of succession to the development of an organism and suggested that the climax community was an "*organic entity.*"

When Clements first proposed his view of succession it was widely accepted, but a vocal critic of the notion of communities as superorganisms was H. Gleason of the New York Botanical Garden. In 1926, he prophetically stated that ". . . every species of plant is a law unto itself."

Gleason argued that succession was not a predetermined process of development, but something much more haphazard; it was dependent upon local growing conditions, the chance scatter of seed, and the vagaries of migration. The truth of this statement has been born out by later paleoecological studies.

Modern ecologists dislike the term *climax* because it carries an underlying notion of stasis: What is going to happen to a climax community? Nothing, because it has reached its climax. Climax is a convenient, but wholly "now-centric" view of the world (our self-centered belief that now is normal).

But our present is just another stage in the great procession of species; it just happens to be the stage that we have documented most fully. Future changes in climate, predation, or pathogen pressures will cause the composition of our plant and animal communities to alter again and again.

Each time we undergo change, the changes in species composition will be roughly proportional to the degree of stress applied, as small climatic or pathogen pressures will be met by small responses in community composition and large stresses will cause entire re-arrangements of community structure. Because change in community composition is normal and stasis is not, the more accurate term of *mature community* is preferred.

Despite the scientific rejection of the idea of ecosystems as a super-organism, this idea has proved attractive to some environmentalists; they refer to ecocide, or killing the environment. The environment is not a living entity, it cannot be killed.

An extreme form of this pseudoscience is presented in the Gaia hypothesis, which states that the whole Earth is a superorganism and that all living things interact to regulate and maintain an equilibrial environment.

According to the Gaia hypothesis, plants emit oxygen and draw in CO_2 to maintain optimal growth conditions for themselves, and they regulate climate locally and globally. Plainly, this is nonsense. Cycles of climate change are sudden, severe, and erratic, and the atmospheric concentrations of gases vary greatly on both millennial and longer time scales.

Earth is not a superorganism, climate and atmosphere are not constant, natural cycles are not regulated by organisms, and all organisms survive or perish in the conditions that surround them; they do not *try* to alter them. The modern view of succession recognizes two discrete processes, primary and secondary succession.

Primary succession describes the colonization and ecological succession taking place on a new surface, such as a lava flow, an explosion crater, a sandbar in a river, the clay left by a retreating glacier, or a sunken ship. *Secondary succession* describes *colonization* and ecological succession following a disturbance.

Secondary succession could take the form of the recovery of vegetation on a land surface where previously existing plants were disturbed, such as an old field, a landslide scar, or a burned forest. Or it could be the rebuilding of a coral reef after it has been hit by a ship.

The essential difference is that primary succession occurs on an area that has never before supported life, whereas secondary succession is the reclamation of an area by organisms after a disturbance. The islands of Krakatau (formerly Krakatoa), Indonesia, provide the best example of primary succession resulting in a complex ecosystem.

ASHES TO FOREST

On August 27, 1883, the largest natural explosion ever recorded was heard from Australia to islands off the coast of South Africa. The island volcano of Krakatau, Indonesia had erupted. A tsunami (tidal wave) generated by the explosion damaged rain forests along the adjacent coasts of Sumatra and Java, claiming the lives of 36,000 villagers.

Scientists visiting the Krakatau island group within a year of the eruption found that more than 20 km^3 kilometers of rock had been blown away and that the old land surface had been buried by hot ash as much as 100 m deep.

A new volcanic landscape had been created. No plant or animal, seed or root, had survived the eruption; the islands had been sterilized. Scientifically, this is very important because the islands offer a definitive time for the start of the succession.

Also, that the islands were virtually free from human disturbance before and after the explosion allowed the regeneration process to proceed naturally. Scientists visited Krakatau regularly between 1883 and 1934, observing the gradual return of a tropical flora and fauna. Within 13 months of the eruption, grasses and blue-green algae were present, and, by the early 1900s, a grassland with scattered trees and shrubs was gradually invaded by a light woodland.

Late in the 1920s, the woodland became dense enough to form a closed canopy and exclude the grasslands on Sertung, Panjang, and Rakata. A new factor then entered the successional history of Krakatau as the islands experienced the first volcanic activity in more than 50 years. Between 1928 and 1932, Anak Krakatau (literally translated, this means "child of Krakatau"), a new active volcano, emerged from the sea in the middle of the volcanic caldera.

Since the 1930s, Anak's frequent volcanic activity has sent dust and poisonous gases onto the islands of Sertung and Panjang. The soil profiles of these islands are sometimes over 2 m deep, most of which is volcanic ash that has fallen onto the islands since 1930.

The forest of Sertung and Panjang has been repeatedly damaged, and what started as a primary succession is now so disturbed as to be a secondary succession on these islands. Only the island of Rakata, where no ash from Anak is found in the soil profiles, has been unaffected by the volcanic activity, and a thin soil just 12 cm deep has formed.

The soil is black with organic carbon, though still gritty from the parent ash material. The centenary of the 1883 eruption kindled researchers' interest in the island group. Since 1979, numerous research expeditions have visited the islands to document the returning plants and animals.

The tallest trees on Krakatau are now more than 40 m tall, and some of them have a trunk diameter of more than 1 m. The forest looks dense and lush, but the succession on Krakatau is far from finished. After more than 100 years, fewer than 300 species of plants have returned to the islands, whereas a similar area of the mainland might support between 1200 and 1400 species of plant.

Because the forest canopy is now closed, it is harder for a new species to compete for resources and grow. Consequently, the rate of forest change will slow down. From the work on these islands, it is estimated that it may take more than 1000 years for Krakatau to become a truly mature forest.

An important aspect of succession is that small differences in habitat type will lead to variations in the species composition of all stages of the succession. A coastal succession will have a progression of salttolerant plants, because salts are carried in the fine sea spray and may affect vegetation some hundreds of meters inland.

A montane succession will have plants more tolerant of steep slopes, cooler temperatures, and increased ultraviolet radiation. A slight variation in soil moisture from one location to the next will enable one species to outcompete another. Thus, succession has a predictable sequence that depends on its stage of development and the growing conditions. However, there is also a random element.

For example, if three species are all equally well suited to become the next major player in the successional game, which one actually moves in may be purely a matter of chance, especially in tropical settings, where there are so many more species to become involved in a successional sequence. Although the type of plant in the next stage can be predicted, often the actual species cannot.

SUCCESSION AND ECOSYSTEM FUNCTIONS

We will concentrate on secondary succession here because it occurs more frequently than primary succession. The scale and nature of disturbance profoundly affect the degree to which ecosystem functions are damaged. In general, the larger the disturbance the more profound will be the dislocation of the processes.

Examples of disturbances that would affect ecosystem function and, ultimately, succession are flooding, erosion, and climatic changes. Each would play a strong role in determining ecosystem function and, in turn, which species could live at each stage in the succession.

Thus, we can think of disturbance as providing a shock to ecosystem functions. The recovery of ecosystem functions, such as the cycling of nutrients, the storage of carbon, or the provision of breeding grounds for organisms, affects and is affected by succession in a continual cycle of positive feedback.

A positive feedback loop is a self-reinforcing series of events. As the loop is repeated, the consequences become more marked. An example of how succession might affect an important ecosystem function is the effect of vegetation on water retention.

In most intact forests, surfacewater runoff is relatively rare, because the inflow of rainwater is slowed by the vegetation cover and absorbed by the soil. So long as plants are photosynthetically active, their roots take water up out of the soil and into the upper portion of the tree, where it is transpired from the leaf surface to the atmosphere.

When there are no leaves on the trees, there is no photosynthesis and no transpiration; thus it is during the growing season that plants lower the water table. In an experiment at Hubbard Brook, New Hampshire, in which trees were removed, the surface-water runoff increased 30%, and dissolved nutrients were washed from the land.

Hubbard Brook was a clear-cut, that is an area from which all the trees have been removed, but increased runoff can also result when the natural vegetation is replaced by plantation trees.

In Malaysia, the replacement of rain forest with palm plantations resulted in a doubling of the peak discharge of water (the flow most likely to cause erosion and floods). In these plantations, the trees are planted in rows and spaced so that the tree canopies will not touch. The ground is weeded and kept bare to ensure rapid growth of the palms.

The effect is that the sparse vegetation cover provided by the palms is insufficient either to absorb all the precipitation or to help prevent rapid runoff after the rain hits the ground. Another factor that will be affected by succession is a change in the temperature and quality of the soil.

Plants and animals have optimal living conditions that form part of their niche and so, too, do decomposers such as fungi and bacteria. These organisms have evolved to live within the normal temperature range experienced in a forest. The problem of changing the soil temperature with habitat disturbance is most acute in moist tropical ecosystems, where the land is shaded by giant trees.

Within an intact forest canopy, the soil temperature scarcely varies between night and day and is an almost constant 24°-25°C. Where a small gap in the tree canopy is opened, a more pronounced midafternoon heating is apparent, with temperatures approaching 30°C.

Such variation is natural within these systems, because forest canopies are continually developing small holes when individual trees collapse. However, the temperatures recorded in a clear-cut, effectively an unnaturally large gap, are almost twice that of the closed forest.

The extreme habitat presented by the soils of the clear-cut will be too hot for the survival of many of the decomposers, and without them the nutrient cycling is slowed. Nutrients, the chemicals essential for plant growth, often exist within the soil in soluble and insoluble forms. If an area has been deforested, it has lost the trees that wick moisture out of the soil.

One consequence is that the water table can remain at, or near, the surface all year. In such a saturated soil, the air spaces are filled with water, the biological oxygen demand (BOD) is still present from microbes, and it is common to find that oxygen concentrations fall to zero. The soil is then said to be *anaerobic*.

The conversion of an oxygen-rich soil to an oxygen-poor soil may cause chemical changes (reduction) to nutrient molecules in the soil. For example, phosphates are released into the soil water as their bonds to iron molecules are broken, while nitrates are converted to gaseous nitrogen or other nitrogen compounds that cannot be absorbed by plants.

If the soil water drains out of the soil or is washed out in a slurry as the surface soil erodes in a mudslide, the nutrients are lost from the system. The movement of soil nutrients either downward through the soil column or laterally out of the system is termed leaching.

On sites that have steep slopes and where the loss of forest does not result in saturated soils, there can still be a substantial loss of nutrients and soil erosion. The loss of topsoil may be slower than the loss of dissolved nutrients.

One explanation is that there is a delay between the cutting of the trees and the washing away of the soil. Initially, the roots would hold the soil in place and so prevent erosion. After several years, the root mat of the dead trees breaks up; as the roots rot, the soil is held less securely and starts to wash downslope.

The steeper the land, the more rapid is the loss of soils. Erosion can be sudden and severe, especially when forests on steep slopes are cut, the tree roots pulled out, and the land plowed for agriculture.

Erosion rates can also be affected by local wind speeds. Early successional and deforested landscapes of bare ground often have high wind speeds close to the ground. A moving stream of air will increase evaporation rates and thus speed the drying of the soil. Once the soil is dry, it can just blow away as dust.

Wind speed close to the ground will often decrease as succession progresses, having an effect on both the soils and the structure of the forest. Wind is also important in the heat budgets of high-elevation or highlatitude ecosystems.

Here an increase in wind speed may prevent bud development and hence hinder the re-establishment of plants. A further influence that wind can exert on a system is through blowdowns. A forest draws much of its physical strength from having a relatively complete canopy. The protective crown and closely spaced trunks create a layer of still air within the forest.

The trees growing in a dense forest effectively hold each other up. The tightly packed individuals prevent neighboring trees from swaying too violently and snapping their trunks. However, individual trees do not have trunks and root systems that can withstand strong winds. If an opening is made in the canopy, wind vortices can be created in the gap.

These high winds knock down trees at the edge of the clearing, turning a small canopy gap into a large one. It is evident that a disturbance to an ecosystem can result in severe soil damage, changes in soil-moisture conditions, and nutrient availability.

The repair of these abiotic systems comes about through the biotic processes of succession. Because the functions of the ecosystem have been altered, the niches available to the species that will colonize the landscape are different from the ones that existed just before the disturbance. Consequently, the species that return will not be the ones that were lost, at least not at first.

From Field to Forest

One of the classic studies of succession was done on the old-field systems of North Carolina by Dwight Billings in the 1930s. By looking at different areas of land that had been abandoned at various times in the preceding 150 years, he was able to piece together a detailed successional sequence for these fields in the Carolinian Piedmont.

The land surface had carried vegetation before, so this was an example of secondary succession. The soils of this area are sandy clays with very little organic content. The abandoned fields had been used for growing tobacco and cotton, crops that drain nutrients from the soil.

Consequently, the starting condition for the succession was bare ground composed of nutrient-poor dry soils that baked hard in the hot, dry summers. Plants colonizing these areas to start the succession would have to prosper in poor soils and be resistant to drought.

The sequence described by Billings is typical, so we can generalize from it. The first plants to occupy the bare ground (called *pioneer species*) are characterized by short life spans, rapid reproduction, and copious seed production. The first pioneer species to invade and build substantial populations on ground like that in Billings's area live for just one year and hence are termed annuals.

These annuals, for example crabgrass, are followed swiftly by ragweed, horseweed, aster, and broomsedge. By late summer, the combination of these species is beginning to cover the ground surface. The pioneer annuals (crabgrass, ragweed, and horseweed) collapse and die with the first frost, and their bodies, leaves, stems, and roots, contribute the first major input of organic matter to the soil.

Aster and broomsedge are biennials; they live for two years, reproducing in the second summer. The seeds produced by the annuals sprout in the second spring of the succession, but they are now competing with the larger biennial plants. By the end of the second summer, aster and broomsedge are beginning to displace the annual crabgrass, but once the biennials have reproduced, they also die.

Progressively, the land is colonized by herbs and shrubs that are perennial: plants that can reproduce multiple times and live many years. With each year, the amount of organic matter falling to the soil surface increases. Worms and other subterranean animals drag the rotting material down into the soil.

The soil gains an organic component, and the depth of the organic horizon increases because of biological activity. These curves represent the changes taking place at a single site. The bumpiness of the curves is a result of chance variations that befell this particular site.

If a large number of sites were studied, the average trend would result in smooth curves for soil depth and species number. As the succession continues and the landscape fills with plants, competition will be increasingly expressed in bigger and deeper root systems to draw on more nutrients and water, larger stems, and more densely packed leaves that catch more sunlight and cast more shade.

A big body thus has a twofold benefit. Increased leaf surface area allows the plant to produce more photosynthetic product, and, by casting shade and draining the soil of water and nutrients, a big plant can prevent would-be competitors from growing close to it.

Tree seedlings with tough leathery leaves or needles can survive in these shadeless conditions. After 5 to 15 years, loblolly pine, shortleaf pine, and sweetgum trees invade the land. The pines and rapidly growing broad-leaved trees are termed softwoods.

The hardness of wood is largely determined by its density or the proportion of carbon to water and air inside the trunk. These softwood trees build big bodies but trade strength for fast growth. Instead of building densely packed cells with a high proportion of strengthening compounds, such as lignin, these trees rely more heavily on the incompressibility of water to give them strength.

Consequently, the timber of softwood trees has less carbon and more water and air than slowergrowing hardwoods. The softwood trees rapidly form a complete woodland cover, shading out most of the herb (nonwoody) species.

Beneath the branches of these trees, there is a new *microclimate* (as used here, defined as the climate beneath or within vegetation). The forest cover casts shade, reduces temperatures and wind speed, restores much of the hydrological budget, and increases humidity beneath the canopy.

These conditions favor the growth of seedlings of late-successional hardwood trees that require relatively rich soils and some shade, particularly when very small. These seedlings need the moist, shaded understory of a forest to protect them from the burning sun.

Seedling oaks and beech, common hardwood trees of mature temperate forests, have large floppy leaves relative to their roots. Having large solar collectors (leaves) is an ideal adaptation for life on the shaded forest floor, where light, rather than moisture, may be the limiting factor.

However, if exposed to full sunlight, these seedlings cannot regulate their temperature and will develop a water deficit. They lose water through their leaves and cannot absorb enough through their roots to replace it. The consequence of the water deficit is that they wilt and die.

Thus the seedlings cannot become established until the earlier successional stages have occurred. The fast-growing pines and sweetgum form dense stands of tall, thin, straight-trunked trees. Short-lived, these trees start to senesce (to grow old) after about 50 years. As these trees age, the hardwoods that have been growing in the understory burst through into the gaps created by falling softwoods.

About 50 years into the succession, the hardwoods become important canopy components as the pines and sweetgums die out. A combination of hardwoods that represents the most mature forest on the modern Carolinian Piedmont is generally reached after about 150 years. Moresubtle changes then take place within the forest.

As the community proceeds toward maturity, the proportions of the various tree species within the woodland community change. Past timber extraction denies us the opportunity to study an undisturbed oldgrowth forest in Eastern forests, but Dwight Billings estimated that the succession from old field to fully mature forest would take at least 350 years.

It is evident that succession is much more than merely changing plant species, it is also a process of soil improvement and microclimate modification. Shortcuts in succession are unusual; a succession must run its full, predictable course.

It is important to understand that almost all of the landscapes that surround us are successional. The pines that flank the highways of the eastern United States, the oak forests of the Midwest, even the chaparral vegetation of California, are on a successional trajectory of change.

For example, the oak forests that stretch from Wisconsin to New England are the product of 100 to 300 years of succession, the time that has elapsed since the earliest settlers logged the land. From historical records, it is apparent that oaks were a minor component of those pre-European forests.

In fact, oaks are generally transitional species that bridge the gap from softwoods to late-successional hardwoods. Not surprisingly, therefore, the forests of New England are changing. The great red oaks that have dominated the forest for the last 100 years are failing to reproduce, and the next wave of hardwoods is growing up underneath.

The species that will replace the oaks are sugar maple, red maple, hackberry, cherry, or sweet birch, according to the part of the country.

Secondary Succession and Seed Banks

The nature, extent, and duration of a disturbance will play a large part in determining the recovery time and pathway of the successional sequence. Recovery from small-scale events will take relatively little time. For instance, a section of forest that was flattened where a tornado touched down will recover quickly.

Root bases of snapped trees may resprout almost immediately, and patches of bare ground will quickly green up as seeds dormant in the soil germinate. These seeds, produced during earlier fruiting seasons and buried in the soil, form the *seed bank*.

The species composition of the seed bank is likely to include all the plants that grew at the site immediately before the disturbance plus others that have been carried onto the site from farther away. For instance, under a closed forest canopy there may be no dandelions, fireweed, or grasses growing because they cannot tolerate the shade.

Although the adult plants cannot grow in the forest, their seeds are blown on the wind and will disperse over a large area. Alternatively, if the forest site is already recovering from a disturbance, the seeds of pioneer plants from years ago may be lying dormant in the seed bank. These seeds can remain dormant for a number of years and will sprout only when the forest is disturbed again.

Therefore, although the parent plants cannot grow at the site, the seed bank may well contain their seed. Following a disturbance that breaches the forest canopy, these sun-demanding species will germinate and grow until they are shaded out. Such pioneer species are often termed opportunists because they have sudden population booms that are dependent on the chance formation of small disturbance sites.

The Survival of Opportunists

The progression from pioneer to competitor is commonly one from shade-intolerant to shade-tolerant species. The herbs are shaded out by birch and pine, trees that grow quickly but cannot tolerate shade. Characteristically, their energy investment in reproduction will be high, although the investment in each individual seed will be small.

Each year they will produce a huge crop of small seeds. In contrast, the slower-growing shade-tolerant species of the mature forest, such as beech or chestnut, produce relatively few, larger seeds. The seedlings of shadeadapted trees have evolved large seeds that are energy-expensive to produce, but provide a nutrient packet for the emergent seedling.

The relationship between seed size and shade tolerance was demonstrated in a study of seedling survival. The seedlings of small-seeded tree species cannot compete for light or water, hence they will do badly in a shaded environment.

Although these small-seeded trees are generally preceded by annual and perennial herbs, they still share many of the same living strategies. For example, in comparison with a large-seeded tree, such as an oak or a beech, the small-seeded trees are relatively short-lived and have a high energy expenditure on reproduction.

A continuum of life strategies is evident from the pioneer herbs, through the early-successional (small-seeded) trees to the late-successional (largeseeded) species. If a whole forest is considered, the persistence of opportunists is a significant contribution to the overall species diversity. All natural systems have some degree of disturbance. Trees die and fall; rivers erode their channels; storms cause blowdowns. Small populations of opportunist species continue to exist within the forest matrix of competitors.

The opportunist populations are always low, always on the move as they colonize a new treefall gap, erosion site, or landslide, but they are readily outcompeted. Not all opportunist species will survive in all forest patches. In any one given area, just a few of the many opportunist species will be able to colonize and reproduce before being shaded out.

However, if all the gaps, streambanks, and disturbance areas in a forest are considered, an almost full complement of opportunist species will be found. Another difference between the early and late successional species is in the way that the trees evolve to spread their seeds.

The tiny seed of early-successional trees often has a diaphanous wing, as in the case of pines or the flat blades of a birch seed. These forms are adaptations to seed dispersal by wind. The construction of a tiny flimsy wing is a relatively cheap energy investment in each seed, but it allows the seed to be blown clear of the parent.

Late-successional trees have fewer seeds, but they invest more energy in each one. The large seed may be supplemented by a tempting bait to attract an animal that carries the seed away from the parent plant. An example is a cherry. The cherry seed is the hard part in the middle; the sugary, juicy flesh of the fruit is the bait to attract a disperser.

It is important to recognize the difference between the flesh of a berry, which is a sugary reward for the animal, and the seed(s) contained in the fruit. The animal may collect the fruit, gnaw off the flesh, and spit out the seeds. Alternatively, it may eat the berry whole, digest the flesh, and excrete the seed.

The seeds of some plants can germinate only after they have passed through an animal's digestive tract. It may seem a strange tactic for a species to evolve to rely on being eaten. Some animals digest and destroy the seeds, in which case they do not help the plant at all.

Other animals-such as squirrels-may be primarily seed-eaters, but, because they drop or deliberately bury so many seeds, they can also be regarded as seed dispersers. Nuts are particularly nutritious seeds that are collected by squirrels, monkeys, and birds. In each crop of nuts, many will be eaten, but some will have been carried to a new location by the animal and will survive to germinate.

Blue Jays and squirrels both stash acorns and beech seeds by burying them. Blue Jays do not appear to return to these hoards, and squirrels rarely seem to remember where they have hidden theirs. The evolutionary reason for these creatures' stash-and-forget behavior is unknown, but two hypotheses have been raised.

First, this behavior could be vestigial; that is, at one time they stashed and did remember to go back to the hoard. But the additional food supply must not have been a significant survival factor. If it had been, there would have been strong selection to remember where the nuts were buried.

This hypothesis concludes that because the behavior pattern is unimportant, it is being lost by degrees. An alternative hypothesis is that although these organisms receive no reward from burying the acorns, they increase the seedling success rate of oak trees. The future descendants of these squirrels may reap the harvest of the acorns so diligently sown.

Such arguments for altruism or foresight among animals are hard to substantiate because there would be just as much benefit to the lineage that did not waste time burying acorns, but kept on eating. This "selfish" line could rely on altruistic neighbors to bury the acorns and provide future harvests, while they worked to increase their individual fitness. Ultimately, the selfish line would "win" and would be the only surviving lineage.

Succession and Animals

Animals play an important part in successional systems as herbivores, seedeaters, and seed dispersers. However, animals are not generally classified according to a successional stage, although most species may be associated with particular successional stages.

Insects such as butterflies that are dependent upon a particular food plant may display a strong association with successional stages. Different bird species are also characteristic of the various stages in a succession, although this association is often as much related to the physical structure of the forest (the size and spacing of trees) as it is to the presence of a particular species of plant.

An example of the changes in bird species that accompanies the succession of fields to forest in the eastern United States.

An example of a bird that can only survive in old growth forest is the Northern Spotted Owl of the Pacific Northwest. This owl needs a particular structure of forest rather than a specific food item. Its niche defines it as a hunter working within a habitat of large trees, some of which are dying. It is a hole-nesting species and must have access to large standing dead or dying trees to provide the nest cavities. It cannot feed and reproduce successfully in other habitats, even though its prey may be abundant.

The Florida Scrub Jay has explicit habitat needs and relies on fire to modify succession. Fire can repeatedly disturb an area and prevent a succession from progressing, periodically kicking the succession back to an earlier stage.

The scrub jay needs this frequent disturbance to maintain open areas that would otherwise become a dense tangle of palms and shrubs. Scrub jays are ground-feeding birds that need about 30% of the ground area to be sparsely vegetated. Yet they nest in slow-growing scrub oaks, trees that reach about 8 m in height.

Hence, the jays need elements of both an early successional stage (the bare ground) and a late successional stage (the presence of hardwood species). Because the jays are strongly territorial and need to be able to forage close to the nest site, the apparently paradoxical needs of both early and late successional elements must be met at one site.

Frequent low-intensity fires that burn the understory, but do not kill the trees, create the ideal habitat for the jays. In Florida, this is a vegetation type that once covered large portions of the state, but has been lost due to fire suppression.

Less frequent fires have allowed the succession to proceed unchecked. The bare ground has been invaded by shrubs denying the birds their foraging areas. When fires do occur they are hotter and more destructive, killing oaks as well as other species. Consequently, the scrub jays are extinct throughout much of their former range and are presently listed as a threatened species.

SUCCESSION AND CORAL REEFS

A succession that is dependent upon a sequence of animals rather than plants is the process of coral reef formation. Corals are small soft-bodied animals that secrete a hard shell of calcium carbonate. Vast colonies of these creatures, each with its own protective coat, form a coral block.

The alga *Halimeda* is a green plant that also builds a body of calcium carbonate, which remains intact when the plant dies. Some reefs have a core of *Halimeda* bodies and an outer coat of coral.

The succession that leads to the recovery of a coral reef is more haphazard than in terrestrial systems because the larvae of the corals are carried by ocean currents. It becomes a matter of chance which species of coral establishes itself first.

For coral reef to develop, the water must be clean, without suspended sediment, and must be above 17°C, with a suitable attachment surface. Once the corals are established, other species such as sea anemones, crabs, and sponges will find niches within the structure of the coral mass. Animals that prey on coral, such as parrot fish and the crownofthorns starfish, will also colonize the reef.

The colonization and development of reefs is relatively slow, so they cannot withstand sustained damage from wave action or human use. Coral reefs are popular with fishermen and divers. Boats anchoring on coral cause immense damage to the living reef, and some fishing techniques, such as the use of explosives and poisons to stun fish for aquarium collection, have led to a degradation of reefs.

Scuba divers and visitors who treasure the reef may also damage these systems, either by collecting coral, touching coral, or disturbing the wildlife of the reef. Where tourism exerts a sustained pressure on the reef, some initiatives have been made to create artificial reefs.

Metal frames or deliberately sunken ships provide a platform for coral attachment. Such attempts to create a reef must be well planned. The engine oil and fuel must be thoroughly cleaned from the hulk and the wreck must be positioned so that it is not a hazard to shipping and will not adversely affect local ecosystems.

The wreck provides shelter for a wide array of fish species, and within a few years some coral growth will be seen. Divers and fishermen are then encouraged to frequent these newly created reef habitats, thus reducing the pressure of human disturbance on the older naturally formed reef.

DISTURBANCE THAT MAINTAINS DIVERSITY

The disturbance inflicted on a reef by divers and anchors is damaging because it breaks large, slow growing structures. The frequency and scale of disturbance can vary both in magnitude and in frequency. Frequent massive disturbances such as volcanic explosions will lead to low local species diversity; however, very rare trivial disturbances do not lead to high diversity.

Consider the experiment run by Paine on the effects of starfish predation. When the predatory starfish (a disturbing force) were removed, the diversity of prey species fell. When released from predation, the most competitive of the prey species excluded other species. In exactly the same way, a plant community that sustained no disturbance would go through a successional process in which a few dominant species prevail.

In 1978, Joseph Connell of the University of California at Santa Barbara proposed the *intermediate disturbance hypothesis.* This hypothesis states that an ecosystem maintains its highest species diversity under conditions of moderate disturbance. Connell argues that all ecosystems are continually perturbed by disturbance events, such as fire, disease, volcanic eruptions, trampling by herds of animals, or climatic change.

Even the death of an old tree is a form of local disturbance. Individual trees collapsing and dying provide an opening, or a gap, that can be filled by pioneer species. The gaps provide a continuous supply of sites to be invaded by pioneers.

If it were not for continuing disturbance, poor competitors, such as pioneer species, would go locally extinct. The continuous change in the forest and the diversity of ages of patches within the forest, reduce the effects of interspecific competition and maintain the niche of early successional species.

If interspecific competition does not develop fully, a superior competitor will not have the opportunity to outcompete and eliminate a weaker competitor. As the plants in the gap mature, they pass through a miniature successional sequence.

This view of the forest emphasizes that the forest is like a patchwork quilt in which each patch represents a different stage of forest regrowth. The intermediate disturbance hypothesis provides a good explanation of why mature ecosystems, whether a forest or a coral reef, maintain high diversity. This model also explains why increasing disturbance beyond a natural level is likely to reduce species diversity.

SUCCESSION AND HABITAT MANAGEMENT

Changes in net primary productivity (NPP) during the successional sequence are important to foresters and conservationists. Bare ground has zero NPP, but productivity increases rapidly as a complete vegetation cover develops.

When herbs colonize the land, their leaves form a single layer covering the ground, and this photosynthetic surface area determines what the NPP will be. A higher NPP can be attained if multiple layers of leaves, all of which are photosynthesizing, can be stacked above a given spot on the ground.

By having vertically spaced branches, trees can have such stacks of leaves, and because photosynthesis can operate maximally even in less than full sunlight, the soft shade cast by the upper leaves does not prevent the lower ones from being productive.

The highest NPP is found in relatively young forests, where every individual is growing vigorously. In older forests, the trees are often spaced farther apart and have bigger gaps in their crowns. Consequently, on average, there are fewer leaves stacked over a given spot in a more mature forest. Also, because some of the trees in an oldgrowth forest are senescent and dying, the NPP for the area will be lower.

Foresters maximize their profits by harvesting timber at the end of the fast-growth period, the peak of NPP in the young forest. In a forest left to mature beyond that point, the rate of increase in log size is decreasing.

In other words, it is more profitable for foresters to cut old trees and replant with young vigorous stock than to let a forest reach maturity. Consequently, forestry stands are filled with young trees. But from a wildlife perspective, an older forest is more valuable than a young forest.

In a mature forest, there are all ages of trees, from seedlings to the dying giants of the forest canopy, and, importantly, there are also dead trees. Large trees, especially dead ones, offer nesting holes and a rich supply of insects and grubs.

Dead trees offer as many niches as do living trees, so a mature forest, with its more diverse age structure, will carry more species than a uniformly young forest. Consequently, conservationists place a priority on mature forests. Thus, foresters and conservationists are likely to remain at odds over the ideal use of a forest.

THE OLD-GROWTH CONTROVERSY

The old-growth forests of northern California, Oregon, and Washington have been a political football for more than a decade. These are the last large tracts of uncut forest in the United States, and they represent the fully mature forests of the northwestern ecosystem.

Although the debate is often phrased as "owls versus jobs," the issues involved run much deeper. The Californian Northern Spotted Owl has become a symbol of the conservation effort. The owl is a cute and endearing logo, easier to sell to the public than the real argument that encompasses the broader issues of biodiversity, erosion, wilderness, deforestation (both domestic and international), and fisheries management. One of the largest issues at stake is the role that the United States can play in international conservation efforts. Until we protect the last of our own virgin forests, what possible right do we have to censure any tropical country for logging its rain forest?

The cutting of the old-growth forests is altering the ecology of the region. Clear-cutting leaves the land surface exposed, and the resulting erosion can wash away the topsoil from clear-cut areas.

The soil washes into local streams and rivers, causing eutrophication and clouding the water. Rivers that have supported salmon and a salmon-fishing industry are now so altered that the salmon will not return. The loss of topsoil also slows the process of natural regeneration.

The Douglas fir will take more than 200 years to become full-sized, and the cycle of succession from clear-cut to mature forest is likely to take at least 400 years. Once the forest has been clear-cut, further human land use ensures that there will be very little chance that the forests ever regain maturity.

Species of the deep forests will be lost from these systems, as only those tolerant of regrowth forests will remain. The felling of the last of these forests would be an act of finality, for they would not, could not, regrow as before. Aesthetic questions are raised: Will we cut the last of our untouched forests? How much is it worth to us to decide that at least some forest in the United States should not be shaped by commerce?

The logging industry argument that conservation is costing jobs certainly has a foundation of truth, but to reduce the issue to owls versus jobs is to hide behind a smoke screen. Until the 1990s, about 30,000 hectares of old-growth forest, representing 4.6 billion board-feet of timber, were being felled each year.

This rate of cutting virtually exhausted old-growth forest as a resource on private lands. By the mid1980s, 90% of old-growth forests between Washington and California had been cut. Past rates of clearcutting could not be sustained, even if the cutting were to include all the ancient forests on federal lands.

If, as some logging industry advocates maintain, it is only the cutting of old-growth forest that is economically rewarding, the industry and all its jobs are doomed anyway within the next 15-30 years. Mismanagement and short-sighted profit-taking both contributed to an industry fighting for survival. Simply put, timber was extracted without being replanted. Extractive logging with no replanting is not a recent phenomenon.

In fact, it was the hallmark of the expansion of Europeans that wherever they went they cleared the forest. Between 1600 and 1920, 98% of the forests of the eastern United States were logged. Uncut forests are virtually absent in the eastern United States, but now that the same philosophy of extraction is to be applied to the last large stands in the Pacific Northwest, there is a public outcry.

Massive reforestation projects for commercial timber have been undertaken in the southeastern United States and also in the Northwest. However, it is still more profitable to fell the old growth than to wait for the planted forests to become old enough to cut. The cutting of old-growth forest was for many years tacitly encouraged, with federal subsidies being granted through the U.S. Forest Service.

Tax money is spent to build logging roads so that trees may be felled from public lands (national or state forests) by private corporations. Tax money is then spent to reforest the land so that it may once again be cut by the private companies. The private companies keep the earnings from the cut, apart from a stumpage fee.

A stumpage fee is effectively a payment made by the logging company for the privilege of cutting the trees. The investment of tax dollars in logging roads and reforestation is not offset by stumpage fees. For every dollar of taxpayers' money spent, as little as 1 cent is repaid through stumpage fees.

In the past decade, subsidies extended to the logging industry have amounted to about $2.3 billion. A further criticism of U.S. forestry policy is that it does not encourage a domestic "finished-products" industry. One of the characteristics of a developing nation is that it ships cheap raw materials for processing to an industrialized nation.

The finished product, an expensive item, is then sold back to the country that furnished the raw materials. The profit to the industrialized nation is the foundation of most economic empires. For years, federal subsidies existed to encourage the export of raw logs to Japan, China, and other trading partners.

The goal was to generate export revenue, but instead the subsidies encouraged the U.S. timber industry to behave as an economic colony, selling cheap raw materials. The results of this trade relationship have been long-term damage to the logging industry, over-exploitation of what should have been a sustainable resource, and the failure to establish a finished-products industry in the Northwest. Caught in the middle, through no fault of their own, are the loggers themselves.

These people have the greatest emotional and personal investment in the forests, and they would adamantly defend their position as environmentalists. For several generations, they have lived, worked, hunted, and fished beneath the great trees.

The foresters see their role as forest stewards-integral to this landscape and equally deserving of consideration as the Northern Spotted Owl. The trees are seen as a resource that will go to waste, taken by fire or eaten by bugs, if they are not harvested.

This is an accurate assessment of the fate of a tree in an old-growth forest in terms of timber production. The forester views the regrowth that follows clearance as a vibrant resurgence of young vigorous trees, promising future harvests-again an accurate assessment.

Threatened with unemployment, the foresters have become vocal opponents of conservation measures. The Clinton administration came to office on a platform of strong environmental measures, but quickly recognized that decisions regarding the northwestern forests have to be politically tenable.

The new policy provides for the continued logging of 1.2 billion boardfeet each year from old-growth forests on federal lands, and it includes $1.2 billion in spending to revitalize the region's sustainable industries. The plan also establishes a series of old-growth reserves to protect forest species and salmon populations.

Like any compromise, it satisfies neither of the adversarial lobbies completely, but it may represent a settlement that is politically workable.

EQUILIBRIUM OR NONEQUILIBRIUM IN OUR MODERN ECOSYSTEMS

Ecological equilibrium implies that all the species likely to grow in a given area have established populations that are fluctuating within normal limits. Thus, even at equilibrium, some changes in species abundance can be expected.

This state of a stable equilibrium has been likened to a ball lying in a hollow. Some change may occur in the population (the ball moves), but the population soon will return to its starting point (the ball rolls back). This view of ecosystems is reasonable over very short time scales of a few hundred years or less.

However, the forests of New England, and even our most mature hardwood forests in the eastern United States (a few remote areas in the Appalachians and isolated stands in the Midwest), do not fit this model. These forests are not equilibrial, and if disturbed they do not return to their starting point. Forests tend not to be equilibrial because they are still responding to the last perturbation and are still successional.

An alternative model of an ecosystem is represented by a ball rolling slowly between low hills. This movement could represent directional climatic change, such as the warming at the end of an ice age or a successional sequence following a volcanic eruption.

As succession proceeds, a chance eventperhaps a disease-affects one of the dominant species, deflects the successional pathway, and results in a different forest type. In the model, this deflection is represented as the nudging of the ball into a different groove. At any time during the succession, a change in the environment caused by factors such as fire, drought, or pollution could set the process back. The setback is represented by the ball moving backward.

As succession starts to repair the damage, the ball will move forward again, but perhaps along a different course. This process continues indefinitely, so that the ball is continually moving but never necessarily returning to any previous position.

As nature is continually shifting the balance of equilibrium, many ecologists believe that, in the long term, ecosystems are essentially permanently nonequilibrial, lurching from one state of near-chaos to the next, albeit in a fairly orderly successional fashion.

9

Effects of Pollution on Vegetables

Very few of the signs or symptoms evoked by infection with parasitic organisms can be said to deserve that much-abused term pathognomonic. There are but a limited number of ways in which the body is able to react to altered conditions, and therefore it is not surprising that few of these reactions are specific.

However, the presence of certain signs and symptoms should alert the clinician to corresponding diagnostic possibilities, while various constellations of symptoms, or syndromes, are to a greater or lesser degree diagnostic.

It must be emphasized that the following is not intended as a complete differential diagnosis of any of the symptoms discussed. Limitations of space do not permit even mention of the various non-parasitic etiologies of many of these conditions.

Abdominal Pain

Crampy abdominal pain may characterize amebic colities, with tenesmus if the ulcerations involve the rectal area. Diarrhea or dysentery is usually present when the infection is symptomatic. If hepatic abscess develops, pain is usually felt in the right upper quadrant (left, if the abscess involves the left lobe), and may be referred to the scapular area.

Pain in giardiasis is usually mild but may occasionally be severe; it is usually crampy and may be accompanied by steatorrhea and a full-blown malabsorption syndrome. Pain is seldom present in intestinal worm infections. Intestinal or biliary obstn3ction (the former primarily in smaller children) can be the result of Ascaris infection, with signs and symptoms which mimic obstruction from any other cause. Strongyloides stercoralis, invading the mucosal wall, may cause a severe duodenitis or jejunitis, with symptoms suggestive of duodenal ulcer disease. A moderate to heavy eosinophilia generally accompaines either these worm infections.

Abscess, Amebic

Amebic invasion of the liver is characterized by tenderness and enlargement of that organ, progressive malaise, an irregularly spiking fever with night sweats, leukocytosis, elevation and fixation of the right diaphragm, and sometimes development of a right lower lobe pneumonitis. With abscess formation, pain becomes more intense and may be referred to the tip of the right (less commonly) the left scapula.

Abscess, Frlarial

Abscesses may develop spontaneously or ,appear' shortly after antifilarial treatment is begun. They occur along the course of lymphatics or at lymph nodes and may be distinguished from pyogenic abscesses by the fact that they are generally sterile when first opened and that fragments of the adult worms may be found in the abscess drainage.

Anemia

Most frequently associated with malaria, hookworm, and broad fish tapeworm infections, anemia may be seen in kala-azar, trypanosomiasis, sclaistosomiasis, fasciolopsiasis and trichuriasis. In falciparum malaria the red cell count may fall to 2.5 to 4.0 million in cases of averege severity, and under 1.0 million in severe infections.

Anemia is usually not severe in vivax malaria and is still less pronounced in quartan infection. The characteristic microcytic hypochromic anemia of hookworm infection is the result of blood loss and is thus proportional to the severity of infection, although adequate dietary intake of iron may prevent its development in light or moderate infections.

The small amount of blood ingested per Trichuris makes anemia rare in other than massive infections. Persons -infected with Diphyllobothrium latum may develop a macrocytic hyperchromic anemia on the basis of vitamin B_{12} deprivation if the worm is attached to the jejunal wall. In kala-azar, and possibly also in Chagas disease, anemia may be a consequence of proliferation of infected reticuloendothelial cells in the bone marrow.

In the other trypanosomiases, schistosomiasis, and certain intestinal helminthic infections such as fasciolopsiasis; anemia may result in part from nutritional causes.

Appendicitis

Amebic ulceration involving the cecal area or appendix may simulate acute appendicits; surgical intervention when there is extensive cecal ulceration may be disastrous. Ascaris may block the lumen of the appendix and give rise to appendicitis; this is reported also for Trichuris. Angiostrongylus costaricensis infection may also mimic appendicitis.

Ascites

Circumoval tissue proliferation leading to extensive fibrosis of the liver in Schistosoma mansoni and S. japopicum infections may lead eventually to a condition clinically very similar to Laennec's cirrhosis, with portal hypertension, splenomegaly and ascites. Although hepatomegaly and splenomegaly occur early in kala-azar, ascites is uncommon. It may occur in chronic cases, probably secondary to a nutritional cirrhosis.

Asthma, Bronchial

Asthmatic attacks may occur is Ascaris infection during the stage of migration through the lungs, or Mater in the course of the infection because of hypersensitization to the absorbed worm antigens. Asthma is not uncommon in visceral larva migrans infections, in which there is usually an -accompaning hepatomegaly and marked eosinophilia. See also tropical eosinophilia, under Eosinophilia.

Blackwater Fever

Calabar Swellings

Circumscribed subcutaneous swellings are seen in loiasis. They are usually intensely pruritic and may be quite painful if they develop in areas where there is little loose subcutaneous tissue. They appear rapidly, developing within an hour or so to a diameter of several centimeters, and persist of several days, or if in an area subject to repeated trauma may last for a week or longer.

Cakjfications, Cerebral

Calcification of areas of intrace rebral infection in congenital toxoplasmosis may be seen no X-ray, and when intracerebral calcifications are round in a patient who has chorioretinitis, a diagnosis of toxoplasmosis ishighly probable. Calcified cysts of Cysticercus cellulosae within the brain may be distinguished by their size and uniform rounded or oval shape.

Chagoma

The hard, reddened, raised primary lesion in, Trypanosoma cruzi infection usually develops on the head or neck and sometimes on the abdomen or limbs, and may persist for two or three months. Although it may occur on or about the eye, the chagoma is not to be confused with the unilateral palpebral edema of Romana's sign (q.v.).

Chorioretinitis

Infection of the retina and choroid by Toxoplasma or (rarely) Entamoeba histolytica may produce visual disturbances, which can be profound if the macula is involved. On ophthalmoscopic examination, a grayish or yellow white area surrounded by exudate is seen early; with healing this leaves a white atrophic patch bordered by pigment deposits.

Chyluria

The formation of lymphatic varices, consequent upon repeated attacks of filarial lymphangitis and obstruction of lymphatic drainage, may lead to the passage of lymphatic fluid in the urine, if varices rupture into any part of the urinary tract. Chyluria usually occurs in attacks lasting a few days the urine way have a milky white colour and contain microfilariae.

Coma

The sudden onset of coma in a patient known to be suffering from falciparum malaria, or in an apparently healthy erson in, or recently returned from, a malarious area, should always suggest cerebral malaria and requires emergency treatment.

While most common as a complication of falciparum malaria, coma may occur with other types of malaria. In African trypanosomiasis, coma develops after a protracted period of increasingly severe symptoms of meningoencephalitis. It is also seen in primary amebic meningoencephalitis, in which a history of rapidly developing fever, meningeal signs, confusion and coma, and of recent swimming or diving in fresh water will often be elicited.

Cerebral cysticercosis may be a diagnostic consideration in persons of Mexican or Latin American origin, or of long residence in those areas, who present with a variety of neurological symptoms including headache, alteration of consciousness, focal seizures, coma and internal hydrocephalus. Diagnosis may be difficlut, and eosinophilia (either peripheral or of the spinal fluid) is not always present. Serological tests are helpful.

Conjunctivitis

Chronic conjunctivitis is seen in onchocercal infections, with hyperpigmentation of the conjunctiva, photophobia and gradual development of corneal opacities; acute =exacerbations of conjunctivitis and photophobia may be associated with attacks of onchocercal dermatitis (q.v.).

The sheep botfly, Oestrus ovis, may lay its eggs in the conjunctivae, and development of the larva in the conjunctival sac is accompanied by considerable pain, localized swelling and conjunctivities.

Convulsions

Focal convulsive seizures of the jacksonian type are seen in a number of parasitic infections that involve the central nervous system. These are discussed under Neurologic Symptoms. Convulsions also may be seen in the malarial paroxysm, in acute toxoplasmosis occuring in newborn children, and in Ascaris infection in children.

Dermatitis

Dermal leishmanoid is a secondary cutaneous manifestation of Leishmania donovani infection, occurring a year or so after supposedly successful treatment of kala-azar. The lesions may be flattened or depressed depigmented macules, or erythematous nodules which, on the face, often occur in a. butterfly distribution reminiscent of lupus erythematosus. Leish manial amastigotes are found in the lesions.

Penetration of schistosome cercariae through the skin causes a localized edema and pruritus, mild in the case of the human schistosomes, more severe in the "swimmer's itch" caused by bird schistosome cercariae.

A similar localized pruritic reaction, occurs with penetration of Strongyloides larvae through the skin; the seaction to penetration of hookworm larvae is somewhat more severe, often with the formation of papules or vesicles; it may last for a couple of weeks or longer if there is a secondary infection.

The cutaneous larva migrans reaction caused by larvae of Ancylostoma braziliense is characterized by a reddened papule at the site of entry; the larva forms a reddened serpiginous tunnel, at first covered with vesicles, later dry and crusted, which advances at the rate of a few millimeters to centimeters a day.

The area itches intensely; without treatment infection may persists for several weeks or months. Strongyloides larvae may produce similar cutaneous lesions, but because of their more rapid subcutaneous movement, they are referred to as "larva currens." Presence of adult Loa loa beneath the skin may be indicated by a thin raised reddened line, a few centimeters in length.

The adult female Dracunculus also may be visible beneath the skin but usually produces no reactior until about to larviposit, when a vesicle forms over the point at which the worm is about to break through the skin.

In onchocerciasis, the presence of microfilariae in the skin sometimes elicits an acute pruritic inflammatory reaction resembling erysipelas and usually confined to the face, neck and ears; repeated acute attacks may result in chronic lichenification, with hyperpigmentation and fissuring.

The migration of Sarcoptes scabiei through the skin produces lesions resembling those of cutaneous larva migrans, but frequently seen in parts of the body that have no contact with soil.

This organisms is highly infectious, and localized hospitall epidemics have been reported. The mites invade the upper layers of the epidermis, in which they form sinuous burrows. They seem to have a predilection for the interdigital, popliteal and inframammary folds the and groin. Intense itching, with formation of small vesicles and crusting of the chronic excoriated lesions, is typical.

The larvae of the horse botfly, Gasterophilus, produce similar cutaneous lesions in man. Pediculosis in hypersensitive persons, usually as a result of repeated exposure, may give rise to a severe localized reaction, with reddish papules at the feeding site, and surrounding vesiculation and a weeping dermatitis.

Bronzing of the affected area may persist following healing. The chigoe flea, Tunga penetrans, produces local pruritus as it lies partly buried in the skin of the toes or elsewhere on the body; secondary infections by clostridia are not uncommon. See also Rash.

Diarrhea

Diarrhea in parasitic diseases may be of diverse etiologies. In kala-azar, infiltration of the submucosa with leishmania-containing macrophages may lead to mucosal ulceration and diarrhea. Plugging of the mucosal capillaries with parasitized red blood cells may lead, in falciparum malaria, to a watery diarrhea so profuse as to suggest cholera.

Blood, containing parasitized red cells, may be found in the stools. The diarrhea or dysentery is usually accompanied by nausea and vomiting. Mucosal ulceration is amebiasis or balantidiasis may produce diarrhea or, if the ulceration is more extensive, dysentery (q.v). Isospora develops within the epithelial cells of the lower ileum and cecum. Infection is self-limited, lasting usually a month or less, and often asymptomatic. In some cases there is mild abdominal pain, nausea and vomiting, and diarrhea.

Giardia infections may be asymptomatic, acco:.ipanied by a mild mucoid diarrhea, or, like Isospora, may give rise to a full-blown malabsorption syndrome with steatorrhea.

Development of the cysticercoids of Hymenolepis nana within the intestinal villi may elicit a mucous diarrhea. Maturation of Trichinella witnin the wall of the duodenum and jejunum produces nausea, vomiting, colicky abdominal pain and diarrhea, starting about 24 hours after infection and lasting up to five days.

In Strongyloides infections there may be mild diarrhea, alternating with periods of constipation, or the diarrhea may be severe and prostrating. In heavy infections ulceration and sloughing of the intestinal mucosa may take place, with dysentery and often with secondary bacterial infection and fever.

Capillaria philippinensis infections may result in profuse diarrhea, malabsorption and a protein-wasting enteropathy. In schistosomiasis mansoni and japonicum, there is diarrhea, presumably of toxic origin, associated with nausea, vomiting, hepatic tenderness, fever, eosinophilia and an urticarial rash, during the period while the worms are maturing in the liver sinusoids.

Somewhat later, with the beginning of egg deposition in the intestinal wall, there may be a profuse diarrhea or dysentery. In persons previously uninfected, the onset of a heavy hookworm infection may be marked by nausea, vomiting, epigastric or midabdominal tenderness, and diarrhea. The diarrhea is presumably caused ay toxicity or hypersensitivity, although mechanical irritation may play some part.

The same may be said of the diarrhea in heavy whipworm infections. In fasciolopsiasis, diarrhea, which usually has its onset about a month after infection takes place, is characterized by the passage of stools containing much undigested food; severe infections are accompanied by symptoms of severe malnutrition, with edema of the face, abdominal wall and lower extremities, ascites and prostration.

The diarrhea sometimes seen in Taenia and broad fish tapeworm infections and in infections with the smaller intestinal flukes may be related to local irritation.

Dysentery

Acute amebic dysentery is characterized by the passage of six to eight or sometimes a dozen or more mucoid blood-flecked stools a day. There may be generalized abdominal pain and tenderness if the entire colon is involved, tenderness over McBurney's point,. nausea and vomiting with cecal infection, or tenesmus, with relief of the accompanying pain after evacuation if the rectosigmoid is the main diseased area.

An untreated attack lasts a few days to several weeks and usually subsides spontaneously to recur after an interval of some days to several years. Between attacks the patient may be constipated. Balantidial dysentery is similar to amebic, and as in the latter disease, many infections are asymptomatic.

Dysentery accompanying kala-azar, falciparum malaria infections, strongyloidiasis and schistosomiasis is mentioned in the discussion of Diarrhea.

Edema

Circumorbital edema, possibly resulting from vasculitis provoked by the migrating larvae, is frequently seen in the early stages of trichinosis; there also may be edema of the bands. Uniiateral circumorbital edema, with local pruritus and sometimes intense pain, results from passage of the adult Loa loa across the eyeball or lid.

Passage of the worm across the eyeball takes from less than half a minute to as long as 10 minutes; the resulting inflammatory changes usually persist for several days. Calabar swellings (q.v.) are also seen in loiasis, while localized edema of the face, neck, ears, etc., accompanied by intense pruritus and erythema, may be recurrent in oncbocerciasis.

Ocular sparganosis is not uncommon in some areas .as the result of poulticing eye lesions with split raw infected frogs. In the subcutaneous tissues around the eye, the sparganum produces a violent tissue reaction with edema; retrobulbar development of the sparganum may cause protrusion of the eyeball and consequent corneal ulceration. Areas of localized bard edema, of uncertain etiology, are frequently seen in 'Chagas' disease, occurring after appearance of the chagoma (q.v.).

The most common type is unilateral edema of the eyelids (Romana's sign) (q.v.). Edematous patches may develop elsewhere on the body, especially involving the abdominal wall, pupic area, scrotum and legs. Of equally obscure origin is the edema of the hips, legs, hands and face that many accompany the acute stage of African sleeping sickness.

Edema of the face and legs, with a pratuberant abdomen, is seen in severe hookworm infections, fasciolopsiasis and diphyllobothriasis, and may be related to malnutrition.

Elephantiasis

Filarial elephantiasis is a chronic enlargement of a limb, the scrotum, a breast or the vulva, with hyperplasia of the connective tissue and skin, a woody non-pitting edema, and thickened, coarsened skin, often with verrucous changes.

In Malayan filariasis, elephantiasis is less severe and generally is confined to the lower limbs. Elephantiasis of the external genitalia in both sexes, and hypertrophy of the femoral lymph nodes, producing a peculiar conditions known as "*hanging groin,*" have been reported from some areas in Africa where bancroftian filariasis is unknown, and are ascribed to onchocercal infection.

In schistosomiasis haematobium, extensive egg deposition may lead to fibrosis, which blocks the lymphatic drainage, and to elephantiasis of the penis.

Eosinophilia

Eosinophilia is a consistent finding in helminth infections, though it may be quite variable in degree. In general, tissue parasites provoke a higher eosinophilia than those that live only in the lumen in the bowel.

As many physicians equate eosinophilia with parasitic disease, it may not be amiss to give the result of a Mayo Clinic study of 418 patients with an eosinophilia of 20 per cent or greater, as quoted by Harris (1979):

Diseases with Eosinophilia of Greater than 20 Per cent (Mayo Clinic 1944)

Disease	Per cent
Atopic diseases (vasomotor rhinitis, asthma,hay fever)	28
Lymphoproliferative diseases (lymphoma)	20
Dermatoses (pemphigus, dermatitis herpetiformis)	10
Nonparasitic infections (principally streptococcal)	11
Periarteritis nodosa (with lung involvement)	10
Parasitic infections	4
Nonlymphatic malignant tumors and leukemia	4
Miscellaneous	13

A marked eosinophilia (20 to 70 per cent or higher) is most frequently seen in trichinosis, strongyloidiasis, hookworm infection, visceral larva migrans, filariasis, schistosomiasis and fasciolopsiasis. Moderate eosinophilia (6 to 20 per cent) often accompanies trichuriasis, ascariasis, paragonimiasis, taeniasis. and eosinophilic meningitis. It must be realized that eosinophilia is an index of host reaction to the parasite therefore, it will vary considerably from one patient to another.

Eosinophilia is not characteristic of any of the protozoan. infections. Tropical eosinophilia or eosinophilic lung disease is characterized by symptoms of chronic bronchitis or asthma, a marked eosinophilia, elevated erythrocyte sedimentation rate, paroxysmal cough or wheezing, malaise, easy fatiguability, anorexia and weight loss.

The chest film may show diffusepatchy motling and transverse branching striations, most prominent in the midlung and basal lung fields, with enlargement of the hilar shadows. Occasionally there may be unilateral densities in the upper lung field which are suggestive of the picture seen in pulmonary tuberculosis.

The disease is reported from such areas as India, Pakistan, Sri Lanka, China, Burma, Thailand, the Philippines, Malaysia and Indonesia, tropical Africa and the West Indies. Its etiology may be diverse. Filarial infection, with human or non-human species, is considered to. be a common cause of this condition.

Other agents may be the pulmonary stages of Ascaris, Strongyloides, Toxocara or other helminths. Treatment with conventional doses of diethyl carbamazine is often effective; antimonial (stibophen) or arsenical drugs (neoarsphenamine) are sometimes effective when there is no response to diethylcar-bamazine.

Epididymitis

An early complication of filarial infection,. often associated with orchitis, and with or without accompanying lymphangitis and fever.

Fever

Patterns of fever may be characteristic in malaria and kala-azar, but it is a mistake to suppose that they must conform to the "textbook" pattern. A quotidian fever is often seen in the initial attack of vivax malaria, with two or more broods of parasites completing their exoerythrocytic cycle at different times, so that there may be a daily fever peak corresponding to rupture of the infected red cells and liberation of merozoites.

Daily fever peaks usually are seen only for a few days; apparently within this time all broods of parasites become synchronized, and thereafter the fever cycle will exhibit a tertian periodicity. Quartan and falciparum malaria may like wise exhibit a quotidian or irregular periodicity during the first few days of the primary attack. Tertian fever is characteristic of vivax and ovale malaria. The paroxysm has an abrupt onset, usually initiated with a chill which varies from a moderate sensation of cold to the intense "*bed-shaking*" chill usually thought typical of malaria.

The chill lasts up to an hour and the fever (to 104 or 105°) for two hours or longer, followed by .a profuse sweat, during the course of which the temperature falls to normal over a period of an hour or so. The sweating stage usually is followed by sleep, and when the patient awakens he usually feels well.

The next paroxysm is initiated approximately 48 hours after the onset of the previous one. Subtertian fever, seen in falciparum malaria, is so called because the cycle may more nearly approach 36 than 48 hours. There is usually no frank chill, and the febrile stage is prolonged, though the fever is not usually so high as in vivax; it may not fall to. normal even in the intervals between paroxysms.

There may be double peaks of fever in each 24-hour period, resembling the fever curve in kala-azar. There is often no well-defined sweating stage, though sweating may be continuous, periodic or completely absent. Quartan fever is seen in malaria caused by Plasmodium malariae.

There is often a regular periodicity from the start; the paroxysms recur at 72-hour intervals; while similar to those of vivax malaria, they are generally more severe. The hot stage often lasts several hours and is frequently accompanied by nausea and vomiting; the sweating stage may be followed by prostration.

Hyperpyrexia may develop as part of an attack of cerebral malaria or in the course of an apperently uncomplicated attack of falciparum malaria; as the result of injury to the heat-control center in the hypothalamus there is a rapid rise in temperature to 107° or higher, and death quickly ensues.

A doubly remittent or "*dromedary*" fever is frequently found in kala-azar. Febrile attacks, which last a few days to several weeks, are separated by afebrile periods of equal irregularity. At some time during the course of a febrile attack, there will usually be one or more days during which a double or triple rise to a temperature of 103 to 105° can be demonstrated during a 24-hour period.

An irregularly spiking fever with hepatic tenderness, suggestive of cholangitis, may be seen in amebic hepatitis, fascioliasis and acute Opisthorchis infections. The initial period of schistosome infection is likewise marked by irregular fever and hepatic tenderness, with nausea and vomitting, diarrhea and giant hives.

An irregular fever, usually with evening peaks and night sweats, is an early finding in African trypanosomiasis, and a high remittent fever, lasting for several weeks, occurs early in Chagas' disease.

A remittent fever, with temperature to 104 or 105°, frequently marks the stage of larval migration in trichinosis. Filarial fever may occur very early in the course of a filarial infection.

There is usually a sudden onset, with fever ranging in the neighbourhood of 102 to 104° and remaining elevated for several hours to a couple of days, and gradually subsiding in the next several days. Attacks of lymphangitis and lymphadenitis (q.v.) usually accompany the febrile episodes.

Funiculitis

Inflammation of the spermatic cord is frequently an early symptom of filariasis.

Hematuria

In Schistosoma haematobium infections, beginning as soon as three months after infection or sometimes not until several years later, there may be intermittent hematuria. There is no dysuria, but there may be some frequency and also bladder pain following urination.

Hematuria is often referred to as terminal hematuria, being limited to the last few drops of urine, blood being forced out as the bladder wall contracts.

Hemoglobinuria

Blackwater fever usually is seen in conjunction with an attack of falciparum malaria, generally in patients who have had previous attacks of malaria. The passage of reddish or red-brown urine signals a bout of intravascular hemolysis, which may occur once or repeatedly and may lead to severe renal tubular damage and anuria.

The cause of blackwater fever is unknown; hypotheses include quinine sensitivity, glucose-6-phnsphate dehodrogenase deficiency in persons treated with primaquine and related drugs, and autohemolysis on the basis of antibodies formed against altered infected red cells.

Hepatitis

Amebic hepatitis has already been described under the heading of Abscess, Amebic.

Hepatomegaly

Any parasitic infection involving the liver may result in enlargement of that organ. Thus, amebic hepatitis or liver abscess, visceral larva migrans, liner-fluke infections and early schistosomiasis are all characterized by an -enlarged and tender lives, which is also seen in. some cases of falciparum malaria and acute neonatal toxoplasmosis as well as in kala-azar and Chagas' disease.

Hydatid infections of the liver and Schistosoma mansoni and japonicum infections may result in an enlarged but usually non-tender liver. The hepatic fibrosis characteristic of chronic schistosome infections produces a clinical picture similar to that of Laennec's cirrhosis, often with splenomegaly.

Those helminth infections involving the liver are characterized also by an eosinophilia. In visceral larva migrans, a leukocytosis of up to 80,000 may be present, with a striking cosinophilia. In amebic abscess of the liver, on the other hand, though the white blood count may be in the range of 25,000, there is no eosinophilia.

Hives

Giant hives and other allergic symptoms, such as bronchial asthma, are commonly seen in ascariasis, and hives often appear during the first few weeks of schistosome infections.

Hydatid Thrill

In large unilocurar echinococcus cysts of the abdominal viscera that are situated close to the abdominal wall, a characteristic thrill may be elicited by quick palpation or percussion.

Hydrocele

This is a common finding in areas where filariasis is endemic, developing, as a sequel to repeated attacks of orchitis. If lymphatic varices develop in the cord and rupture into the scrotal sac, a condition known as lymphocele results.

Hydrocephalus

Although not so intimately associated with congenital toxoplasmosis as are chorioretinitis and cerebral calcifications, hydrocephalus or microcephaly is commonly seen in this condition.

Hyperpigmentation

Kala-azar derives its name from intensification of the pigmentation of the skin over the cheeks and temples, and around the mouth. It is most obvious in darkskinned races.

In onchocerciasis, repeated attacks of allergic dermatitis may result in hyperpigmentation of the area, usually on the face, neck or ears. Bronzing and induration of the affected skin areas may oceur in chronic pediculosis (vagabond's disease).

Jaundice

Obstructive jaundice may be seen in severe liver fluke infections but is not characteristic of light infections or those of moderate intensity. The symptoms of the falciparum malaria syndrome known as bilious remittent fever include acute epigastric pain, nausea and vomiting, marked enlargement and tenderness of the liver, with jaundice appearing on about the second day. Diarrhea, a high remittent fever and oliguria are usually seen, and death may result from renal or hepatic failure.

Kerandel's sign

Noted in the stage of central nervous system involvement in African sleeping sickness, this sign may be elicited by pressure on the palm of the hand or over the ulnar nerve and consists of severe pain which occurs shortly after the pressure has been relieved.

Leukocytosis

Leukocytosis seldom continues throughout the course of any of the parasitic infections. In amebic hepatitis or abscess there may be a white blood cell count of 25,000 to 30,000, with 70 to *80* per cent polymorphonuclear neutrophils.

In visceral larva migrans. a leukocytosis of up to 80,000 has been reported, with an eosinophilia of 20 to 80 per cent. Trichinosis may be characterized by a white count of 30,000 early in the infection, and strongyloidiasis by one nearly as elevated; these usually decline and may be followed by leukopenia.

Leukocytosis early in the course of infection, followed by leukopenia with a relative monocytosis, is common to many protozoan and helminth infections.

Leukopenia

A white cell count of 4000 or less, with a relative monocytosis, generally is seen throughout the course of kala-azar, sometimes terminating in agranulocytosis.

In malaria, a leukopenia of 3000 to 6000, with a relative monocytosis, characterizes the afebrile periods, while there may be a leukocytosis during the paroxysm.

Lymphadenitis

In filariasis the femoral and epitrochlear nodes are most commonly involved, as are the axillary and inguinals. The nodes are enlarged, painful and tender during an acute attack of lymphangities and tend to remain enlarged between attacks. A condition resembling infectious mononucleosis sometimes is seen in the acute stage of toxoplasmosis, with fever, weakness, malaise, generalized adenopathy and sometimes a rash.

There may be generalized lymphadenitis without fever or other symptoms. In the early stages of African trypanosomiasis there may be generalized adenopathy; the glands of the posterior cervical triangle are most conspicuously affected (Winterbottom's sign). Generalized adenopathy is seen in the acute stage of Chagas' disease.

Lymphangitis

Acute lymphangitis is an early symptom of filarial infection. It usually is accompanied by fever and may affect'the limbs. breast or scrotum. When it occurs on a limb, it is usually centrifugal in development, starting at a lymph node and progressing distally.

The course of the lymphatic is readily seen because of local distention and erythema. Centrifugal spread of the lymphangitis is the reverse of that seen in bacterial lymphangitis (blood poisoning), in which the infection extends proximally from the point of origin.

Lymphocytosis

A relative or absolute lymphocytosis, unusual in parasitic infections, is, however, generally seen in Chagas" disease. Initially there may be a slight leukocytosis, usually followed by leukopenia.

Lymph varices

Dilatations of the lymphatic vessels may occur secondarily to lymphatic blockage in filariasis. They are most frequently seen in the inguinal and femoral areas, or other lymphatic tracts may be affected. The soft lobulated swellings may rupture and drain. When this occurs on the scrotum, a chronic condition known as lymph scrotum may develop.

Helena

Upper gastrointestinal bleeding of a degree sufficient to produce melena is rare in parasitic disease; it is mentioned here primarily with strongyloidiasis in mind.

Infection with Strongyloides stercoralis may run the gamut from a complete lack of symptoms to those infections of the duodenum and jejunum which are so extensive as to produce ulceration of the mucosa. with blood loss to the point of clinical anemia, and with melena.

Especially in immunosuppressed patients, the coincidental finding of anemia with melena' and a significant eosinophilia should stimulate a thorough search for this sometimes elusive parasite.

Meningoencephalitis

Invasion of the central nervous system by trypanosomes is characterized in African sleeping sickness by increasing symptoms of meningoencephalitis. There may be quite variable sensory and motor changes, personality disorders, headache, confusion, drowsiness and finally coma.

Similar but milder symptoms are seen in Chagas' disease. Minor neurologic symptoms are seen during almost any attack' of malaria (i.e., headache, disorientation), and cerebral malaria may develop as a complication of any type of malaria.

It is characteristic of falciparum malaria, however, and may develop slowly with increasing headache and drowsiness over several days or may present as a sudden coma or other acute mental disturbance. There may be signs of meningeal irritation; symptomatology is quite varied, depending upon the brain areas affected.

If the cord is affected, the symptoms may be suggestive of multiple sclerosis. Amebic meningoencephalitis, caused by invasion of the central nervous system by ordinarily free-living ameboflagellates of the genus Naegleria and possibly other amebae, is an acute, rapidly progressive infection, apparently acquired while swimming or diving in fresh-water lakes or pools.

It is characterized by fever, headache, mental confusion and coma, and death frequently occurs within a few days of onset. Eosinophilic meningoencephalitis, seen in various parts of the Pacific area in recent years, is believed, on strong epidemiologic grounds, to be symptomatic of infection with Angiostrongylus cantonensis and thus a form of larva migrans infection. It is characterized by fever, headache, stiff neck, and increased cells (mainly eosinophils) in the spinal fluid. It is generally a mild and self-limited infection.

Microcephalus

Monocytosis

A relative or absolute monocytosis is a frequent finding in both protozoal and helminthic infections.

Myocarditis

Myocardial infection is characteristic of Chagas' disease and is seen in about 50 per cent of chronic cases. Cardiac failure may come on slowly, although in infants it tends to occur in the early acute stage. There may be pericardial effusion. Congestive heart failure also has been reported in African trypanosomiasis the probably in the Rhodesian form of the disease. In African typanosomiasis the etiology of the heart failure is not as apparent. Myocarditis, occasionally severe enough to cause death, has been reported. inntrichinosis.

It is the result of migration of the larvae through the myocardium, in which they do not encyst. Myocarditis also may be seen in acute toxopla3mosis in both infants and adults, the result of invasion of the myocardium.

Myositis

Although myositis is a nonspecific symptom of many febrile illnesses, severe myositis is characteristic of the stage of larval migration in trichinoses. If accompanied by circumorbital edema, eosinophilia and a history of consumption of improperly cooked pork, the diagnosis may be made with some certainty.

Myositis, usually involving a single muscle group, may also occur in Sarcocystis infection.

Neurologic symptoms

Neurologic symptoms in trypanosomiasis, malaria and amebic and eosinophilic meningoencephalitis are discussed under Meningoencephalitis. Variable neurologic symptoms may occur in schistosomiasis when eggs carried by the bloodstream to the central nervous system lodge there and provoke a granulomatous reaction.

Neurologic and other symptoms caused by embolization of eggs are more common in Schistosoma japonicum infection than in the other two species, while in S. mansoni and S. haematobium, eggs are found more frequently in the spinal cord than in the brain, perhaps because of ectopic wanderings of the adult worms.

In S. japonicum infection, there may be severe neurologic symptoms, including coma and paresis, during the incubation period or first few weeks after infection. Transitory neurologic symptoms of a variable nature may be caused by the migration of ascarid and trichina larvae in the central nervous system; hemiplegia and focal epileptic attacks have been reported in trichinosis.

Hydatid, coenurus and cysticercus cysts may develop within the central nervous system, where they may produce symptoms related to a space-occupying lesion or, if within the ventricular system, internal hydrocephalus.

Cysticercus larvae may give rise to epileptiform seizures, as may Sparganum proliferum and adults of Paragonimus westermani that have gone astray.

Nodules, subcutaneous. Lipoma-like subcutaneous nodules include onchocercomas (q.v.) and cysticercus and coenurus larvae. The cysticercus larva of Taenia solium develops most frequently in the subcutaneous tissues, where it forms nodules 0.5 to 3.0 centimeters in diameter.

In almost half the recorded human cases of coenurus infection, the larvae have been found in the subcutaneous tissues; others have been recorded from the brain, spinal cord and eye. Echinococcus cysts also may be found in the subcutaneous tissues.

Spargana also form subcutaneous nodules, somewhat elongate and several centimeters in length, which may resemble lipomas, but they may move through the subcutaneous tissues at irregular intervals and often cause pain.

Sparganum proliferum may develop as branched or multiple nodules and invade the viscera. (See also Edema for a discussion of ocular sparganosis).

Larvae of the botfly Hypoderma migrate through the subcutaneous tissues, finally coming to rest beneath the skin, where they produce elongate nodules several centimeters in length.

Considerable pain may accompany migration, but the resting nodule is seldom painful or pruritic. The human botfly, Dermatobia hominis, burrows into the skin and subcutaneous tissues, producing an intensely pruritic papular lesion, which has the appearance of a furuncle.

There is a small central opening, from which comes a serous exudate and through which the posterior end of the larva may protrude from time to time. Secondary infection is common.

Obstruction, intestinal

Ascaris, especially in children, may produce complete intestinal obstruction, with accompanying abdominal pain, vomiting, distention and hyperperistalsis. Partial or complete intestinal obstruction may also characterize infection by Angiostrongylus costaricensis.

Ocular Symptoms

Onchocercoma

Adult worms of Onchocerca voleulus lie in coiled masses beneath the skin, completely enclosed in a fibrous tissue capsule. They are from a few millimeters to several centimeters in diameter, generally freely movable, and resemble lipomas.

In Mexico and Guatemala they frequently occur beneath the patient's scalp; in Africa most of them occur on other parts of the patient's body.

Orchids

Filarial orchitis may occur early in the disease and at times in the absence of lymphangitis or fever; repeated attacks lead to hydrocele.

Pain

Abdominal pain, generally vague or ill-defined, is said to accompany many of the intestinal parasitic infections. The presence or absence of such tenuous pains is of no value from a diagnostic standpoint. Epigastric pain, sometimes with nausea and vomiting, may be seen in giardiasis, trichinosis and strongyloidiasis; it is related to the duodenitis and jejunitis provoked by these infections.

Moderate to severe abdominal pain is seen in acute amebic colitis; it may be confined to the cecal area or may be generalized. Angiostrongylus costaricensis may give rise to similar symptoms. In ascariasis, severe pain may signal intestinal obstruction (q.v.), perforation and peritonitis (q.v) or bile duct blockage.

Muscle pain in trichinosis is discussed under Myositis, and the delayed pain sensation seen in African trypanosomiasis under the heading of Kerandel's Sign.

Peritonitis

Penetration of Ascaris through the wall of the intestine usually leads to generalized peritonitis, with pain, marked distention, generalized abdominal tenderness, and free air under the diaphragm, detectable by X-ray. In severe amebic dysentery, ulcers may erode through the wall of the intestine and cause peritonitis.

Pneumonitis

Pneumonitis is characteristic of severe Ascaris infection and is caused when the worm larvae break out of the capilliaries into the alveoli, whence they are coughed up to be swallowed, beginning the intestinal phase of the disease.

Symptoms and signs are first noted one to five days after the eggs are ingested and consist of cough, fever, respiratory distress and the physical and X-ray signs of a bronchopneumonia; in severe cases there may be complete consolidation of one or more lobes.

The pneumonitis usually clears within a week or two; it may be accompanied by high eosinophilia and an urticarial rash. Similar signs and symptoms may accompany the corresponding stage in strongyloides infection, although the pneumonitis is generally not so severe.

In hookworm infection there is seldom a clear-cut pneumonitis at this stage, but a cough is frequently present. In schistosomiasis there may likewise be a transitory cough, sometimes with hemoptysis and frequently with dyspnea, during the stage of migration through the lungs. Pneumocystis carinii causes an interstitial plasma cell pneumonia, mainly in newborn and young children.

Some cases have been reported in adults. The X-ray picture is that of bronchopneumonia. Pneumonitis may be a part of acute toxoplasmosis in infants during the neonatal period, and more rarely in adults.

Atelectatic pneumonitis may be seen in amebic abscess, the result of pressure from the elevated right diaghragm the abscess may erode through the diaphragm to produce a right lower lobe infection, infrequently an abscess may develop primarily in the lung.

If there is erosion into a bronchus, there may be expectoration of abscess material, a light reddishbrown,. or "anchovy paste," colour.

Proteiunria

In falciparum malaria, proteinuria, with hyaline and granular casts in the urine, is common. Rarely there maybe oliguria or anuria, usually accompanying an attack of blackwater fever (q.v.). The nephrotic syndrome, with proteinuria, issometimes seen in quartan malaria.

Pruritus ani

The nocturnal pruritus that accompanies pin-worm infection varies considerably in degree, probably depending upon hypersensitivity of the host. In some persons there is no noticeable itching, whereas in others it may be sufficiently severe to interfere with rest. Anal pruritus may be associated with active migration of gravid proglottids of Taenia saginata, out of the anus.

Pulmonary symptoms, chronic

In all three types of schistosomiasis, but especially in S. haematobium infections, ova may be carried to the lungs, where pseudotubercle. formation around them may produce a radiological picture suggestive of miliary tuberculosis, and increasing fibrosis may lead to cor pulmonale.

Paragonimiasis is characterized by chronic cough, the production of thick blood-specked sputum or sometimes frank hemoptysis, and increasing dyspnea. X-rays may show patchy infiltrates, rounded shadows suggestive of coin lesions, calcifications and pleural thickening or effusion.

In pulmonary echinococcosis, cough is usually the first symptom. There may be increasing dyspnea; with erosion of blood vessels there will be hemoptysis, and with obstruction there results secondary bacterial infection and fever. If the cyst ruptures into a bronchus, the contents may be coughed up, or the patient becomes asphyxiated.

Rash

An allergic urticarial rash or hives (q.v.) is often seen in the early stages of schistosome infection and in ascariasis. A macular or maculopapular eruption may occur early in the course of a trichina infection, and one of the variants of acute toxoplasmosis is a typhus-like fever, with a macular rash, prostration, and sometimes stupor and cardiac decompensation.

During attacks of fever in the early stages of African trypanosomiasis there may be an irregular blotchy rash, often annular in appearance. The individual patches may be several inches across; they tend to fade in a few hours, and reappear at irregular intervals.

Retinochoroiditis

Roman's sign

Unilateral palpebral edema, involving both upper and lower eyelids, appears only in the course of an infection with T. cruzi. The edema is hard and non-pitting; it may remain confined to the eyelids or may spread down to -involve the cheek and neck. It may subside promptly or persist for weeks or month.

Shock

When shock complicates falciparum malaria, the patient is pale, with a cold and clammy skin, thin fast pulse, and low blood pressure. There is often acute abdominal pain, vomiting and diarrhea.

The etiology may be one of primary adrenal failure, through parasite-induced ischemia or infarction or it may be secondary to reduced blood volume and blood pressure caused by widespread vascular injury. Rupture of an echinococcus cyst may lead to anaphylatic shock.

Splenomegaly

As part of the generalized lymphoid hyperplasia in both African and American trypanosomiasis, splenomegaly may be observed. In kala-azar the spleen is said to enlarge downward about an inch per month, and it may extend into the pelvis. It is non-tender and reverts to normal size after effective therapy.

The spleen enlarges during an acute attack of malaria and is usually palpable within two weeks after onset. Between attacks it may regress in size, and in adults it may become fibrotic and smaller than normal. In children, repeated attacks may lead to great enlargement of the organ, which may reach the pelvis.

The "splenic index" as a guide to endemicity of malaria, obtained by examination of a population for evidence of enlarged spleens, obviously must be derived only through examination of children. The spleen ii usually tender during an acute attack of malaria, and tenderness may be apparent before the organ can be palpated. Splenic infraction or rupture occurs rarely.

In Schistosoma mansoni and S. japonicum infections, splenomegaly is secondary to hepatic fibrosis brought about by egg deposition in the liver, and portal hypertension.

Splinter hemorrhages

Sometimes occurring during the stage of active larval migration in trichinosis, these hemorrhages are a sign of vascular injury.

Steatorrhea

Malabsorption, characterized by the presence of fat in the stool, is seen in certain parasitic infections. The most common of these is giardiasis, which may make its presence known by flatulence and the production of foulsmelling fatty stools. The less common and self limited Isospora belli infections are also characterized by seatorrhea,-as are those caused by Capillaria philippinensis.

Tachycardia

A fast pulse is noted' early in both African and American trypanosomiasis. In Chagas' disease it persists into the subacute and chronic stages, where it may be associated with heart block, Stokes-Adams syndroma and fibrillation:

Ulcers, cutaneous

In leishmanial and trypanosomal diseases there is a primary multiplication at the site of infection. In Leishmania tropica-complex infections there is first a papule at the site of infection, which gradually transforms into a shallow ulcer with raised edges.

The Chiclero ulcer of Southern Mexico and Central America is similar to oriental sore, except when it occurs on the eat, where it may erode the pinna. L. braziliensis first produces cutaneous ulcerations, which may, through extension or metastasis, come to involve the nasal mucosa, the soft and the hard palate, the nasal septum, the pharynx and the larynx.

In blacks, granulomatous rather than ulcerative lesions are generally seen. In African sleeping sickness there may be a firm tender raised lesion, up to *3* cm. or 'more in diameter, at the site of infection. This "trypanosomal chancre" is painful or pruritic, but like the chagoma (q.v.) it does not apparently ulcerate unless secondarily infected. Ulcerative cutaneous lesions rarely are seen in amebiasis, either in the perianal region or in the skin surrounding fistulas or surgical drainage incisions from hepatic obscesses.

A rounded ulcer, 2 mm. to several centimeters in diameter, marks the place at which the guinea worm discharge its larvae. In the centre of the ulcer, a portion of the worm may be visible. There is often secondary infection, and a painful localized reaction may persist until discharge of the larvae is complete.

Urethritis

Trichomonas vaginalis has been found in up to one third of cases of "nonspecific" urethritis in the male.

Vaginitis

A prolific, irritating, green or yellowish, thin discharge is seen in Trichomonas vaginalis infection; the vagina may be diffusely,-congested, or punctuate hemorrhagic spotsmay be seen.

The organisms may be present in asymptomaticindividuals. Pinworms may migrate from the angus and enter the vagina, where they produce a temporary, intense pruritus in some children.

Visual difficulties

Associated with parasitic disease include circumorbital edema (q.v.), conjunctivitis (q.v.) and chorioreti nitis (q.v.). Ascarid larvae (both those of Ascaris lumbricoides. and Toxocara) may invade the eye, producing iritis or other symptoms.

Patients infected with Onchocerca actually may beaware of the. intraocular movement of the microfilariae, and lesions of the anterior chamber, iris, ciliary body, choroid, and retina, developing-in this condition, may lead to diminution of vision or total blindness. Cysticercus and coenurus larvaemay develop within the eye. Ophthalmomysiasis may occur.

Winterbottom's Sign

X-ray evidence of parasitic disease

Amebiasis: Amebic granulomas of the large bowel simulate carcinoma in barium. enema studies. Cecal amebiasis tends to produce a funnelshaped deformity of that portion of the bowel as seen in barium enema studies. In amebic abscess of the liver there may be elevation of the right diaphragm and sometimes. right lower lobe pneumonitis.

Intravenous sodium diatrizoate (Hypaque) infusion and tomography of the liver may show the wall of the amebic abscess. Giardiasis: Evidence of intestinal malabsorption. Toxoplasmosis: Intracerebral calcifications. Pneumocystosis: Pneumonitis, typically sparing lateralmargins of the bases. Dracunculiasis, filariasis and loiasis: Calcified worms may be seen in the tissues.

Ascariasis: Pneumonitis. Adult worms may be seen as cylindrical empty spaces in the barium-filled bowel in a small bowel series. Strongyloidiasis and hookworm infection: Pneumonitis. Loss ofmucosal markings and a tubular deformity of the duodenum and jejunum may be seen in small bowel studies on patients withh strongyloidiasis.

Cysticercosis: Calcified cysts in the subcutaneous tissues, muscles, brain. Echinococcosis: Well-defined, rounded masses may be seen in the lung parenchyma; sometimes a fluid level is visible within them. Hepatic cysts are visible only if calcification of the wall has taken place. Sometimes calcified daughter cysts are seen.

(Hepatic photoscanning with the use of radioactive isotopes will reveal non-calcified cysts as well.) Hydatid cysts of bone produce extensive intramedullary erosion, demonstrable by X-ray. Paragonimiasis: Patchy infiltrates or rounded densities in the parenchyma, pleural thickening, or fluid.

Schistosomiasis: Pulmonary fibrosis, or a picture suggestive of miliary tuberculosis. Corpulmonale with dilatation of the pulmonary artery and its main branches, right ventricular hypertrophy. S. haematobium infections: Calcification in the wall of the bladder, hydronephrosis, hydroureter.

10

Ecological Niches

In this chapter a close look at species packing in parasite communities will be undertaken in an attempt to resolve the divergence of opinion. Attention is limited to the literature on helminth parasites of vertebrates because it illustrates the full range of types of coexistence seen in any taxon and it contains some of the most celebrated examples of coexistence of parasites, some incredibly rich communities within one organ system, excellent experimental work revaling the fundamental and realized niches of parasities and is deserving of much more attention by ecologists.

In the review by Schoener (1974) on resource partitioning in ecological communities covering 80 studies, none on helminths is included. Some studies are summarized in Table elsewhere in this chapter with a statemen t on the predominant type of coexistence in the community. The kind of evidence provided in the studies is also listed with a check indicating quantitiative data or experimental manipulation.

The general pattern of coexistence is clear. The vast majority of cases indicates a predominantly non-interactive niche occupation (no substantial shift from fundamental to realized niche in presence of another species), either in nonover-lapping niches or in strongly overlapping niches.

In the latter case all species occur in the alimentary canal and are usually members of very rich helminth faunas. Although studies have not gone far in determining how these species coexist while overlapping so broadly along the length of the alimentary canal, it is clear that other niche dimensions must be considered. Schad found in the genus Tachygonetria in the tortoise gut that some species occur near the gut mucosa while other can be found throughout the gut lumen. Some species feed on large particle sizes, others specialize on bacteria, and others imbibe purely liquid food.

Given the great physico-chemical diversity of the gut, many other parameters may be involved in the niche diversification in these gut parasites. Thus the group of studies showing predominantly overlapping but noninteractive niche occupation illustrate overlap only on the most obvious dimension of gut length, which has been the most, commonly studied.

Since niche divergence on other gradients is evident, this group of studies should be classed with the other non-interactive examples making 18 studies out of the total of this type. In the nonoverlapping class some studies have been placed that show seemingly insignificant amounts of overlap (30 per cent or less), again making the distinction an arbitrary one.

Holmes (1973) also found many examples of what he called. selective site segregation of niches where niche occupation was uninfluenced, by the presence of other parasite species. As in Table elsewhere in this chapter he supplied many examples of niche segregation of this type and only few where coexistence involved reduced realized niches in the presence of competitors, i.e., interactive site segregation.

He concluded that the majority of parasite communities are mature because the residents have evolved discrete niches without competition. That is, communities have reached the evolutionary phase in Wilson's (1969) concept of community development and have presumably passed the earlier noninteractive, interactive, and assortative phases.

The fact that there are two phases, in community develop-ment with predominantly noninteractive niche occupation, and these at the two extremes of community . age,, should make us pause before reaching conclusions from the observation that many parasite communities are predominantly noninteractive.

The concepts stressed in this monograph favour the conclusion that parasite communities are in an early stage of development. Noninteractive niche exploitation is common because resources remain unutilized since species have not evolved to use them.

Communities are largely in the noninteractive. and interactive phases of development and seldom have the assortative and evolutionary phases been reached. Each species is specialized to a narrow range of resources because of coevolutionary demands other than competition. A closer look- at the helminth com-munity literature, which follows in the next two sections of this chapter, justifies the latter conclusion in my opioion.

Of course, competition can be observed among helminth gut parasites, but I contend that it affects a minority of species. The influence of immune responses may also prove to be important, but, again, evidence is wanting that large numbers of species interact via the host's immune system.

Crompton (1973) reviewed the literature on 252 species of helminth in the alimentary canal of vertebrates, but he cited no clear examples of interspecific interaction through immunological responses and only four examples of niche shifts through interspecific competition.

But eight examples were provided for the extension of niche breadth in response to intraspecific competition as parasite populations. increased in a host, suggesting that interspecific constraints on niche expansion were absent.

Particularly in the gut, but perhaps elsewhere also, resources may be replenished by a host so rapidly that they are not limiting except at the most extreme parasite densities (when the host is likely to die with the consequent death of the parasites).

NONINTERACTIVE COEXISTENCE

There is little evidence to suggest that competition has been an organizing force in the studies indicating nonoverlapping, non-interactive coexistence of parasites. In mink pulmonary tissues, Stockdale (1970) reports three species of metastrongyle nematode each with a very distinct niche Perostrongylus psidhami in alveolar ductsand terminal - and respiratory bronchioles; Filaroides marits in peribronchial connective tissue; Crenosoma hermani in bronchi. Stockdale notes that pulmonary tissues provide a diverse array of resources available to nematodes: alveoli and alveolar ducts, terminal and respiratory bronchioles, bronchi, lamina propria of the bronchial bifurcation, peribronchial connective tissue and pulmonary arteries.

In a range of animals all these sites have been colonized but in the mink little more than three of the six sites are utilized. The nematodes are loosely packed, almost twice as many species could coexist in the pulmonary community, and it is most unlikely that competition could cause such complete divergence of ecological niches.

Two species of blood flukes in rockfishes had fundamental niches that showed a similarity of 7 per cent and when together this similarity was reduced by only 3 per eent. Indeed, the species could not overlap significantly because they are adapted in fundamentally different ways to lodge in different parts of the vascular system.

Aporocotyle macfarlani is a squat fluke that wedges into the walls of blood vessels, largely in the gill arches. Psettarium sebastodorum is a longer, narrower fluke that loops its body and is so held largely .in the chambers of the heart.

These species have a grossly different body form that preadapted them for coexistence. Divergence of niches once both species had colonized that host was probably miniuscule. Similar examples are described by Llewellyn (1956), Williams (1960), and Uglem and Beck (1972). In the snake Coluber constrictor three species of Kali-cephalus can be found: K. inermis in the anterior part of the esophagus, K. costatus in the duodenum, and K. rectiphilus in the rectum.

Species packing is so loose it could not be created by competitive interaction but rather by the demands for specialization, leaving resources available for other species to colonize. Three species of Apocreadium occupy largely nonoverlapping niches: A. balistis the first third of the intestine, A. uroprocto-ferum the second third, and A. coili the rectum. Had competition been a force in organization we should expect more overlap even to the extent that some species have Hutchinsonian niche differences of only 20 to 30 per cent.

In the literature describing species with largely overlapping niches the evidence for competition commonly acting as an organizing force is also very unimpressive. Schad (1963b) claimed that the pinworm communities in tortoises showed non-overlapping niche occupation with the inference of tight species packing.

But this claim was based on correspondence of relative abundances to Mac-Arthur's (1957) broken stick model that can be derived from very different assumptions and is thus dis-credited as a means of distinguishing organizational influences in a community.

Based on Schad's studies, we could reasonably expect in the tortoise gut a group of species specialized to each of at, least four sections of the gut, each group segregated into those in the lumen and those mostly against the mucosa, and within these subgroups species feeding on large and small particles and liquids.

Even at this moderate scale of specialization 24 species could be expected in the gut whereas Schad, Kuntz, and Wells (1960) found only

10 species of Tachygonetria. Holmes (1973) chose to emphasize the complementary distributions of Atractis actyluris with Mehdiella uncinata and Tachygonetria dentata found by Petter (1966) in tortoise guts.

But of the 14 species of common nematode studied in detail by Petter, A. dactyluris was the only species possibly involved in competitive interactions, and it became dominant only in older tortoises when many oother factors could be changing in the gut.

Of the 43 species of helminth in the scaup alimentary canal, Hair and Holmes (1975:253) concluded that the community is "composed of a chance combination of ecological specialists." Where they claimed to find inierspecfic competition, only a pair of species was involved and the mean overlap between them was only 14 per cent, but in some cases large numbers of each species coexisted over 20 to 30 per cent of the intestine, suggesting that competition was not the mechanism leading to the small mean overlap value.

In one gut Hymenolepis abortiva was abundant but completely overlapped by H. spinocirrosa. For the 13 parasite species in one scaup gut (data for which were given in detail), there was a significant correlation between population size and the number of segments of the gut occupied indicating niche expansion under population pressure unimpeded by other species.

The abundant species were not competitive dominants !as there was no sign of comple-mentary abundances in the 10 scaup guts examined, even between 11. abortiva and H. spinocirrosa (which showed a positive but nonsignificant correlation in abundance). Hair (1975) concluded that the majority of helminth species in the scaup responded individualistically to gradients in the gut, which I interpret as indicating a lack of positive or negative relationships between parasite species.

Chubb (1964) noted no interactions between Echino-rhynchus clavula and any other parasitic helminths in the guts of fish. Thomas (1964) also concluded after a very extensive study of brown trout parasites that competition between parasites occurs only rarely.

In pairwise partial correlations between six helminths over four years and twice a year (165 pairwise comparisons), he found many more positive than negative significant correlations.

In a similar set of correlations involving only the four helminths in the alimentary canal whose distributions in the gut largely overlapped, but with up to three seasonal samples per year (264 pairwise comparison) he found only 14 cases that were significantly and negatively correlated (whereas 13 such cases should be expected by chance) and 12 cases showed significant and positive correlations. Although the three intestinal trematods of the mole show some differences in distribution along the gut, the probability of colonization for each species was so low that they hardly ever interacted.

Less than one per cent of the moles studied had more than one species of the three, and Frankland noted that the distribution of each species, even within an area where it occurs, is very patchy and local. He also found that the presence of these flukes had no effect on the other intestinal helminth parasites of the host.

INTERACTIVE COEXISTENCE

Interactive niche occupation is defined as the substantial shift by one species from ffundamental to ;realized niche in. the presence of another species. The cases in 11.1 involving inter-active coexistence concern relatively few species: three studies on pairs of species and one study reporting co-existence of three species of grill parasite but their exclusion by a fourth.

Holmes (1973) provides other example, particularly of competitive exclusion, but the examples in the table are snfficient to illustrate the types of interactive coexistence to be found and the questions raised by such studies.

Three of the four studies showing interactive coexistence involve acarithocephalans. In these parasites all nutrients are absorbed through the integument, as in tape-worms, and carbohydrate . shortage can be severely limiting.

Therefore, these species may be particularly susceptible to exploitative competition for soluble nutrients. The cases studied by Chappell and Holmes are particularly convincing examples of competition. In the former case the fundamental niches of the two parasites in stickleback showed a percentage similarity (PS) of 46 per cent, but when occurring together their realized niches had PS=17 per cent.

In the rat, the two parasites had Lfundamental niches, that were 64 per cent similar, but in concurrent infections the realized niches were only 10 per cent similar. The excellent experimental studies of Holmes also raise some important questions. The same pair of parasites in rat showed strong niche shifts, particularly by Hymenolepis diminuta; but in hamster there was no indication of competition.

Proportional similarities of distributions along the gut were 45 per cent in single infestations and 46 per cent in con-current attacks. Also in rat H. diminuta had the broader niche on the gut-length dimension while in hamster M. dubius had the broader niche.

It becomes necessary in order to understand coexistence of parasites and their community organization fully to study the full range of coexisting hosts since parasite species and species pairs behave differently in each host. Also where host tissues are damaged and/or immune responses triggered, infection may be transient and a rapid succession of species may be expected.

Niche occupation and community development in time may be extremely dynamic. The,dynamic nature :to be-expected in some parasite com-munities is fully realized in the gill parasitic community of carp studied by Paperna (1964). The community is composed of four species of monogenean trematode in the genus Dactylogyrus: D. anchoratus, D. extensus, D. minutus, and D. vastator.

Dactylogyrus extensus and D. anchoratus were the better colonizers because they could be infective throughout the year. Thus if young carp hatched early in the year when water temperatures were cool, they were rapidly colonized by these spccies, and significant numbers began to build up on the gill surfaces.

However, as water temperature increased, D. vastator became infective and colonization was much niore extensive. This species caused gill damage and rapidly made conditions unsuitable for the early colonizers, and they were usually pushed to extinction on the majority of hosts. They survived only 10 to 20= days in the presence of D. vastator.

As the gills became seriously damaged by D. vastator, con-ditions on the host became unsuitable for it, and after a relatively brief tenure of 44 to 45 days per host, the populations, became extinct.

The gills gradually healed and again became available for colonization by the parasities. But a specific immune response to D. vastator eventually developed, the species was eliminated permanently from the community, and the gills were available to the other gill parasites.

They very dynamic, non-equilibrium state of the populations and community are also illustrated in Figure elsewhere in this chapter, where fish length is closely correlated with fish age.

This example contains the important elements of non-equili-brium coexistence within patches identified by Skellam and Hutchinson (1953) and is similar in some respects to the transient competitive displacement observed by Istock (1967). The competitively inferior species are the better colonizers and appear to have a lower reproductive capacity.

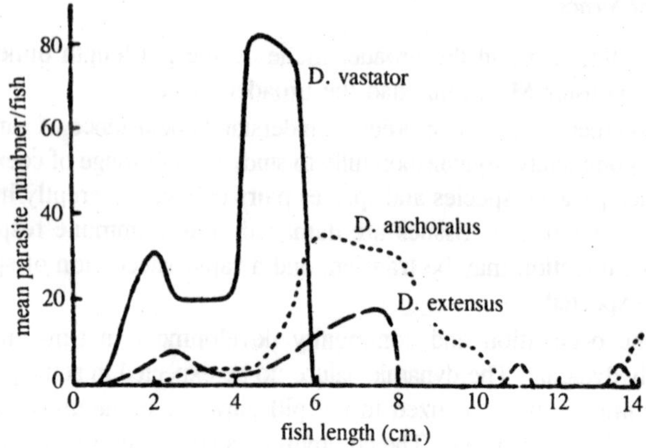

Figure 10.1: Mean number of parasites per fish for the species Dactylo-gyrus vastator, D. anchoratus, and D. extensus in relatign to fish length.

New sites are continually becoming available for colonization. Sites rapidly become unsuitable for the competitive dominant, so its competi-tive edge is repeatedly lost.

Many other examples in the parasitology literature many fit this scenario of transient competitive interactions, but in the absence of good experimental work interpretation of the mechanisms that produce complementary distributions is impossible. For example.

Cucullanus heterochrous is evenly distributed in the flounder gut from November to May, but from June to October it is found predominantly in the rectum when C. minutus is present in the intestine. As the authors point out, we cannot tell if this is a competitive effect or an age effect on C. heterochrous.

Rohde has made a particularly intensive study on species packing in monogenean ectoparasites of fish. He has repeatedly concluded that many resources remain unexploited, that co-existence is noninteractive, and that "segregation of sympatric species may be due to random selection of niches". His evidence is convincing.

Monogenean flukes usually exist at low population densities, and although there is a latitudinal gradient of increasing diversity toward the tropics, there is no change in host specificity along this gradient or specificity in site selection on a host.

Monogen an species show highly restricted site selection on hosts even when only one species occurs or a host. When several species coexist, niche overlap is frequently minimal or nonexistent. A comparison of niche occupation on temperate versus tropical hosts yielded the conclusion that most micro-habitats utilized by tropical parasites remain empty on fish in cold seas.

The mechanisms that result in such narrow niches on a host, even in the absence of competing species, are not fully understood, but the great topographic diversity on fish, particularly on the gill where many monogenean species live, and the considerable complexities of water flow no doubt demand extreme site specificity.

This seems to be at least as important as site specificity as a mechanism for increasing population density and the probability of cross-fertilization, an explanation favoured by Rohde. Community ecology has been dominated by Gause's principle that species cannot coexist for long if they exploit a very similar set of resources.

The evolutionary pressure exerted by competition has been regarded as the major organizing influence in communities. But for the majority of parasites listed in Table elsewhere in this chapter competition appears to be uncommon in the present and to have played an insignificant role in their evolutionary history. Where competi-tion exists, it may frequently result in non-equilibrium transient competitive displacement, a distruptive influence in community development.

Based on parasities of plants and animals, fully support these generalizations. For such highly specialized organisms as parasites living in complex environments with. steep gradients of resources, even small, randomly generated. differences in physiology, behaviour, and morphology may. result in optimal exploitation of very different sites in a host or very different hosts. Resources available are so diverse it is importable that a new colonist carries a niche exploitation. pattern very similar to a resident species.

11

The Ecology of Desert Plants

The laws of human behaviour are very much in dispute, largely because there are no obvious experimental approaches to them. But animal and plant behaviour can be studied both in nature and in the laboratory, and the science of their ecology should. eventually be helpful in the understanding of human relationships, for the basic laws which govern the interrelations among organisms in general must also underlie human behaviour. Ecology is an extremely complex study.

The desert is an ideal area for research. It is usually unspoiled by the encroachment of civilization. Its plant life is sparse enough to be studied conveniently in detail, and it shows clearly and primitively the effects of the physical factors at play in the environment.

Most important of all, the desert climate is violent: winds sweep over it unchecked, and its temperature and rainfall swing between wide extremes. Rainfall may vary fivefold from year to year. There are so few rainstorms that the effects of individual rains can be measured.

The desert's sharply contrasting conditions can be reproduced in the laboratory for convenient experimental investigation of the germinationand growth of plants. And the desert has an unending lure: for the botanist; in the spring it is a delightful place.

The most extreme desert in the U.S. is Death Valley. "Screened off from the nearest source of water vapour-the Pacific Ocean-by the tall Sierra Nevada, the valley bottom has an average annual rainfall of only 1.35 inches. It has almost no surface water-only a few springs bringing up the scanty runoff from the dry surrounding mountains. Since it is sunk "below sea level, Death Valley has no drainage.

As a basin which holds and collects all the material that may be washed into it from the mountain canyons, it has accumulated salts in its central part. Seen from above, this salt bed glistens like a lake, but a traveler on foot finds it a dry, rough surface, studded by sharp salt pinnacles which crackle and tinkle as they expand or contract in the heat of the day and the cold of the night.

In the salt plain no green plants can grow: there are only bare rocks, gravel and salt. But on the fringes of the plain plant life begins. Here and there are patches of a lush green shrub-the mesquite. With their tender green leaflets, which suggest plenty of water, the plants seem completely out of place.

Actually they do have a considerable source of water, but it is well underground. The mesquite has roots from 30 to 100 feet long, with which it is able to reach and tap underground lenses of fresh water fed by rain percolating down from the mountains.

The mesquite is the only shrub that can reach the water table here with its roots. But a mesquite seedling must send its roots down *30* feet or more through dry sand before it reaches this water.

How, then, does it get established? This is one of the unsolved mysteries of the desert. Most of the mesquite shrubs in Death Valley are probably hundreds of years old. Some are all but buried by dunes of sand, piled around them over the years by the winds that sometime blow with great force through the valley.

There are places where dozens or hundreds of stems protrude from a dune, all probably the offshoots of a single ancient shrub rooted beneath the dune.

Another Death Valley plant endowed with a remarkable .root system is the evergreen creosote bush. It has widereaching roots which can extract water from a large volume of soil.

Thecreosote' bush is spread with amazingly even spacing over the desert; this is especially obvious from an airplane. The spacing. apparently is due to the fact that the roots of the bush excrete toxic substances which kill any seedlings that start near it.

The distance of spacing is correlated with rainfall: the less rainfall, the wider the spacing. This probably means that rain leaches the poisons from the soil so that they do not contaminate as wide an area. We commonly find young creosote bushes along roads in the desert, where the road builders have torn up the old bushes.

During prolonged periods of drought creosote bushes lose their olive-green leaves and retain only small brownish-green leaves. Eventually these also may drop off, and the bush then dies unless rain comes soon afterward.

However, it takes a really long drought to kill off all the creosote bushes is an area, They have suffered severely in some areas of the southern California deserts during the drought of the past five years. Because a killing drought tends to remove them wholesale, there are usually only a few age classes of creosote bushes in an area; each group springs up after a drought or during a period of unusual rainfall.

There are other shrubs that master the harsh conditions of the desert, among them the lush green Peucephyllum, which seems to be able to live without water, and the white-leaved desert holly, which grows in fairly salty soil.

Two prime factors control the abundance and distribution of plants: the number of seeds that germinate, and the growing conditions the seedlings encounter while they seek to establish themselves. In the case of the desert shrubs the main controlling factor is the growing conditions rather than germination,. for though many seedlings may come forth in a rainy season, few survive long enough to become established.

The story is. entirely different for the annual plants in the desert blooms with a magic carpet of colour. In the spring of 1939 and again in 1947 the nonsalty portion of the valley was covered with millions of fragrant, golden-yellow desert sunflowers, spotted here and there with white evening primroses and pink desert five-spots.

The bursts of flowering are not necessarily correlated with the year's rainfall. For instance, the wettest year in Death Valley was 1941, when 4.2 inches of rain fell, but there was no mass flowering that year or the following spring.

If Death Valley is to bloom in the spring, the rain must come at .a certain time-during the preceding November or December. There will be a mass display of spring flowers if November or December has a precipitation of well over one inch: in December of 1938 and in November of 1946 the rainfall was 1.4 inches. Rain of this magnitude in August, September, January or February seems ineffective.

Let us consider these annual plants in greater detail. Probably their most remarkable feature is that they are perfectly normal plants, with no special adaptations to withstand drought. Yet they are not found outside the desert areas. The reason lies in the peculiar cautiousness of their seeds. In dry years the seeds lie dormant.

This itself is not at all amazing; what is remarkable is that they refuse to germinate even after a rain unless the rainfall is at least half an inch, and preferably an inch or two. Since the upper inch of soil, where all the viable seeds lie, is as wet after a rain of a tenth of an inch as after one or two inches, their discrimination seems hard to explain. How can a completely dormant seed measure the rainfall?

That it actually does so can easily be verified in the laboratory. If seed-containing desert soil is spread on pure. sand and wet with a rain sprinkler, the seeds will not germinate until the equivalent of one inch of rain has fallen on them.

Further'more, the water must come from above; no germination takes place in a container where water only soaks up from below. Of course this sounds highly implausible-how can the direction from which the water molecules approrch make any difference to the seed? The answer seems to be that water ;leaching down through the soil dissolves seed inhabitors.

Many seeds have water-soluble germination inhibitors in their covering. They cannot germinate until the inhabitors are removed. This can be done by leaching them in a slow stream of water percolating through the soil, which is what happens during a rainstorm.

Water soaking up in the coil from below of course has no leaching action. Some seeds refuse to germinate when the soil contains any appreciable amount of salt. A heavy rain, leaching out the salts, permits them to sprout. Other seeds, including those of many grasses, delay germination for a few ways after a rain and then sprout if the soil is still moist-which means that the rain probably was fairly heavy.

Still other seeds have inhabitors that can be removed only by the action of bacteria, which requires prolonged moisture. Many seeds preserve their dormancy until they have been wet by a series of rains. In the washes (dry rivers) of the desert we find a completely different vegetation with different germination requirements.

The seeds of many shrubs that grow exclusively in washes (paloverde, ironwood, the smoke tree) have coats so hard that only a strong force can crack them. Seeds of the paloverde can be left in water for a year without a sign of germination; but the embryo grows out within a day if the seed coat is opened mechanically.

In nature such seeds are opened by the grinding action of sand and gravel. A few days after a cloudburst has dragged mud and gravel over the bottom of a wash, the bottom is covered with seedlings. It is easy to show that this germination is due to the grinding action of the mudflow: for instance, seedlings of the smoke tree spring up not under the parent shrub itself but about 150 to 300 feet downstream.

That seems to be the critical distance: seeds deposited closer to the shrub have not been ground enough to open, and those farther downstream have been pulverized. Smoke-tree seedlings form about three leaves, then stop their above-ground growth until their roots have penetrated deep enough to provide an adequate supply of moisture for the plant.

Thereafter the roots grow about five times as fast as the shoots. Few of these seedlings die of drought, but a flood will destroy most of them; only the oldest and biggest shrubs resist the terrific onslaught of rocks, gravel, sand and mud streaming down the wash.

The ability of the smoke tree to make the most of the available moisture was demonstrated by the following experiment. Cracked smoke-tree seeds were sown on top of an eightfoot-high cylinder containing sand moistened with a nutrient solution. Rain water was then sprinkled on them for a short time.

Six seeds germinated, and five of the plants survived and have grown for 18 months in a high temperature with only a single watering midway in that period. Indeed, they have grown better than seedlings which were watered daily!

We have studied the control of germination in great detail in our laboratory at the California Institute of Technology. We have learned, for instance, that two successive rains of three tenths of an inch will cause germination provided they are given not longer than 48 hours apart.

Rain in darkness has a different effect from rain during the day. Most amazing is the seeds' specific responses to temperature. When a mixture of raintreated seeds of various annuals is kept in a warm greenhouse, only the summer-germinating plants sprout; the seeds of the winter annuals remain dormant.

When the same seed mixture is kept in a cool place, only the winter annuals germinate. From this it is obvious that the annuals will not germinate unless they can survive temperatures following their germination-and unless there has been enough rain to allow them to complete their life cycle.

Since these desert plants cannot depend on "follow-up" rains in nature, they germinate only if they have enough rain beforehand to give them a reasonable chance for survival. A very small percentage of seeds (less than 1 per cent) germinate after an insufficient rain. Such seedlings almost invariably perish before reaching the flowering stage.

On the other hand, more than 50 per cent of all seedlings than have sprouted after a heavy rain survive, flower. and set seed.

And here we find a remarkable fact: even though, the seedlings come up so thickly that there are several thousand per square yard, a majority of them grow to maturity. Though crowded and competing for water, nutrients and light, they do not kill one another off but merely fail to grow to normal size. In one case 3,000 mature plants were found where an estimated 5,000 seedlings had originally germinated.

The 3,000 belonged to 10 different species. All had remained small, but each had at least one flower and produced at least one seed. This phenomenon is not peculiar to desert plants. In fields of wheat, rice and sugar cane, at spots where seeds happen to have been sown too thickly, all the seedlings grow up together; they may be spindly but they do not die.

It is true that in gardens weeds, often crowd out some of the desirable plants, but usually this happens only because these plants have been sown or planted out of season or in the wrong climate. Under those conditions they cannot complete with the plants fully adapted to the local. growing conditions-plants which we usually call weeds.

We must conclude, then, that all we have read about the ruthless struggle for existence and the "survival of the fittest" in nature is not necessarily true. Among many plants. especially annuals. there is no struggle between individuals for precedence or survival.

Once an annual has germinated, it matures and fulfills its destiny of forming new seed. In other words, after successful germination annual plants are less subject to the process of "natural selection." Very likely this accounts for the fact that so few of the desert annuals seem to show adaptations to the desert environment.

This does not mean that the plants have avoided a solution. but the evolution has operated on their seeds and methods of germination rather than on the characteristics of the grown plants. Selection on the basis of germination has endowed the plants with a remarkable variety of mechanisms for germinating, and at the same time it has made them show to germinate except under conditions insuring their later survival.

The opposite is true of the cultiva·ed plants that man has developed: has selection has favoured the plants that germinate most easily and quickly. This ha given us the wrongperspective on the significance of geraiuiatto.i in plant survival.

We return now to our original theme: Can the ecology of plants in the desert teach us anything about human ecology or human relations?

At least one moral stands out. In the desert, where want and hunger for water are the normal burden of all plants, we find no fierce competition for existence, with the strong crowding out the weak.

On the contrary, the available possessions-space, light, water and food-are shared and shared alike by all. If there is not enough for all to grow tall and strong, then all remain smaller. This factual picture is very different from the time-honored notion that nature's way is cutthroat competition among individuals. Actually competition or warfare as the human species has 'developed it is rare in nature.

Seldom do we find war between groups of individuals of the same species. There are predators, but almost always they prey on a different species; they do not practice cannibalism. The strangler fig in the tropical jungle, which kills other trees to reach the light, is a rare type [see "Strangler Trees," by Theodosius Dobzhansky and Joao MurcaPires; Scientific Ame-ican, January, 19541.

Even in the dense 'forest there is little killing of the small and weak. The forest giants among the trees do not kill the small fry under them. They hold back their development, and they prevent further germination. In a mountain forest in Java it was observed that the small trees living in the shade of the forest giants had not grown after 4.0. years, but they were still alive.

Hundreds of different species of trees, large and small, grow in a tropical: jungle. This diversity of vegetation is one of the jungle's most typical characteristics. Some trees grow faster, taller or wider than others, but these growing characteristics; which we have always considered as useful adaptations in the, struggle for existence, do not really control the trees survival.

If they did, we would find very few species of trees in a jungle, and there would be an evolutionary tendency for these.trees to 'become taller and taller. Actually the tallest trees are found not in jungles but in more open forests in temperate climates; remarkably enough, tropical jungles often have no particularly high or large trees.

All this shows that selection does not work on the basis of growth potential. It works on the ability of plants to grow and survive with very little light. In our minds the struggle for existence is usually associated with a ruthless extermination of the less well adapted by those better adapted-a sort of continuous cold war.

There is no cold war or even aggression in the desert or jungle. Most plants are not equipped with mechanisms to combat others. All plants' grow up together and share whatever light or water or nutrients are available. It is only when the supply of one of these factors becomes critical that competition starts. But it appears likely that in the jungle, as in the desert survival is taken care of by the control of germination. Competition and selection occur during germination, and we can speak of germination control of the plant community-comparable to birth control in human society.

Apparently evolution has already eliminated mostt of, the plant types that are unable to compete successfully. Fast-gros'ing, show-growing or tall plants all have the same chances once. they have germinated.

The struggle for existence is not waged among the well-established plant forms but tends to eliminate new types which germinate at inopportune times, have a decreased ability to photosynthesize or are less frost-resistant. This expiaitisi why so few plants die in the desert from drought or in the jungle from lack of light or in cold climates from frost.

As a general moral we conclude that war as man wages it finds no counterpart in nature, and it has no justification on the basis of evolution or natural selection. If we went to describe the process of control of the plant population in human terms, we should talk about birth control.

12

TERRESTRIAL ECOSYSTEMS

To understand the biosphere, we must examine major biomes and ask not just how *communities* differ but why. Although no single factor defines an environment, *environmental* extremes may *dramatically* limit options. Consider, for example, the earth's poles. These ice-covered regions that the *penguins* and *polar bears* call home are the least hospitable areas of the earth.

They are, cold most of the year because of the pattern of sunlight, water currents, and wind: The brief summers are never warm enough to melt the *accumulated* ice packs. As a result, rooted plant life is impossible. In the north the food web is based on the producers of the Arctic Ocean.

The presence of a continent at the South Pole results in an environment with little life. A well-developed food chain is present only on the edge of the continent. In the arctic north, the land of permanent ice is edged by a *tundra* that develops where more *moderate*, day lengths and increased solar radiation leave the soil bare and soft for a few short months. Conditions permit *terrestrial* food chains to develop.

Large, *nomadic animals*, such as *reindeer* and *caribou*, *graze* on the low, hardy vegetation but must range widely to find enough food. *Predatory* wolves and foxes follow the great herds or hunt lemmings and other small rodents that bottrow in the ground. Although tundra soil is frozen much of the time, sunlight thaws the surface each spring.

Suddenly plants burst into flower as the *desolation* of the dark, *snowy winter* is broken by the long, warm days of arctic summer. Black flies, mosquitoes, and other insects emerge in great swarms. Migratory waterfowl, shore birds, and song birds arrive from thousands of miles away to nest and feed on hordes of insects from *temporary ponds* and *thawing rivers*.

Father south, cold is not so pervading here the land form :and rainfall becvnte important variables. As a result, the earth is blanketed with biomes like a giant patchwork quilt. *Forests*, *grasslands*, and *deserts* are *scattered* about.

No two are alike, and of course, none remains untouched by human hands. Some we have only exploited. Others we have manipulated beyond all recognition. The story is at the same time fascinating, inspiring, .and sad.

TEMPERATE DECIDUOUS FORESTS

European colonists found most of the eastern seaboard of North America covered with deciduous trees-trees that shed their broad leaves in the fall. Similar forests once blanketed most of Europe, the temperate coasts of Asia, and smaller areas of Australia and South America.

The Plant Community

Mature deciduous forests often contain dozens of tree species, but in any given area one or two kinds of oak, hickory, chestnut, maple, basswood, buckeye, or beech are common enough to give the forest their name. Big trees dominate the community by providing most of the food supply and by modifying the physical environment through shade and windbreak action.

The largest trees are widely spaced, but the forest includes individuals 'of all ages. Such a forest is a stable community that can xnain'tain itself through continued reproduction. Under the trees of a deciduous *forest*, *shrubs* and *herbaceous* (nonwoody) plants are scattered about, but few are abundant except in clearings.

The density of the leafy canopy overhead and the time each year that the canopy is present regulate growth of understory (below the canopy) plants. Many of these are small herbs or "*spring flowers*" that grow rapidly as days lengthen.

They reproduce and carry out much of their photosysnthesis before the tree leaves open and reduce the sunlight available on the forest floor. Soils of some deciduous temperate forests are brown and rich-looking, but most of the available minerals cycle. through the plants each year. Only a small portion of the minerals absorbed are retained in the wood of the tree. The remainder returns to the ground as twig and leaf litter. Not all the returned materials can be reused the following year, because decomposition takes a long time.

Of the minerals released from the litter, some invariably leach away in rainwater. Humus from decomposing leaves and twigs helps hold both water and minerals. Temperate deciduous forests are highly productive, and they support a large number of organisms, as suggested by Table elsewhere in this chapter. Such forests are also quite diverse.

An often overlooked part of the community lives in the litter on the forest floor. Much of the forest enters this decomposer food chain yearly. Litter decomposition involves the activity of multitudes of tiny animals and microorganisms. Insects such as springtails and other near-microscopic arthropods eat dead leaves.

These primary consumers absorb less than 10 per cent of the nutrients in the litter. However, as a result of their digestive process, the remains that become feces are easily attacked by bacteria and fungi. Animals not only consume and alter litter they also mix it into the soil. Earthwarms are among the most active litter mixers. The carnivores that eat the litter feeders also stir litter and mix it into the soil as they endlessly seek their prey.

Adaptation to Climate

Temperate deciduous forest have moderate temperatures and rainfall (about 70-100 cm or 28-40 in./yr) but are characteristically subject to forest. Shedding leaves in the fall protects the trees against cold damage. Otherwise the large leaf surface that favours transpiration and photosynthesis during the warm season would allow heavy evaporation and severe water loss during the winter.

You will recall that the absorption of water by roots relies on diffusion, as well as on energy-consuming activities of root cells. Both are slowed by cold, and of course, frozen soil yields no water. Cold weather can dehydratc plants more than hot weather, especially when it is combined with strong winds.

Furthermore, leaves are difficult to protect against freezing. Deciduous trees have evolved an effective -strategy to prevent damage from winter cold. First they concentrate sugars and other organic compounds from their leaves into roots and stems.

Here these large molecules lower the freezing point of cell fluids and prevent formation of ice crystals that could rupture cells. Then the trees simply shed their leaves. Leaf fall is a preprogrammed process coded into the genetic structure of the plant and only slightly affected by the weather any particular year.

In response to a decrease in auxins, an abscission (cutting off) layer forms where the leaf stalk joins the stem, and the cement between the cells in that area softens. In the absence of strong intercellular cements, the short cells of the abscission layer separate, permitting the leaf to drop off or blow away in a gentle breeze.

The colour changes that foretell leaf drop in deciduous forests result from cessation of chlorophyll formation. Because chlorophyll breaks down spontaneously in light, leaves remain .green only through continued synthesis of chlorophyll.

With the coming of fall, chlorophyll manufacture ceases, and this green pigment gradually bleaches in sunlight. In the absence of chlorophyll we see yellow or reddish pigments, mainly carotenoids that aid in light absorption for photosynthesis. Another source of red colour results from interruption of phloem by the developing abscission layer. This causes sugars to accumulate in the leaves, where some are converted into reddish compounds.

Community Succession in Deciduous Forests

When the vegetation in an area is destroyed, it is usually replaced. Often the new vegetation is different from what was. dertroyed.. And in most cases, this new vegetation is gradually replaced with another and then another.

The sequence for any particular area is always the same. Eventually the vegetation becomes stabilized. This permanent, stable vegetation is said tobe the climax vegetation for that particular region. The replacement of one vegetation, and then another, in a predictable· sequence is known as succession.

The fact that successional stages and climax vegetations differ from place to place results from differences both in the environment and in the history of the vegetation present. Obviously, a particular species can appear in a successional vegetation only if there is a seed source. The seed may be present in the ground or provided by patches of successional vegetation.

Because climax vegetation is susceptible to destruction by fire, flood, or some other catastrophe, no area is long without successional growth. Most human societies continually disrupt natural vegetation. Consequently, the vegetation people see daily is successional rather than climax vegetation. Examples may be found in roadsides fence rows, neglected yards and fields, and cut-over land.

Table 12.1: Average Numbers of Organisms/2.6 km² (1 Square Mile) of Temperate North American Deciduous Forest During the Summer

Plants	
Trees 7.5 cm (3 in.) or more in diameter	75,000
Tree seedlings	78,600
Shrubs	281,000
Soft-stemmed plants	345,000,000
Animals	
Invertebrates (insects, snails, centipedes, millipedes, earthworms, etc.)	2,688,000,000
Pairs of small nesting birds	768
Large predatory birds (owls and hawks)	2 to 5
Mice	240,000
Gray squirrels	1,500
Flying squirrels	1,500
White-tailed deer	40
Wild turkeys	20
Gray fox	3
Black bear	0.5
Mountain lions	0.2

When first visited by Europeans, much of the Americas supported climax vegetations. Because the forests seemed untouched by humans, they came to be known as virgin forests. Usually what the layperson calls a virgin forest the biologist recognizes as the local climax vegetation.

The common ternL second growth most often refers to a successional forest. The factors controlling successional patterns differ from place to place, and they are often poorly understood.

Most studies have involved land that was cleared for agricultural use and then, later, abandoned. Whenever bare ground is left undisturbed. rapidly growing annuals (plants that set seed the first year and then die) may appear.

Although there is a characteristic first-year vegetation in each plant community, irk many places these plants are replaced by introduced annuals that everyone calls "weeds." This is one example of the fact that the history of an area affects the pattern of succession.

During the first year, biennial (two-year) and perennial" (many-year) plants also get started. The second spring these plants draw on reserves, usually stored in their roots, and make such rapid growth that they crowd out the young annuals.

Many biennial species have their early leaves in a whorl close against the ground. These leaves create dense shade around the base of the plant and contribute to suppression of nearby annuals. The dandelion is a biennial with this characterist!e grawth pattern.

Although the details vary for one reason or another, one stage of succession leads to another. The growth habits of annuals and biennials may explain which are dominant the first and second year in certain biom.s, but many other factors can be involved.

Shade tolerance at various stages in the life cycle differs among tree species and may determine the pattern of forest succession.. In much of the deciduous forest biome, pines precede the climax vegetation. Most pines are particularly vulnerable to shading. Lower limbs die as the pine forest grows dense, and pine seedlings never survive in deep forest shade.

The onks, maples. beeches, and other memb.,rs of the climax forest are more shade-tolerant. Small trees become tell and thin in heavy shade but survive and eventually grow taller than the pines. Soon shade from the deciduous species kills the pines.

The seedlings of the deciduous trees also survive in the shade of larger ones, so there are always small trees in the understory. When a tree is blown over, others quickly replace it in the canopy. Thus shade tolerance helps explain why the deciduous trees replace the pines and also why the deciduous trees are the climax vegetation.

For details of succession in a well-studied part of the deciduous forest biome. The series of vegetational stages that follow destruction of a climax vegetation, as we have just described, is often called secondary succession. Note that secondary succession begins when soil is available.

Primary succession is a series of events whereby plants colonize an area of barren rock, such as fresh lava. Presumably this process has occurred at least once wherever there is now vegetation. In many instances primary successions have been associated with the evolution of species and have required millions of years.

However, we see examples of the early stages of primary succession today on rock outcrops. The original colonizing plants are usually lichehs that produce acids. The acids dissolve certain minerals in the rocks.

This process roughens the surface, so the lichens can attach better, and it also makes minerals available for lichen growth.

Over the years, mineral grains released by' the acids and decaying lichen components create a small amount of soil. Other plants, particularly mosses, may grow in the lichen soil and so constitute the second stage of primary succession. Later events depend on the environment and the species present, just as we noted with secondary succession.

What Humans Have Done with Deciduous Woodlands

Most of Europe was once covered with climax deciduous forests except at high elevations and in places where standing water created marshes. The forest canopy was so dense that, it has been said, a squirrel could travel from central Russia to the Atlantic coast without ever touching ground.

On much of the continent the dominant species were oaks, but in some regions elms, beeches, and birches were prominent. Fire and Axe. Many of these forests succumbed to fire or the flint axe. At first people cut trees mainly to obtain building material or fuel, but sometimes trees were felled merely to clear the land.

Initial clearings were often abandoned and recovered by forest, as has been shown by the study of pollen buried in the mud of nearby lakes and bogs. Decreases in pollen of oak ivy (a native understory vine) mark the first clearing of the forest.

This stage is followed by high levels of weed pollen, which indicate a period of cultivation. Later peaks in hazel pollen show when these shrubby trees, took over fields that must have been abandoned. Vast tracts of climax forest still flourished in Roman times.

Throughout that period the forest edge expanded and contracted with wars and other changes in human fortunes. Eventually, the relentless demand for plowed land and forest products doomed the woodlands. As commerce and trade grew, more and more timber was needed for shipbuilding.

Glass and soap manufacture required wood ashes as 'raw materials. The smelting of tin, lead, copper, and iron depended on charcoal made from wood. By the eighteenth century these industries had scalped the forests of England, and the British had turned to digging coal.

The woodlands of western Europe disappeared a short time later. Such drastic alteration of the landscape naturally had far reaching effects. Rains began to wash the soil from the naked land. It is no coincidence that several British seaports filled with silt during the twelfth and thirteenth centuries and were abandoned when their waters were no longer deep enough to float seagoing vessels. Erosion is still evident in parts of England.

Some fields have been farmed with the same hedgerow boundaries ever since the land was cleared. In places where the hedges run across the middle of slopes, the soil is as deep as six feet on the upward side of the hedgerow but so thin on the lower side that rocks lie exposed.

We have no idea how much more soil eroded away entirely and washed into the ocean. Domestic animals prevented regeneration of most British woodlands. A great sheep industry thrived in England during. the Middle Ages grazing was so heavy that the seedlings had no opportunity to grow out of reach of livestock.

As sheeprearing decreased, rabbits, introduced from the Continent, increased dramatically. The rabbits stripped bark from the young trees and did so much damage that few seedlings survived. Conversion to Grassland and Moor. In many deforested areas of Britain the climate, soil, and grazing animals interacted to create a habitat favourable to coarse grasses.

Manure from the sheep and rabbits returned minerals to the soil, established an efficient nutrient cycle, and permitted the formation of a crumbly soil that supported a heavy turf. Not all the deforested British lands went to grass. On some soils the loss of trees raised the underground water level enough to create bogs.

There is a simple explanation for this drastic change. Each day during the leafy season, large trees transpire tremendous volumes of water. Deforestation reduces this drain. on the groundwater.

Therefore cutting certain forest can lead to their replacement with bogs or wet, peaty moors that support low shrubs.

Fate of the Forests

Wherever civilization flourishes, forests are destroyed. The history of other forests differs little from that of European forests. The Chinese began clearing ground for* crops at least four thousand years ago. The Mediterranean forests were already seriously damaged by Plato's times.

As a rule, few forests remain where civilization has long thrived. Although we must infer much of the history of Eurasian vegetation, we know a great deal about what happened in North America. Along the East Coast, the abundance of land and the need for a lightweight crop the could be traded in Europe promoted slash-and-burn tobacco farming. Not only did cutting and burning the trees clear the land, but it provided ashes that contained sufficient minerals to support a few crops of tobacco.

However, these minerals were soon lost from American soil. The mineral-rich tobacco leaves were shipped to Europe and converted again to ashes, this time in foreign. pipes. The broken nutrient cycles and rapid erosion quickly ruined the tobacco plantations.

Whenever that happened, the owners merely moved westward and cut another area. In this way the forests around Chesapeake Bay were destroyed before the American Revolution. So much soil washed into streams and rivers and settled into the bay that the shorelinewe know is quite different from the one the early settlers found.

Wherever the tobacco fields, were abandoned, the vegetation began to regenerate. Probably some fields in Virginia and. nearby states have been cleared three or four times over as many centuries. A few bear climax vegetation today, but because of the chestnut blight, we have not a single forest just like those the first planters cut down.

Chestnut blight is a fungus introduced into New York early in this century on disease-resistant Chinese chestnuts. Soon the blight swept through the eastern part of the United States leaving great stands of dead trees. Some old chastnuts still have live roots that send up new shoots, but there are no new trees, because the blight is lethal to sprouts.

CONIFEROUS FORESTS

The conifers are gymnosperms that bear seeds in cones instead of within fruits as do the flowering plants. Familiar conifers include pines, spruces, firs, cedars, and redwoods.

Boreal Forests

A wide band of conifers girdles Eurasia and North America north of the deciduous forests and grasslands. Most of these conifers retain their leaves the year around and shed one set only after the next is in place.

Persistence of the leaves permits conifers to take immediate advantage of good weather, since they are able to begin photosynthesis without waiting to develop new leaves. This is a distinct advantage to ward the poles, where the warm season is short. These conifers also tolerate low temperatures.

One reason is that they have stiff, wax-covered leaves known as "needles." When cold winds blow through the forests, the thick layer of wax retards water loss through evaporation. Of course, the leaves do dehydrate, and they would wilt if they were not rigid. Thus the stiffness of the needles, due to tissues with exceedingly thick cell walls, prevents damage that would otherwise be caused by wilting.

The leaf structure of conifers clearly suits them to subarctic regions, where winter winds sweep across the landscape. Coniferous communities have fewer species than do deciduous forests. One reason is that the ever-present shade, of the year-round canopy restricts photosynthesis by understory plants.

As a result, the ground is nearly bare except for a deep carpet of slowly decomposing needles. Slow decomposition coupled with leaching of the soil by acids from the needle litter results in low fertility. Conifers generally have root fungi, known as mycorrhizae, which aid in accumulation of minerals.

Trees without these symbiotic partners are at a disadvantage. A boreal forest usually consists of one species of high latitudes. The major differences are in the length of the day and the intensity of sunlight. Where mountains are at temperate latitudes, organisms experience a day length typical of the tem-, perate zone.

But because mountains stand above much of theearth's atmosphare, the sun's radiation is more intense here than at lower attitudes. (This results from the fact that the atmosphere absorbs part of the radiation that reaches it.) Yet mountains cool quickly at night because of loss of radiant heat through the thin atmosphere.

This and exposure to winds make high altitudes colder than those in adjacent lowlands. The cool weather of high altitudes creats environments resembling those toward the poles.

Southern Conifers: A Fire Climax

The same adaptations that fit conifers to winter dryness in cold climates suit many to hotter areas, especially where the soil is sandy and the water supply is unstable. In the southeastern United States, pines colonize abandoned fields and form major forests.

Perhaps their initial success depends on mycorrhizae since these soils are usually poor. Left undisturbed, many such pine forests are replaced by oak, hickory, or magnolia. Apparently fire set by lightning or by humans maintains thesepine forests, since they tolerate fire, whereas the broad-leafed trees do not.

The pines have a thin trunk bark through which ' new buds sprout if existing limbs are destroyed. A thick tuft of needles protects the terminal bud of the southern longleaf pine and makes it extremely resistant to fire. As a matter of fact, longleaf pine seedlings seldom survive in the absence of fire, for they are sensitive to crowding and shading.

Only when other vegetation is burned back can the little pines get enough light to grow. If southern pine forests are burned every few years, the fires do little damage to wildlife, because the animals can escape by running through of flying over the low fire line. In fact, occasional burnings of patches of pine forest increase the population of bob-white quail and wild turkeys.

These birds find food and shelter in the successional stages that follow the fires. We are not suggesting that fire is always beneficial even in these forests. In contrast to the low, cool surface fires of frequently burned regions, fires in pine forests that have not burned recently blaze up high and hot.

Over many years without fire, a thick blanket of needles and fallen limbs accumulates on the ground. Once this litter is on fire, it provides so much fuel that the heat is sufficient to ignite the tree-tops and produce ,great crown fires. Such fires destroy the plant community and much of the wildlife.

GRASSLANDS

Most temperate grasslands have long since succumbed to the cow and the plow. Only a few retain the unmodified vegetation of the plains, prairies, steppes, velds, or pampas. But whether they bear, native vegetation or support the highly selected grasses we know as grains, these grasslands supply the bulk of human food.

Cattle and sheep graze on their grasses cattle, hogs, and chickens fatten on corn grown on former grasslands; .and most of our cereals, especially wheat, are produced on soils that once supported native grasses.

Biology of Grasses

All the grasses belong to one large family and share distinctive characteristics that fit them to their environment and make them of particular use to humans. Many people are surprised to learn that grasses are flowering plants. Open grasslands are windy, and it is the wind that pollinates grass flowers.

Among these wind-pollinated plants, natural selection has favoured those that have conserved resources by producing small, petal-less flowers.

Therefore, grasses and some other wind-pollinated species lack the showy petals that other plants use to attract animal pollinators.

A single head of oats or other grass contains numerous flower. Each tiny flower can form a single fruit called a grain, or kernel. The overian tissue of the fruit fuses with the single seed inside in such a way that they become one continuous structure.

Adapted to Withstand Grazing

As grasslands evolved, their :abundant thin leaves offered a bonanza to herbivorous animals. As a result, there evolved a large group of grass-eating mammals, including the ancestors of today's cattle, sheep, and horses. The selective pressures of these grazers promoted evolution of traits that resist grazing damage.

For one thing, grasses store nutrients in their roots. As a result, loss of stems does not substantially reduce their reserves. Another factor is the presence of silica, the substance we know as glass, in grass cell walls. Of course, grazers have evolved excellent grinding teeth. But grasses take their toll.

Tooth wear is so severe that many old herbivores eventually starve to death. The growth pattern of grasses has several distinctive characteristics that many also adapt them to withstand grazing. Grass leaves originate singly at prominent nodes along the stem.

The lower part of each leaf forms a sheath that surrounds the stem for considerable distance before bending sharply outward as a flattened blade. The leaves retain a meristematic growth region at the base of the sheath and another at the base of the blade.

If the blade is cropped back, these meristems resume growth and lengthen the leaf to compensate for lost photosynthetic tissue. Thus grass leaves grow from the base rather than from the tip. You can see this growth pattern in any lawn.

Until time to flower, the grass stem remains short, and the leaves grow upward beyond the tip of the stem. Thus the stem tip is protected from damage as long as possible. Only when it is time to reproduce does the stem elongate between several nodes and the tip stretch skyward. Here the flowers develop where they are exposed to the winds that pollinate them.

Binding the Soil

Grasses bear abundant roots. Most are adventitious roots, which arise not from the primary root formed by the embryo but from the lower nodes of the stem. The sod-forming perennial grasses have extensive stems lying just on top of the soil or in the upper soil layer; these serve .both to hold the soil and to spread the plant.

From rhizomes (underground stems) arise adventitious roots and occasional branches that penetrate to the surface, giving rise to what appear to be new plants. Quackgrass, a garden pest across the northern half of the United States, often reproduces through rhizomes.

Plowing or cultivating disrupts and scatters the quackgrass rhizomes. Each piece with an intact node may form a new plant. Often grasses have stolons, stems that lie on the ground and root at intervals.

Each rooting node may give rise to aerial branches. Rhizomes and fibrous roots constitute over half the mass of a grass plant. Together they form a network penetrating throughout the soil and binding it into a nearly inseparable plant-soil complex known as sod.

Neither wind nor water can erode a healthy sod. Growing roots and rhizomes break the soil repeatedly and contribute to the characteristic crumbly texture of grassland soils. Many of the roots of perennials die each year and are replaced by new roots. Decay of dead roots supplies humus and leaves speces that aerate the soil.

Decaying roots return minerals to the soil, where they are immediately reclaimed by other roots. This process is part of the rich and efficient nutrient cycle of grasslands. Dead stems and leaves provide an extensive ground cover in most grasslands.

Unmowed grasses accumulate as much as 10,000 kg of humus per hectare (about 9000 lb/acre) each year. It takes three of four years for litter components to decompose. Hence the litter forms a deep layer that shades the ground and lessens evaporation due to the wind. The litter also holds rainwater and aids its penetration into the soil.

Because the water soaks in, there is no surface runoff and therefore little. erosion. Except in the most moist grasslands, the rainwater selom soakss deep enough to join the groundwater. Instead, the extensive root system picks up most rainfall while it lies in the upper layer of the soil.

Then the xylem carries the water immediately to the leaves, where it is transpired back into the atmosphere. Because little water percolates down far into grassland soils, minerals are not leached away; instead, they remain near the roots.

Retention of minerals contributes to the richness of grassland soils. This and the crumbly texture produced by the roots make grassland soils excellent for agriculture.

Grassland Communities

The factors that limit forests and permit grasslands to develop are hard to determine. Some biologists maintain that grasslands develop only where there is insufficient rainfall to support trees that could shade out the grasses.

On the other hand, there is both historical and experimental evidence that many grassland edges, such as those between the American prairies and the eastern deciduous forest, were maintained by fire. Where forests and grasslands meet, burning usually favours grasses over trees. Variations in climate and accidents of grazing have resulted in complex and dynamically balanced grassland communities.

Contrary to popular belief, the American prairies were never a uniform sea of grass ranging from the deciduous forests of the East westward to the Rocky Mountains. Mixed in with the grasses there were other herbs, especially members of the aster family and legumes, such as the lupines.

Nitrogen fixation by symbiotic bacteria in the nodules of the legume roots contributes to the fertility of the soil and the vigour of the community. The roots of various species extended to different levels and were best developed in specific regions of the soil. Concentration of roots of one species at a particular level reduces competition between species.

But because each level is populated by roots of some type, resources are fully exploited. The grassland landscape is even more varied along the moist borders of streams, rivers, marshes, lakes, and ponds. Where inland waterway pass through grasslands, groves of trees and shrubs thrive, along with other organisms ordinarily associated with woodland communities.

Grassland Animals

A large and diverse animal community lives in every grassland. The deep soil that covers rocks and the absence of woody vegetation limit aboveground shelter, except where grasslands 'merge with woodland or along rivers and streams.

Thus most small animals depend on the soil for protection. Numerous little mammals burrow beneath the sod. Prairie dogs, rodents related to squirrels, are symbolic of the short grasslands or Great Plains of North America. Stockmen exterminated most of the prairie dogs, believing that these animals competed with livestock for forage.

Undoubtedly the selective grazing of prairie dogs on grasses favoured the growth of other plants. -Pronghorn antelopes, which were once almost as numerous as 'bison and are now few in numbers, relied heavily on the broad-leaved vegetation of prairiė dog "towns."

Elimination of prairie dogs also resulted in near extinction of ·one of its predators; the black-footed ferret. This handsome, weasellike animal hunted in the prairie dog burrows. Because vast numbers of prairie dogs are necessary to support even a tiny breeding population of ferrets, this species is now extremely rare or perhaps extinct except for a few in captivity. Prairie dog burrows and those of gophers, pocket mice, kangaroo rats, and ground squirrels provide shelter for other animals, including, grass-hopper-mice and snakes.

At least one third, the burrowing owl, relies on old rodent burrows for nesting sites. So do cottontail rabbits. Beetles and camel crickets also use burrows; the dung, fungi, and hoarded vegetation afford these insects a ready food supply. Ants are abundant in grassland soils; some species build huge mounds surrounded by a zone stripped clean of all visible life except for the ants themselves.

Animals that dig underground benefit the grasses, because they aerate the soil and mix in humus from the surface. Even those that are underground transients contribute fecal material where it is directly available to the roots. Some animals, such as grasshoppers, are found only aboveground. Nevertheless, they depend on the soil for shelter.

The female grasshopper uses the tip of her abdomen to penetrate deep into the soil and bury her eggs. The adults perish in the rigour of winter, but the species continues because the developing embryos of the next generation lie safely protected in the soil.

A number of nedium-sized animals that live in the surface vegetation face danger from predators. Rapid movement through thick grasses is very difficult, and vision is limited consequently, it is easy for predators to stalk their prey. Escape must be fast and sure; otherwise it comes too late.

Consider how grasshoppers, jackrabbits, and jumping mice meet this challenge. Huge aerial leaps permit such animals to clear the top of the vegetation, get an unimpeded view for a moment, .and then drop some distance away without leaving a trail.

No Hiding Place

In wide-open habitats large animals find little or on shelter. Under these circumstance "predator control" becomes as group activity, and the animals aggregate together. The pronghorns, bison, and muskoxen of North America, the kangaroos of Australia, the saga antelopes, wild horses, and asses of the steppes of Russia, the gnu and zebra and even the ostriches of Africa show herd instincts.

In a group there are many eyes to watch for predators, and alarm spreads rapidly. Frightened pronghorns raise their tails and display a large white patch on their rumps. The flash of white rump and white flaglike tail on a running pronghorn starts every other pronghorn in sight on its way! Mixed herds, such as are common in Africa, cooperate in watching for danger.

Ostriches are taller than most mammals they herd with and are usually'the first to sound alarm. Large grassland animals are exceedingly fleet; they have long leng that cover the ground quickly. The faster runners in the world inhabit grasslands.

The American pronghorn, our fastest native animal, can do 60 miles an hour. At this rate the pronghorns leave a solitary predator or a pack of wolves so far behind that no amount of strategy or cunning can lead to another encounter until the pronghorns have had time to feed and recuperate from the original confrontation.

Of course, natural selection has also promoted evolution of fast-running grassland predators. In Africa, the cheetah has been clocked at 65 miles an hour. It is known to accelerate from a stand-still to 45 miles an hour in a few seconds. Grassland herbivores rely on the group not only for detection of predators but also for defense.

When threatend, bison form protective head-outward circles. The young are securein the center of the circle. Herding is itself a defensive measure. Predators are confused by large numbers of running animals. Thus if the individual a predator is following loses itself within the herd, the predator stops in confusion.

For this reason, most predators kill only aged, diseased, deformed, and very young animals that are unable to keep up with the herd. These same. animals are especially vulnerable, because they are also weak.

Grazing and Overgrazing

Each grassland is a balanced ecosystem of producers and consumers. The native herbivoures have evolved with the plantsand are adapted to the vegetation and to one another. Likewise. grasslands are adapted to withstand grazing by certain animals.

Unfortunately, domestic animals often have destructive effects on ecosystems in which they did not evolve. The abuse of natural grasslands by domestic animals arisess from two factors. First, the domesticated grazers, with few exceptions, are from other parts of the world.

Hence local grasses are not adapted to circumvent their feeding patterns. Domestic sheep, in parlicular, can graze more closely than native North American herbivoures can. Most grasses arevulnerable to extensive loss of stems and leaves.

Second, overgrazing by domestic animals is common. The usual population controls that limit wild grazers are nearly if not totally absent from populations of domestic animals. Humans do their best to protect their animals from severe weather, predators, or temporary food shortages.

When they slaughter animals for food, people carefully select surplus young adults, particularly excess males. Very young animals, which have a period of rapid growth ahead of them, pregnant females, and females of good breeding age are seldom killed.

In almost all cultures, people exploit their understanding of animal growth and reproduction to maximize the number of animals and obtain as much food as possible. Unfortunately, most societies lack a similar understanding of the ability of grasslands to support animals for long period. Perhaps this difference in understanding animals compared with grasslands results from the fact that the life cycle of the animals is comparatively short.

Each human has the opportunity to see many generations of cattle grow up and reproduce. In comparison, the effects of overgrazing may appear only over decades and sometimes require several human generations to become acute.

Damage from Overgrazing

Repeated close cropping of grass blades reduces the photosynthetic potential of the plant .and hence the energy that can be stored in the roots to support the following seasons' growth. In response to grazing, most grasses undertake a compensatory growth.

The leaves elongate at their meristems, and new branch stems arise near the ground. Both results from the loss of auxin-producing tissue at the tips of leaves and stems. Under excessive grazing some grasses continue to make new growth until their underground stores are exhausted.

Heavy grazing prevents the stems from growing out, blooming, and setting seed. Sometime the supply of new plants is cut off completely. Close cropping of leaves and stems also inhibits normal growth of roots that must occur to replace old, dying roots, to ensure absorption of water and minerals, and to bind the soil against erosion.

If all leaves are gone, the grass crown (base of the stem) lies exposed to physical damage from freezing or trampling. Finally, overgrazing harms hams the soil directly. Reduced vegetation and surface litter increase evaporation and reduce water absorption.

Much of the rain simply runs off along the surface, eroding the soil. Overgrazing has accelerated erosion of the deep gullies and arroyos of the arid Southwest. Heavy grazing also changes the soil texture. Continuous tramplingcompacts barren soil and thereby destroys spaces between the particles.

This reduces ability of the soil to hold air and water.

Range Management

Except for the constant pressure for short-term economic gains, range mangement is quite simple. Grasslands must be permitteded to set seed. The manager can achieve this goal by dividing the land into plots and rotating the grazing so that each plot remains ungrazed every few seasons until after the seed has ripened and dipersed.

If overgrazing on the other plots is to be prevented, more land must be available for a herd of a given size, or the total number of animals must be reduced. Another problem arises from the fact that grazing animals never use available forage uniformly.

They always prefer some areas, especially those near water holes. Sometimes judicious placement of salt blocks can balance the distribution of grazing.

Natural Checks

If range use must be so carefully managed, how did the thundering herds of bison live in equilibrium with the native grasslands of North America? The answer is quite simple there really were not many bison in relation to the amount of grassland.

The highest estimates of bison populations suggest that there was only one animal per 20 acres of range. Although the bison traveled in herds, raising clouds of dust with their hoofs and trampling the vegetation badly in places, most plants went many seasons without a single bison passing their way.

Some pond and stream margins did suffer repeated damage, and these probably supported successional vegetation. But in general the grasslands werelightly used. Natural checks limited the bison population. Although only grizzlies from the western mountains could have killed healthy adults, the young bison and ill ones were prey for wolves and perhaps coyotes.

Weather may have been another limiting factor. According to Indian tradition, a large herd of bison disappeared from. Illinois during a terrible blizzard late in the eighteenth century. Always some bison became trapped in river muds, and some surely died from disease or parasites.

But the best animals usually survived, and numbers were in balance with the food: supply. However, there can be little doubt that there were times when drought brought starvation to the bison and damage to the grasslands.

Drought, Dust, and Deserts

The moderateAy dry climate of grasslands carries the constant risk that fluctuation in rainfall will create droughtTwenty-three separate droughts have been recorded in theRussian steppes alone during the past. century and a half. But the geassland community survives, because the plants are adapted to the ravages of drought.

Overgrazing reduces the resistance of grasses to drought, and plowing the sod can lead to erosion that will nearly destroy the entire ecosystem. Let us examine the history of American grasslands and the effect of humans and drought on them.

The Dust Bowl

The late 1920s and early 1930s were marked with increased rrainfall that permitted tall grasses to to flourish on the American prairie. The seven-year drought that struck in 1933 drastically altered the species composition of the unplowed prairies, most of which had been subjected to heavy grazing.

Dry-adapted grasses quickly replaced those requiring more moisture. The big bluestem grass that could grow nearly eight feet high almost disappeared only a deep root system and underground food reserves permitted some plants to survive.

Even more drastic changes occurred in the normally drier Great Plains to the west. Grazed ares were badly damaged, but ranchers were reluctant to reduce their herds. One study in western Kansas showed less than half of the ground covered with vegetation in 1935 and only five per cent in 1936.

Great dust storms were both the cause and the result of the decreased vegetation. High temperatures and low rainfall prevented crop growth on plowed fields. Dry winds raised clousd of dust from these fields and from the poorly covered grassland when the dust fell from the air, it drifted like a horrible dark snow.

A deposit of only an inch was often sufficient to smother short gasses and produce another field of unstable soil. Stressful as the great drought was, no species is known to have been completely eradicated. All survived in favourable habitats or as ungerminated seeds.

Such survival would be expected, for only a small portion of the seeds of wild plants will sprout upon encountering favourable conditions. Nor will all the remainder sprout in any one season. So after several years in which all germinating grass seedlings shrivel from lack of water and die, there will still be live seed left in the ground.

When a normal year finally comes, a few seeds will sprout and begin to replenish their kind. Although no species were lost in the drought, the effect on the soil was another story. The rains that followed the drought fell on loose, naked soil that eroded into steep gullies.

Turning Grasslands into Deserts

The drought of the 1930s was certainly not the first one Americans had known, nor was that the first time dry weather and overgrazing had damaged the grasslands and hurt the ranchers. Increasing herds of sheep and cattle during the latter part of the nineteenth century had culminated in starvation of stock and disastrous economic losses when drought struck in the 1890s.

Following the Spanish pattern of migratory sheep grazing, some regions of the West have been overgrazed for several centuries. By moving the animals continuously, mainly to higher elevations in the spring and back downwards in the fall, ranchers can maintain large herds on very poor land. Arid western lands often show the effect of this practice.

The hills are terraced by continuous rows of sheep paths. Except on the highest peaks of the Sierra Nevada and the Rockies, the vegetation has been altered, perhaps permanently, by such practices. In some regions natural grasslands have been replaced by weedy desert vegetation. In western North America sagebrush now dominates many of what were once cool, short grasslands.

To the south, creosote bush, cacti, and mosquite have replaced other grasses. It is important to recognize that these "new deserts" lack the diversity and complexity of old "true deserts." But once overgrazing has produced bare sports, the mesquite thrives. It sends roots out literally, as well as deep into the soil, sometimes as far as 8 meters (25 feet).

Overgrazed grasses with poor root systems cannot compete for water with mesquite. Soon the grasses die back further, and the mesquite expands. Hungry cattle feed on the fleshy mesquite fruit pods, but mature seeds pass unharmed through the cattle. Thus cattle scatter mesquite seeds about, especially in the trampled areas where they congregate.

Fertilized by the cattle dung, the mesquite seeds are well planted in the barren but hospitable soil. American cattlemen have no monopoly on the conversion of grasslands to deserts. It has long been said that the Sahara Deserts marches farther south each year.

During the early 1970s drought coupled with high human and cattte populations led to loss of herds and massive starvation among the people of the sub-Saharan or Sahel grasslands. Some climatologists trace this disaster to major weather trends, but drought, overgrazing, and disaster are not strangers to these or most other arid grasslands.

DESERTS

The story of the desert has one theme-water. The distribution of water in time and space determines the nature of fragile .desert ecosystems. An average rainfall of less than 25 cm (10 in.) a year will produce a desert; but each desert is different, just as. are each forest and each grassland.

Relative humidity, temperature extremes, the underlying rock and drainage-all contribute, to the uniquenses of each desert. Deserts are never totally dry; there is always some water. Although dew can be of considerable importance in the water budget of certain organisms, most desert life relies larger on sporadic rainfall.

Particles of desert soil hold surface layers of water, as do other soils. Any excess water flows downward to collect over impenetrable layers of rock. Ground-water lying near the surface produces springs and oases.

Substantial layers of groundwater underlie many deserts; some are believed to represent the accumulations of thousands or even millions of years, Perhaps this "fossil water" can be traced to rainfall during. periods when these lands that are now deserts had more humid climates.

Or groundwater from regions with higher rainfall (such as adjacent mountains) may feed into the rock layers under deserts. In any case, water can be drawn from desert wells faster than it is replaced. Only rarely does vegetation carpet the desert. Consequently, rains create flash floods that dig deep gullies and carve rugged landforms in the desert.

Some desert soils developed where we find them; the wind has carried others hundred of miles from their origin. Desert soils are surprisingly fertile; many support substantial vegetation after a good rain or when irrigated.

Desert Plants: Many Solutions to One Problem

Plants have evolved seemingly endless adaptations to desert conditions. Individuals divide the water supply so efficiently that they tap almost every drop.

Most desert plants exhibit special modifications to gather and conserve water, but many merely become dormant during dry periods. For example, lichen on desert rocks are active only *intermittently*. When dehydrated by hot desert days, these lichens suspend most life functions and for a time tolerate extremely high temperatures (to 80°C or 176°F).

But after being dampened by night *dews*, these same plants revive and resume photosynthesis at dawn.

When the Rains Come

Although no higher plants withstand the severe dryness that lichens undergo, many live through. drought as seeds, bulbs, or other low-moisture structures. Such, plants usually have shallow roots that grow laterally through the top soil for considerable distance.

The wide distribution of roots permits them to adsorb substantial amounts of water from a light shower. In more moist deserts, seeds of annuals germinate every year, and the plants bloom predictably, usually within a few weeks in early spring.

But in many deserts, bloom is irregular. Certain species appear only every 10 to 20 years. They survive because their seeds remain alive but inactive in the soil. Seeds of some desert plants germinate any time there is sufficient moisture, but others rely on one or more of such additional cues as light and temperature.

The short-styled sedge of the Negev in Israel responds to rain in another way. Although the old leaves lie dead on the surface of the ground, their base remain alive and start to grow right after a rain. The desert becomes green immediately with new sedge leaves, but each supports dead material at its tip.

Every Drop Counts. Root systems of perennial desert plants vary markedly. Some rely on extensive near-surface roots, especially when growing on hills or ridges far above the groundwater. Others, particularly plants near dry stream beds, produce long taproots that reach far into the soil and rock.

Plants of stony deserts may send a single root under each nearby rock. This way they can absorb water that condenses from vapour during the cool desert nights.

Some cacti sprout new roots within a few hours of a heavy rain. Once the water is absorbed and stored in the thick fleshy stem, the new roots shrivel and dry up.

Around many desert shrubs, such as the creosote bush and sagebrush, lie areas barren of vegetation. These species secrete toxins that accumulate 'in the soil and inhibit other species. Thus these shrubs can use all nearby moisture without competition.

. Many succulent (fleshy) desert plants, such as sedums and aloes of Africa and agavas of North America, store water in thick, permanent leaves. But whether the water storage tissue is modified leaf or a stem, as in cacti, it is usually green with photosynthetic pigments.

In bright, unshaded deserts, sunlight penetrates to the deepest cells. Packing the photosynthetic tissues in stems or thick leaves petmits sufficient photosynthesis and reduces the surface area from which water can evaporate.

Few desert perennials have large leaves. Some, like the gray sagebresh, grow bigger leaves in the moist season and progressively smaller ones with the coming of dry weather. The last leaves formed are mere scales.

Other species, such as crown of thorns of Africa, the ocotillo of the U.S. Southwest and the boojum tree of Mexico, send out ordinary leaves during the moist season but drop them completely as soon as water is in short supply.

Special mechanisms doubtless regulate stomata in many desert plants. For example, agaves open their stomata only at night; during this time they absorb carbon dioxide and store it for use the following day.

This is the reverse of the common pattern; plants of moist environments open their stomata during the day and close them at night. Much dry-adapted vegetation bears spines or hairs. The adaptive value of these structures has been the subject of speculation.

Obviously spines deter some animals from feeding on the water-rich tissues. Spines also shade and insulate the plant. When hairs are dense, they interfere with air movements near the surface. This reduces evaporation and holds an insulating layer of air that can slow transfer of heat to the plant as the environment warms.

Perhaps these spines and hairs also provide a surface on which water vapour condenses into dew. Despite all these adaptations, desert plants can suffer severe water deficits during midday temperature peaks. Such daytime deficits are made up during the night but they may actually be beneficial as physiological acclimatization to extreme heat.

It is well established that enzymes are less sensitive to denaturation by heat in dry than in most environments. Perhaps midday dehydration permits desert plants to tolerate temperatures that would "cook" other vegetation.

Animal Adaptations to the Desert: A Tale of Water Conservation

Desert animals obtain their limited water rations from dew, occasionally from drinking water, but very largely from the water released during cellular respiration. In fact, this may provide the entire water supply of kangaroo rats. (You will recall that the respiration of glucose yields both carbon dioxide and water.)

Birds that eat insects may also obtain sufficient water from their food, But those with a diet of dry seeds fly many miles daily to reach drinking water.

Mammals, too, search for water. Some, such as the ibex and gazelle, will dig deep into the bottom of dry springs or temporary stream beds to reach groundwater.

Whatever their water source, desert animals have evolved strategies to conserve water. Many, including some reptiles and a multitude of small rodents, are nocturnal.

They spend their days in cool underground burrows, where they waste little water in evaporative cooling. Although desert birds are active during the day, they seek shelter in the shade of rocks, cliffs, or plants.

The camels, donkeys, sheep, and goats that people raise in -arid lands grow thick woolen coats that insulate these animals from the desert sun. Both donkeys and sheep keep their body temperatures in check through evaporation associated with painting.

Consequently, they must tolerate tremendous dehydration, because they use so much water in evaporative cooling. In fact, a well-dried-out donkey can guzzle a quarter of his body weight in water within only a few minutes. Instead of using water in panting, goats and camels tolerate a rise of several degrees in their body temperatures.

They accumulate heat during the day and dissipate the stored heat during the cool desert night. Most desert rodents excrete as little water as possible with their wastes. Perhaps you have. noticed the milky urine of a pet hamster. These natives of the Syrian deserts reabsorb to much water from its kidney tubules that the minerals precipitate and give its urine a milky appearance. A large surface area-to-volume ratio could make dehydration a serious risk for desert insects that are active during the day.

Many such species have evolved water-conservation adaptations that parallel those of desert plants. A thick waxy cuticle covers the bodies of many desert insects, just as desert plants have an extremely thick waxy cuticle on their leaves.

All insects have multiple openings for gas exchange, .not unlike the stomata of plants. But the gas exchange openings of some deserts are recessed in pits, just as are the stomara of desert .plants.

CHAPARRAL

Variations in terrestrial environments seem endless. Grasslands naturally merge into deserts, and a little abuse will make deserts out of dry grasslands. Similarly, deserts grade into forests. Indeed, dry-adapted trees, such as pistachios and acacias, characterize certain deserts. Some dry, warm environments support thorn forests.

The shrubby, leather-leafed plants that now cover much of the North Africa and Southern Europe are similar to the chaparral of the south-western United States. As far as can be determined, chaparral is the climax vegetation along the coast of Central and Southern California, where summers are dry but where winter can bring up to 50 cm (20 in.) of rain.

In this mediterranean-type climate the chamise, manzanita, and other shrubs bear leathery leaves the year around. Severe dehydration during the dry season is largely avoided by simply closing the stomata. Nevertheless, the plants suffer water shortages during the summer. Extensive root systems penetrate as far as 8 meters (25 feed) into the soil.

Fire sweeps the chaparral regularly, destroying all vegetation above the ground. The roots of many plants survive, and new sprouts appear quickly, attesting to the availability of water in the soil. In other species, heat activities seed germination.

The chaparral community is apparently a fire climax. Most of the minerals of this ecosystem are converted into ashes during periodic fires. Minerals leach from the ashes when it rains. This loss keeps the soil poor. Almost all chaparral plants have mycorrhizal associates that gather minerals, and many have nitrogen-fixing symbionts.

Chaparral soils are subject to heavy erosion. Homes built in chaparral areas many survive a fire, only to be washed out in a sea of mud and water when rain falls on the denuded soil.

LAND AND PEOPLE

Terrestrial ecosystems vary in their resilience, that is, in their ability to withstand abuse and to grow back when the abuse ceases. If protected from unusual erosion and loss of seed sources, most temperate forests can support successional stages and reestablish themselves in a few centuries.

Grasslands seem more fragile, perhaps because it is so difficult to prevent erosion in semiarid areas. Although we have less data concerning the resilience of tropical forests and tundra, they are apparently even less stable ecosystems.

In any case, it is sobering to realize how drastically people have altered terrestrial environments. The degree of destruction in most areas seems roughly proportional to the length of time that agriculture has been practiced and to the state of industrial development.

During the past 10 years, timber shortages in temperate areas have stimulated heavy logging of tropical forests. Also, well-intended but misguided attempts to increase food production have promoted clearing of tropical forest lands.

Meanwhile, development of such arctic resources as petroleum is creating traffic that gouges up the tundra. All these assaults on terrestrial ecosystems trace to increasing human populations. More people require more food and more lumber and more raw materials.

In evaluating the impact of growing human numbers, we must include overall effects on the biosphere. Since the continents are a major portion of this great, worldwide ecosystem, reduced resilience in terrestrial ecosystems must contribute to a generally less stable biosphere. This reason alone is sufficient to cause concern. If people are to survive, we must take care of our precious terrestrial ecosystems.

INDEX

C

D

E

F

G

H

Q

R

S

T

U